Praise for *Written i*

"I was immediately caught up in the book's story-telling momentum and emotional power. A wrenching, unblinking depiction of all the terrible and wonderful things Carol Flake Chapman experienced in the wake of her husband's death, *Written in Water* is a book that strikes universal chords of heartbreak and hope."

— Stephen Harrigan, author of *The Gates of the Alamo*,
Remember Ben Clayton, and *Water and Light*

"*Written in Water* cleanses two important doors of perception: grieving without getting lost in the process and connecting with a larger perspective through the healing balm of Nature. This is a deeply moving and transformative read."

— Will Taegel, author of *The Mother Tongue*,
Dean of the Wisdom School of Graduate Studies

"Reading *Written in Water* took my skin off and revealed new skin underneath. This astonishing book has been a profound companion for me."

— Sarah Bird, author of *Alamo House*, *The Yakota Officers Club* and *Above the East China Sea*

"A finely honed investigative reporter, Carol Flake Chapman opens portals of life's mysteries many of us never reach. Reflecting on the man she loved being taken in his prime becomes the catalyst for a journey of discovery. The breadth of her voyage through grief to her rebirth takes the reader from the marrow of bone all the way to the penumbra of the moon."

— Larry Winters, author of *Brotherkeeper* and
The Making and Unmaking of a Marine

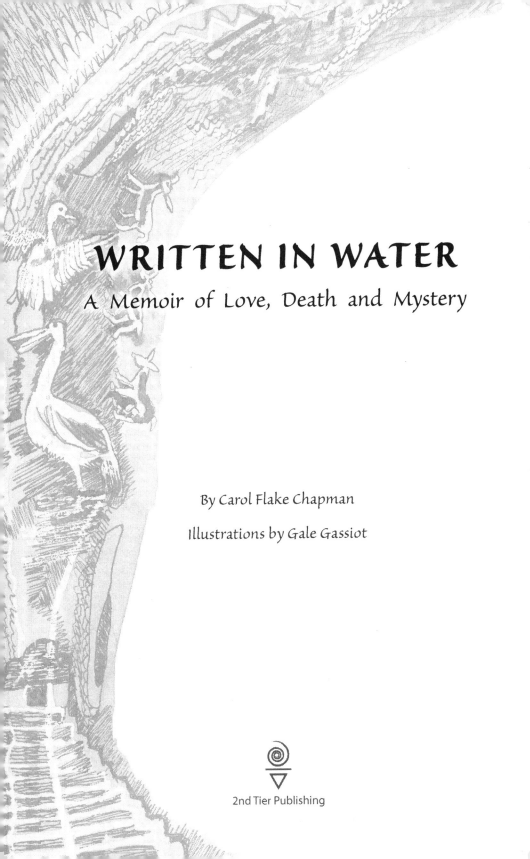

WRITTEN IN WATER

A Memoir of Love, Death and Mystery

By Carol Flake Chapman

Illustrations by Gale Gassiot

2nd Tier Publishing

Published by:
2nd Tier Publishing
13501 Ranch Road 12, Ste 103
Wimberley, TX 78676

ISBN 978-0-9862290-2-2

Illustrations by Gale Gassiot
Book design by Dan Gauthier

The soft bonds of love are indifferent to life and death.

~ Isaac Asimov

Table of Contents

Part III
Slow Grief

Part IV
When the Light Came Back

Acknowledgments

I can't imagine how I would have gotten through the time following Gary's death without the help of the necessary angels who kept showing up at the right time with the right words, who somehow knew just what I needed at certain moments, who were there for me with all manner of comfort. I thank my family for their sustaining love and support. My mom and dad were there for me in a big way, as were all my siblings, particularly my sister Ellen, who stayed close with deep understanding. I thank Ben Kvanli, Barry Day and Steve Smith for their heroic actions above and beyond the call of duty during a traumatic time. Thanks to all Gary's colleagues, friends and students at the LBJ School for their comfort and support. Thanks especially to Bob Hutchings for providing both expertise and kindness when I needed to get Gary back home. I thank Pete and Kathryn Lewis, Elizabeth and Jerele Neeld, Grant and Margot Thomas, Ruth and Jamie Pennebaker, Sarah Bird and George Jones, Emily and Berthold Haas, Josephine Sacabo and Dalt Wonk, Bill and Sally Witliff, Nancy Mims and Rodney Gibbs, Severo Ornstein and Laura Gould, Marcia Ball and Gordon Fowler, Jack and Jill Nokes, Sherri Greenberg, Patsy Clark, Jennifer Vickers, Katie Hafner, Brenda Bell, Peggy Weiss, Jamie Galbraith and Yin Tang, Annie and Don Hudson, and Larry and Roberta Wright and their daughter Caroline for surrounding me with love, food, music and practical help at times when it really counted. Thanks to Joseph Moore, Greg McDonell and the Women's Circle of Central Presbyterian who went the extra mile in bringing comfort. I am grateful as well to the women of my book club and to my kind and thoughtful neighbors who helped in so many ways. Thanks to Andy and Nona Sansom who were there always with loving kindness and who, along with Louie Bond, brought me back to writing. I want to thank Lodis Rhodes, Diego Latella, Sharon Strover and Darwin Horn for extending their friendship with Gary to me and for helping me understand who Gary was. I thank Steve Harrigan, Will Taegel, Peter Zandan and Jim Hornfischer for their wise perspectives and encouragement in the writing of this book. Thanks to the American Academy in Rome for allowing me to finish the book in such glorious surroundings and amid such good company. I am grateful to Dan Gauthier and Shiila Safer for their creativity, caretaking and guidance in the design and production of the book and to Gale Gassiot for her beautiful, visionary illustrations. I thank Gary's father Art Chapman for his stoic kindness and generosity in helping to point the way to a meaningful future. I thank his aunt Laura for her insight and wisdom. And most of all, I thank my beloved Gary for a love that passeth all understanding.

Prologue

After my husband died suddenly on a river in Guatemala, I had little thought of writing about his death or about the time of grief and consolation that followed. I was simply trying to survive from moment to moment, and I couldn't imagine that I would ever emerge from my state of shock and bereavement. I had been a writer for more than 30 years, but after Gary died, I couldn't envision writing anything of significance ever again. My heart was broken, and so was my will to write, which was entwined with my will to live.

Out of habit, however, because I had worked so many years as a journalist, I kept notes along the way, which for me was almost like breathing. Often my notes were scribbled on scraps of paper at hand, even on the backs of grocery receipts. In my more coherent moments, I found myself thinking of the familiar line from T.S. Eliot's "Wasteland," which had gained an unexpected relevance: "These fragments I have shored against my ruins."

Because of the extraordinary things that were happening and because I realized that I was submerged in a kind of altered state, I knew it would be important to remember details and events later, to recollect in tranquility—assuming that I would get there one day. Even in my lowest moments, I knew I would want to remember. But for months I was unable to write little more than a sentence without considerable pain.

When I eventually realized that the time following Gary's death had begun to take the form of a journey, I became more conscious of trying to shape my experience of mourning into a kind of pilgrimage, which meant that much of what had seemed random and coincidental came to have a sense of direction—that is, if following instincts and impulses could be said to imply direction. I can't say that I had much command of my wits when I began my improvised pilgrimage, and at times, I was grasping at straws. But the straws often seemed to point in a certain direction.

While at first my aim was simply to find a way out of bottomless grief, to find a reason to stay alive for another day, I began to look for more. I wanted more than just to live and breathe, more than just being able to get up in the morning. I wanted to find at least a possibility of regaining my footing in a world where I no longer seemed to have a home. Grieving in place wasn't working. I became a seeker as much as a pilgrim, venturing from the fraying edges of life as I had known it into unknown territory that was at once strange and familiar. Despite my numb despair, I wanted to find a way to recover the sense of joy and meaning in life that Gary and I had shared for much of our lives together—and that I would need to find on my own.

Gary was in many ways the kind of husband that women dream of—kind, considerate, and loving beyond measure. And he was charismatic. He was a thinker and motivator who mattered mightily in his work. Theoretically, as the gospel tells us, you're not likely to be accepted as a prophet in your own hometown—and certainly not in your own backyard. People close to home either knew you when or know you now too well. But Gary was a remarkable human being—a teacher of extraordinary influence and a persuasive visionary of the implications of technology. Though he was skeptical of anything overtly spiritual, I sometimes thought of him as a bodhisattva—in Buddhism, an enlightened or heroic being whose purpose is to bring enlightenment to others.

We had once expected happiness-ever-after in our marriage. For most of our years together, we had been as lucky in love as anyone could ever be. But in the months before Gary's death, long-unexamined tensions and conflicts in our lives had begun to surface, which I think we both feared could drive us apart. When Gary died without warning, we had been cheated not only of the chance to say goodbye, but also of the chance to figure out a way to come to terms with our growing differences.

My pilgrimage of consolation eventually became a quest to try to put together some missing pieces of the puzzle so that I could understand and honor who Gary was, even as his mark on the earth became a matter of memory and imagination. It was also the beginning of a journey to find out who I could be without him. Though I often felt that it was Gary who should have survived rather than me, that my loss would have mattered less to the world, I was the one who remained.

Somewhere along the way I began to accept that while I could hold and cherish him in memory, I couldn't take Gary's place nor could I carry on his work, no matter how much the world needed him. I had neither his vision nor his practical skills. And certainly not his charisma. I couldn't even begin to trace all the ripples he had sent out into the world with his work and with the students he had inspired. But I did have my own work to take up again when I was able and my own path to follow when the light returned.

One day, a year and a half after Gary died, I was walking the circular stone-lined labyrinth at a church retreat center deep in the Texas Hill Country. The retreat center, called Mo Ranch, sits on a particularly beautiful stretch of the upper Guadalupe River. There was no threat of getting lost, for unlike a maze, with all its blind alleys, a labyrinth, despite its twists and turns, always leads to the center. In the Cretan maze that Theseus conquered with the help of Ariadne, the minotaur, the mythic beast, part man and part bull, lurked at the center. But in medieval times, walking a labyrinth was a substitute for a pilgrimage to Jerusalem.

The procedure in approaching a labyrinth is to ask a question or to open your heart and mind and simply start walking. Maybe you'll get an answer, maybe not. It could be an answer you might not want to hear. But you keep walking. And listening. Even for skeptical walkers, putting one foot in front of the other, along a path patterned like the ones pilgrims have walked for centuries, is soothing in some archaic way. I wondered, though, if there could be something ominous lying in wait for me at the center. Or worse still, nothing at all.

As I plodded along, my feet heavy as lead, I heard, "You are no longer a wife." Okay. I know that. It hurts. Ouch. I could see that I was heading toward the center, but then I was moving toward the outer perimeter.

Never going to get there. Then back toward the center. Then I heard, "But you are a writer." Well, okay, but I haven't been able to write in the way I used to write. I used to be a writer, I thought, just like I used to be a wife. Thud. I kept plodding. And then I heard, "Telling stories can change the way people look at the world." Pause. Plod, plod, plod.

I reached the center of the labyrinth, and I heard the rush of the current of the Guadalupe as it sang over the rocks. For that moment, I felt at peace. There was no past, no future, only the present. And in the song of the river, I felt an inkling of purpose. I did have a story, though I didn't know yet what to make of it.

How could I possibly explain some of the inexplicable things that happened to me after Gary's death? I couldn't explain them to myself, much less to someone who has never been in a state of profound grief. As a journalist, I knew that in telling my story I would be stepping out of the usual bounds of credibility and venturing into the land known to skeptics as woo-woo.

In my journey, I often found myself in the "thin places," as the Irish have dubbed them, in the realms where the boundary between heaven and earth, between reality and dream, becomes porous. Along the way, there were anomalies: the timely appearances of necessary angels; songs popping up mysteriously from a cosmic playlist; a succession of hawks; a spider, a black deer, and an owl bearing messages. Really? Where was the proof? Where were the reliable sources? Was I a reliable witness to my own story, given that I had been driven half-crazy by grief? And by the way, was there a story worth telling? Was there a story there that could make sense of a sudden, senseless death and a life turned upside down?

Was there a story that could shift the way people look at death and grieving and consolation? Was my story, which often seemed so strange and unreal, actually a story that connected me to the universal stories of life and death that have been told for centuries and generations? Was it a story that connected me to a reality that was more mysterious and yet more intimate in its reach than I had ever imagined?

Many of my experiences were so beyond the ken of ordinary life I hesitated even to talk about them, much less consider writing about them.

But eventually I didn't really care if people looked at me as though I had been on some kind of mystical bender. When I did begin to talk to friends and acquaintances about Gary's death and about my time of mourning, I realized that the terra incognita where I found myself was a place that everyone traverses eventually, one way or another. I found that people wanted to know what it was like. As I began to find consolation in unforeseen ways and in unexpected places, I wondered if my experiences might offer some hope and cast some light in the dark places that seem to have no clear way out.

What did it mean to go into "mourning," as women used to call it when they threw away their clothing of many colors and donned black as their official uniform of loss? As I contemplated the fate of disappearing into the shadows, I made a conscious decision to move toward the light wherever I could find it.

Partway into my journey of grieving and consolation, a friend asked me what I was looking for. "Glimmers," I said. Glimmers of meaning, glimmers of comfort, glimmers of connection, glimmers of joy, glimmers of a love that lives on after death. And I found them all along the way—from friends, family, strangers, music, poetry, birds, butterflies, animals, rivers, cloud formations, cities, God's grace.

Gary and I were aficionados of the cultural movement called Slow Food, which advocates the unhurried preparation and savoring of food that embodies the essence of the places where it is grown and produced. And so I began to think of my time of intense grieving, as I sought the consolations of different places, some bitter, some sweet, as Slow Grief. There was no single place or significant moment that eased my sorrow, but rather a kind of cumulative consolation that very slowly brought me back to life.

Death and loss are universal. But finding consolation, I learned, is highly personal. Ours is a culture that forces us to improvise a way of grieving, and there is no single way to heal or recover from loss. My own way of consolation grew out of experiences in my life that are not common to everyone, and so I would hesitate to use my own journey as an actual guideline for anyone else. Traveling had been a way of life for me as a writer, and so it was a natural way for me to seek healing. Women with young children, with demanding full-time jobs or without the means to travel would find it difficult to spend a year of pilgrimage as I did. The same would be true of men who are in mourning.

Sometimes, though, a pilgrimage can mean traveling inward. And often the thin places of transcendence and the necessary angels of consolation may be no further away than a slow walk down a moonlit path or an unexpected conversation with a helpful stranger. As the scripture tells us, we may entertain angels unaware.

Part I

To the Bottom of the Ocean

In the middle of the journey of our life, I came to myself
In a dark wood where the straight way was lost.

~ Dante

Chapter 1

Lost in the Current

The call from Gary's father came about four o'clock on a Tuesday afternoon, December 14th, 2010, as I was mentally crossing off items on a to-do list for my kayaking trip to Guatemala. Start series of anti-malaria pills. Check. Hope Malarone doesn't make me as crazy as last time I took it. Check. Change some dollars into quetzals. Check. Get extra battery for iPhone. Check. I hadn't succumbed yet to the usual last-minute packing frenzy, as I had gotten such a good start and still had a couple of days to get everything together.

I had even finished my Christmas shopping, since Gary and I would be spending the holidays off the grid. I was relieved at the idea of catching the waning light of December as far away as possible from traffic-jammed shopping malls and inflatable frontyard Santas.

Gary was already in Guatemala with his small group of paddling buddies, and he had texted me that morning about their progress. They had finally reached the put-in spot for the Rio Cahabon, high up in the region known as the Alta Verapaz. They'd soon be testing the churning waves of the crystalline Cahabon on its turbulent course through the jungle canyons of Guatemala's remote eastern highlands.

They'd encounter rapids with names like Rock and Roll, Entonces and Las Tres Hermanas. They'd be dancing on the river, their hips swiveling their boats in a daring tango with an unpredictable partner. Amazingly, there was wifi at the backpacker stronghold of El Retiro, where the group unloaded their kayaks on the riverbank and prepared for a day of go-for-it paddling.

I could tell from his succinct texts that Gary was itching to finally hit the water. I sensed that his anticipation of a comradely challenging adventure had been dented somewhat by the reality of dealing with the complications of travel in the developing world. A long, tiring drive from Mexico, a series of bureaucratic hang ups on the border and a flat tire on a road still rutted from Hurricane Agatha's deluge six months earlier put them a day behind schedule. They spent the night camping near the Mayan ruins of Tikal and left for the riverside village of Languin at dawn.

"Tikal spectacular," Gary texted. "On top of pyramid at sunset."

Gary was characteristically stoic about the problems on the trip so far, but I could tell that it had been a more frustrating, exhausting journey than he expected. He was concerned about whether I should join him, as we had planned.

"Reluctant to put you through this," he texted. "Requires a lot of patience and endurance."

I was to meet him two days later for the second and more leisurely leg of the two-week adventure trip led by his ace kayak guru Ben Kvanli. I would be bypassing the unrelenting rapids of the Rio Cahabon and catching up with the group on the slow-moving, aptly named Rio Dulce, the sweet river, for tranquil sight-seeing and swimming with manatees.

Gary had seemed unusually stressed in the previous weeks, as he adjusted to the unfamiliar pressure of being constantly on call as the new graduate advisor at the LBJ School of Public Affairs. His great strength and joy in his work at the LBJ School had been teaching, and he was now locked into a position that kept him desk-bound and tied to his iPhone far more than he was used to. The tinnitus that had been plaguing him for the past few years had worsened, so that he needed sleeping pills every night to find respite from the high-pitched ringing in his ears. It made him uncharacteristically touchy and irritable and sometimes so depressed I made him promise he wouldn't do away with himself. The only place where the ringing stopped, he told me, was on the river.

We both thought of the trip to Guatemala, despite all the potential hassles, as a chance to let the river take us away from it all for a while. But we bickered early on about whether I'd find the trip too demanding, and Gary was still clearly having doubts. I was taken aback by his apparent lack of confidence in my ability to deal with hardship, and it troubled me. It continued to prickle.

"I still want to go," I insisted that morning in a text to Gary.

As a journalist and travel writer who'd taken plenty of risks over the years in pursuit of a story, or of a book chapter, I felt that I could rough it in just about any situation. After all, I had driven alone across remote stretches of Mexico in search of Monarch butterflies and of hidden hideaways for adventurous travelers; I had climbed the Virungas of Rwanda in search of mountain gorillas; I had galloped on a racehorse across the desert in Dubai; I had helped send a potentially vengeful mob-connected horse killer to jail.

Admittedly, my riskier adventures sometimes gave me sleepless nights. But foolishly, I thought of myself as fearless, and I resented the implication that I wasn't up to a challenge. I was full of prickly bravado. Gary's doubts seemed to hold larger ramifications about our life together, and I was all the more determined to prove him wrong. We texted back and forth, debating the best way for me reach the rendezvous point Ben Kvanli had planned in Flores, the capital of the state of Peten and gateway to Tikal.

Gary suggested that I become Facebook friends with Ben, who was able to get online on a computer at the campground, so that we could communicate via Facebook messages about the arrangements. I didn't hear from Ben, but finally decided I'd take a bus from Cancun, which I'd reach by plane, to the city of Chetumal, which straddled the Mexico-Belize border, and then switch to a bus line operated by the Batty Brothers of Belize to get to Flores.

"It will be worth it just for the photo," I texted.

It was my last message to Gary that morning, and I didn't get a reply. I assumed he was already on the boulder-strewn river, taking on the rapids that came so quickly, one after the other, that they were known as wave trains.

I was feeling a little smug that I had already packed my new kayaking gloves and a small dry bag for my iPhone that I could clip to a belt. I knew I wouldn't be facing any serious whitewater on the Rio Dulce, and the only splashing would probably come from clumsy paddling, but Gary's penchant for spiffy sporting equipment was contagious. This time, I was going to match him with cool stuff.

I sent him one more text that day, telling him I would be having dinner with our friends Marcia Ball, the musician, and her artist husband Gordon Fowler. Gordon was making duck gumbo, and I wanted Gary to feel a little envious. I was missing him badly and wishing that I had decided to brave the big rapids along with him.

Chapter 2

Light and Shadow

I was already familiar with that splendid view over the jungle from the pyramid known as Temple IV, the tallest standing pre-Columbian structure in the Americas. I still have a photo of myself at the top waving grandiosely to a friend at the base. The massive temple was built to honor a Mayan ruler with the flavorsome name of Lord Chocolate, and I could picture Gary standing atop it with arms proudly akimbo, just as I had done nearly ten years earlier.

Theoretically, I would be there in Tikal with Gary and the gang a few days later. Part of the inducement of the trip, at least for me, was arriving at the epicenter of Mayan civilization at the solstice on December 21st, when the shadow of Temple IV would edge across the plaza and creep up the steps of the temple facing it, a kind of slow consummation in light, shadow and stone. What's more, the solstice would mark two years before the "end" of the Mayan calendar in 2012, a point in time that had stirred speculative frenzy about a possible end of the world.

On December 12th, I posted a picture I had taken of Temple IV on Facebook, with the caption, "Gary will be camping here tomorrow night...I'll be there soon in time for the solstice, when really strange and mysterious things happen."

The next day, on December 13th, I posted a photo of a silly bumper sticker I had spotted on a car in Austin: "Palin 2012: 10,000 Mayans can't be wrong." A Palin presidency, it implied, would usher in the apocalypse.

Of course, I didn't really think the world was going to end in 2012. And from what I could tell, neither did the Mayans. It was simply the end of the 13th *baktun*, or time period, in a Long Count calendar inscribed on a set of tablets discovered in the archeological site of Tortuguero in the Mexican state of Tabasco. But Guatemala had a way of getting under my skin, even without predictions of doom. The Mayans hardly had a monopoly in the ancient world on torturing their captives, but there are few scarier-looking devices than the carved stone chacmools, the altars on which they had placed sacrificial victims to be sliced up.

I told Gary when we were first planning the trip that I felt that Guatemala has a dark side that made me uneasy.

"It's like an undertow," I said. I didn't know how else to describe it.

Gary was thinking of rivers and rapids, and I was thinking of great beauty shrouded in a legacy of blood.

Gary had not been to Guatemala before this trip, but I had spent time in the country back in 2001, staying with a family in Antigua while I took classes in Spanish at a school in the center of town. As a journalist, however, my lessons soon became much deeper than learning useful tenses. My teacher and I became so *sympatico* that one day, for reading material, she brought in a red spiral-bound book recounting the murders of priests and activists over the years that were finally being documented. We spent time traveling to markets in the hills around Antigua, where she introduced me to women's weaving cooperatives. She taught me, too, the ways certain verbs were conjugated in Guatemala to reinforce positions of dominance and servility.

Later, I traveled with my Mexican friend Gloria to small villages around glistening Lake Atitlan, near places where some of the worst atrocities had taken place, and where the lingering sense of damage and loss was still tangible, despite a burgeoning tourist industry. One day we climbed a steep hill to a small smoke-filled hut in the village of Santiago de Atitlan, where young women hoping to find a husband were making sacrificial offerings of money, tobacco and alcohol to a sinister-looking effigy known as Maximon, a wooden idol sporting a black sombrero and draped in a brightly colored serape.

Despite the cigarette protruding from his mouth, the oddly debonair idol looked as bloodthirsty as any Mayan despot. We were asked to pay ten dollars each for the privilege of being in Maximon's presence. But we both sensed a vaguely evil, hostile presence, and we backed out of the hut so fast I stumbled over a rough stone on the floor and nearly fell. Maximon seemed to embody the dark side of Guatemalan history — the bloody excesses of the Mayan, conquistador and military tyrants that had left many a grave in Guatemala.

I had my own doubts about going to Guatemala, but they were different from Gary's, and I tried to brush them off. I wasn't worried about roughing it or contracting a touch of *turista*. My misgivings had to do with a vague apprehension that Guatemala, despite its allure, held hidden dangers that we, as outsiders, might not anticipate or comprehend. I felt, though, that Gary badly needed this trip, and I had encouraged him to go.

Ordinarily, we would have thought of Italy, Gary's favorite place in the world, when we needed a getaway, but the country of the good life, *il buon vivere*, didn't seem the right place at the time to work out some of the issues and tensions that had been building in our lives. Gary was yearning, I thought, for some of the physical challenges and brotherly bonding he had experienced in the army in his twenties and which he seemed to find in his new kayaking adventures.

I knew there would be risks involved in kayaking a wild river in the remote reaches of a country never far from violence. But Gary felt utter confidence in Ben Kvanli, the leader of the group, who had not only grown up in Guatemala as the son of missionaries, but who had once competed for the country as a kayaker in the Olympics. Gary talked about Ben in the same way he talked about his idols Springsteen, Puccini or Machiavelli, with utter reverence.

Ben had been a U.S. national champion in double canoe, and he had just won one of the toughest whitewater kayaking competitions in the country, the U.S. freestyle championship. Also along on the trip was a burly Cajun oilfield troubleshooter named Barry Day, whose exploits on a whitewater trip to Mexico the previous year had Gary talking for days. Barry, who was based in Nigeria, was well into his fifties, but according to Gary, he was strong and fearless. The third member of the trip was a soft-spoken doctor from Corpus Christi named Steve Smith. Although Gary towered over the slightly built physician, Steve was the more experienced kayaker. And he also happened to be an emergency-room specialist.

If anything happened, Gary assured me, he could hardly have better companions. And despite my misgivings, I believed him. As I still do. What's more, Gary had just undergone a complete checkup at the Austin Heart Hospital, and his doctor had told him that he "couldn't be in any better shape" at his age. He had scored zero on a cardiac MRI to check for atherosclerosis, putting him in the lowest-risk category at his age for a heart attack, as he proudly told his father in a letter.

Gary's own survival skills, developed in the military, were formidable. He had served as a Green Beret, trained as a combat medic, and he had taught jungle survival training. Even after years in the confines of academia, he exuded a kind of effortless Hemingway-esque grace under pressure that came across as utter calm in the midst of chaos. Although Gary was a latecomer to kayaking, I felt that his skills would be more than adequate for the Cahabon. He had spent much of the past summer working on his "rolls," the counter-intuitive maneuver that allows a swamped kayaker to go under and pop back up again, using the paddle as a kind of lever.

He had been laser-focused on getting better. He watched video after video of legendary experts like Eric Jackson, and he drove down to San Marcos three mornings a week to train on the rapids there with a nationally ranked 16-year-old whitewater prodigy named Andre Sanborn. He bought a whitewater kayak designed by Eric Jackson that he felt was more suited to the Cahabon than the beginner model he had started out with. He had even ordered U.S.,

Mexican and Guatemalan flag stickers to affix on the prow of his new boat the week before he left.

Even before he finished packing, Gary had already dropped off his newly embellished boat, as well as my own sit-on-top, at Ben Kvanli's rambling riverside headquarters in San Marcos, where Ben had added them to the collection of kayaks he was planning to haul through Mexico on his way to the expedition's rendezvous point in Cancun.

I drove him to the airport early Saturday morning, on December 11th, along with all his neatly packed kayaking gear and camping equipment, and kissed him goodbye through the open window of my car.

Impulsively I got out of the vehicle to give him a hug. He had gotten up at 4 am to finish a recommendation that one of his graduate students had requested, but he looked as fit and happy as I had ever seen him. I watched him walk away, with his usual strong stride, his big duffle bags weighing on his broad shoulders. Neither one of us noticed the shadows that were gathering around us.

I was meeting my friend Ruth Pennebaker for lunch that day, and we agreed to get together the next night for a movie, *Black Swan*, which I knew Gary would have hated. For some reason, as we ate our salads, I started telling Ruth about a terrible December day not long after Gary and I moved to Austin 16 years earlier. Susan Hadden, Gary's colleague and closest friend at the LBJ School, had gone with her husband Jim to Cambodia as a birthday holiday. Shortly before she left, Gary said goodbye to her in the LBJ School parking lot, and he had felt a dark moment of apprehension, as he told me later, that he would never see her again.

Such an irrational thought was very unlike Gary, who generally scorned all things psychic or supernatural. He asked Susan if she was sure she wanted to go, hoping she would change her mind. Ten days later, he opened up the Sunday *Austin American-Statesman* as we were drinking our morning coffee, and he set the paper down, put his head in his hands, and began crying softly. Susan had been murdered by bandits while driving to a remote temple, and Jim had been badly injured.

As I described that morning to Ruth, I began weeping as though the shock and the wound were still fresh.

"I'd know if something like that was going to happen to Gary," I said, through my tears.

That afternoon, I opened up the latest copy of the *New Yorker* that had just arrived, and I began reading Joyce Carol Oates' harrowing story of her husband's unexpected death from pneumonia. While I marveled at her ability to write so vividly about something that would leave most women without words, I thought smugly that surely there would be better ways to cope with sudden widowhood. And how could she have left the hospital the night he died, leaving him to die alone, I wondered. How could she not have sensed what was going to happen?

And yet on that cool December day, just four days later, as Gary approached the undertow and the shadows, I was preoccupied with my wretched list. By late afternoon, I thought, Gary must be paddling the last set of big rapids for the day, maybe already pulling his stubby red Jackson Super Hero out of the emerald green water onto the jungle riverbank. I envisioned him unhooking his life jacket, unstrapping his helmet and exchanging booties for sandals, feeling waterlogged but adrenaline-pumped, surrounded by toucans and butterflies, ready for a beer.

Because Gary had taken up kayaking so late in life, he had embraced it with the full-hearted passion of the newly converted. Finally getting on the river must have been a thrill and a relief, I thought. A kind of baptism.

Chapter 3

Chacmool

I couldn't imagine why Art Chapman would be calling at this time of day, as he knew that Gary was already in Guatemala and that I would be busy packing, getting ready to join him.

"Are you sitting down?" he asked.

I thought he must be joking, since I assumed that people only say those words in the movies. Art's sense of humor is as dry as the Sahara, and I've learned to wait for his punchlines. But this time he sounded calm. Too calm. He's a satellite designer, an aeronautical engineer, trained to anticipate trouble, and this was a practical question.

"Gary has passed away," he said flatly.

And at that moment it didn't matter whether I was sitting down or standing on my head because the words didn't compute. They made no sense. I wasn't going to collapse, as Art might have feared, because the words just bounced off my brain like bullets off a shield. Art might as well have said that a tsunami was on its way from the Gulf of Mexico to Austin, and I should head for high ground.

I didn't believe him. It simply wasn't possible. Surely I would have known if something had happened to Gary. I still had his text messages from that morning on my iPhone as evidence. He had to be alive. Of course he was alive. Gary, my strong and tender warrior, was invincible. No. Life couldn't change that fast, from open to shut in a matter of hours, from promise to finish before the sun had set.

Art recalls that I told him at that point that he was lying. But
what I remember saying is, "No. He can't be dead. There has been
a mistake."

I do know that I shifted instantly and rudely from dutiful daugh-
ter-in-law into my default mode of skeptical journalist. Art didn't
know what he was talking about, I thought. He's well into his 80s,
and his hearing isn't the best. Maybe the group was robbed, though
I couldn't imagine a gang of thieves or kidnappers managing to
hijack kayakers on a fast-moving river.

"What happened?" I asked. "How do you know?"

Art said that he had gotten an official call from the American
consul in Guatemala City, who had notified him that Gary's death
had been reported. It wasn't clear who had done the reporting, but
someone had called the consul to inform him that Gary had died
and had given Gary's full name, date of birth and passport number.
Art's name and phone number had apparently been on file as Gary's
next of kin. Art didn't know any more details, and I couldn't imagine
why he would accept something so terrible, so unbelievable, something so completely unlikely, on so little evidence.

"Well, obviously someone must have stolen Gary's passport," I
said. "I'm going to find out what's going on," I said resolutely.

I got the consul's number from Art as well as the number of the
person who had purportedly called to report Gary's death. It must
have been a landline, I thought, since Gary's iPhone had been out
of range once the group had gotten on the river. I called Gary's
number anyway and frantically sent text messages into the ether.

"Where are you?" I typed, my index finger finding the right letters although I was finding it harder and harder to focus.

"Please let me know where you are."

It was closer to prayer at that point than texting.

As far as I knew, Gary was the only one in the group who had
a working cell phone with him on the trip. He had joked about
having to lend his phone to everyone in the group. Ben Kvanli's
phone had been stolen, along with his money, while he was hauling

the kayaks for the trip through a rough stretch of road near Vera-cruz. Oddly, the robbers had not taken the kayaks, but had taken the ownership papers for the boats, which had caused the lengthy delay at the border when the van and trailer reached Guatemala. I couldn't call the doctor, Steve Smith, either because he had made an agreement with his wife that he would stay off the grid during the trip. Gary had asked me that morning to send Steve's wife Shelley a message that the group was safe.

I called the number Art had given me for the American consul, who answered his phone right away. Not a good sign, I thought.

"David Chang speaking," he said.

"This is Gary Chapman's wife," I said, forcing myself to speak slowly and deliberately. "Gary's father Art Chapman called me and said that you had called him to report that Gary has died."

I could hear Chang clearing his throat, but I continued on in a rush, my voice getting shrill and shaky.

"But what evidence do you have? He can't possibly be dead," I said.

I was starting to lose it.

"We were just texting each other. What on earth is going on?"

"We have his passport number, his full name and his date of birth," said Chang, his voice quiet but matter of fact. "Gary Brent Chapman. Born August 8, 1952."

Chang suggested that I call the other number Art Chapman had given me for someone named Lee, and I hung up abruptly. Looking at the number I had scrawled on the back of an envelope, I punched in the digits, with no idea who I was calling. The phone rang a couple of times, and a woman answered in Spanish.

"*Bueno*," she said.

My Spanish was rusty from disuse, but I retrieved the simple words I needed. Words I had first learned in Guatemala but never thought I would have to use.

"*Busco mi esposo*," I said. I'm trying to find my husband. "*Se llama Gary Chapman.*"

I could hear her rapid uptake of breath, and she didn't answer for a moment.

"*Si*," she said, and there was a world of meaning in the word.

The other Spanish words I needed were there for me, retrieved from some part of my brain that was still functioning.

"*Está muerte?*"

Is he dead? Somehow I remembered the odd quirk in Spanish that in describing the condition of being dead, one uses the verb *estar*, the temporary state of being, rather than *ser*, which suggests a permanent state. Is Gary temporarily dead? I was asking. Is he dead at this moment?

"*Si*," she said. "*Lo encontraron flotando in el rio*," she said. They found him floating in the river. Yes, at this moment, he is dead.

She explained that she was in an office and she gave me yet another number to call. I got no answer from that number, but as the phone rang and rang in the unfamiliar beeping of a foreign exchange, I knew in my heart, if not my mind, that there had been no mistake, that this looming nightmare was real. I wasn't going to wake up the next day relieved that Gary and I had endured a bad scare.

I remembered an ominous call I had gotten on the morning of my birthday three years earlier. Gary had left for work, and I was cleaning up the breakfast dishes while thinking about the next post on my website. Gary made the commute on sinuous Bee Cave Road from our house in the hills west of Austin to the UT campus five mornings a week, and traffic had gotten frustrating as population swelled in our semi-rural neighborhood.

When I answered the phone, the stranger who called spoke too quickly and nervously to be a telemarketer and not officiously enough to be in law enforcement. The stranger was doing his best, but it was one of those calls that women dread and yet anticipate somewhere in the deep reaches of our danger-fraught hunter-gatherer brains every time our beloved climbs into a vehicle, on his way to hunt the hairy mammoth, and drives away.

"Mrs. Chapman, your husband has been in an accident," said the stranger, a Good Samaritan who had stopped to help and who never did give me his name. "But don't worry," he said. "He's going to be OK."

Gary's SUV had been struck by another vehicle on Bee Cave Road just in front of the Church of Conscious Harmony, he said. I had attended the church on occasion, and I knew the exact curve in the road he was talking about. I don't remember thanking the stranger or even hanging up the phone. I ran out to my car, leaving the front door ajar, and drove like a demon until I encountered stalled traffic that had backed up for miles. Without braking, I moved into the breakdown lane, zooming past idling cars, ignoring the patrolman who was trying to set up warning cones. I stopped my car and hurried up the road in the house slippers I had neglected to change. I headed toward the barrage of lights from patrol cars, fire trucks and ambulances.

I felt mired in slow motion as I came upon a scene out of an apocalyptic Mad Max movie, with three vehicles badly smashed up, still smoking from the impact, and metal debris everywhere. One of the vehicles had been cut in half, with the back half lying halfway down the slope, beyond the guardrail that it had broken through. Gary's Nissan Pathfinder had been stopped by the guardrail, but it was crushed, with shards of glass and shorn-off parts lying all over the road.

The stalwart 10-year-old SUV had been hit broadside on the driver's side of the vehicle by a speeding, out-of-control Mercedes sedan. The sullen, wild-eyed 22-year-old at the wheel apparently escaped unscathed from the remaining front half of his parents' Mercedes and was sitting on a guardrail, flipping the bird to the EMS attendant who was urging him to get to a hospital. Gary was lying on a gurney, with his head strapped down, as two EMS attendants prepared to heft him into the waiting ambulance. Before I could panic, he waved and beckoned me over. Small pieces of shattered glass were embedded in his bloodstained face, and I could see a big bruise on his shoulder. He smiled ruefully as I grabbed his hand.

The police report would later state that the Mercedes was going between 60 and 70 mph when it hit Gary's Pathfinder. Two women in the third vehicle, a BMW sedan, which was also struck by the speeding Mercedes, had been severely injured and had been hospitalized. But Gary was able to crawl out of the crushed SUV on his own, with his only apparent injuries being the bruises from the airbag and the shoulder strap of his seat belt. Later, when I looked at photos taken of the totaled Pathfinder for insurance purposes, I couldn't imagine how he had survived. I told Gary that God had given me a miracle for a birthday present.

This time, though, there would be no reprieve, no miracle. Our luck, and our life together, had run out. Gary had been taken from me for good, although I didn't know then whether he had been taken by the river, by bandits, by God, by a glitch in his heart, or by the spirits of the ancient Maya still looking for high-ranking captives to sacrifice. I did know, however, that it was not Gary who was strapped on a cold stone chacmool to have his heart cut out. It was me.

The Good Journey

Finally someone answered the number the woman gave me. The mysterious Lee turned out to be an expatriate American named Lee Beal, based at Lake Atitlan, who had been helping Ben with his expedition and who had been on the river with the group. It was a woman working in his office in Panajachel who answered my earlier call.

Lee was surprisingly brusque as he answered my questions. Yes, Gary was dead. He had overturned in his kayak and had come out of the boat, as kayakers routinely do when they can't manage to right themselves. But he had not surfaced right away, and he had not been breathing when Steve Smith managed to pull him out of the river with Ben Kvanli's help. No, it had not been a particularly turbulent stretch of the river, he said. Such a mild stretch of rapids it had no name.

I remember being baffled that no one else in the group seemed to be willing or able to talk to me, but I'm not sure if I was actually speaking coherently at that point. I hung up not really knowing what had happened or why.

What I didn't realize then was how fast everything had happened and that just moments earlier, Steve Smith was still administering CPR to Gary, trying futilely to revive him, while Ben was trying to figure out a way to transport Gary's body out of the steep jungle canyon. The men must have been functioning in a state of shock, although Steve was able to call on his emergency medical training as well as a surge of adrenaline to try to save his friend. It was the

Cajun oil worker Barry Day who later described the desperate scene to me as Gary's kayak brotherhood dealt with the sudden death of a tall, solidly built man in a remote reach of the river, surrounded by jungle, hours away from a town or village.

Barry was leading the pack, paddling ahead of Gary, when he suddenly saw Gary's boat float past him and then his paddle. Barry assumed Gary had come out of the boat during a roll, and he angled up to the boat to secure it. When he turned around, he saw Steve Smith, who had been following Gary on the river, throw a rope to the spot where Gary had slipped out of the overturned boat.

Steve, I knew, had quick reflexes, and he was a master of rope throwing. Gary had told me about a time when he and Steve were paddling a turbulent stretch of the upper Guadalupe River behind a clumsy young kayaker, who was suddenly flung from his boat as he hit a rock. The powerful current trapped the boy against a boulder, and he flailed helplessly as he began to slip below the surface. Steve threw him a rope and pulled him to safety before the boy even realized how close he had been to death.

When Steve realized that Gary would not be coming back up to the surface on his own, he scrambled out of his boat and swam toward the spot where he saw Gary go under. Surprisingly, it was not Ben Kvanli, with all his strength and physical prowess, but wispy Steve, who probably weighed a good 70 pounds less than Gary, who was the one to reach Gary first. Steve reached under the water and managed to grab hold of Gary's life jacket and pull him up from what Steve later said was a "hole," a spot in the river where the onrushing current can trap a kayaker.

Ben, who had been trailing them, hauled them both to shore. But Gary was already gone. Steve worked on him for more than an hour after he and Ben pulled his limp body out of the water and onto the riverbank, where Barry joined them as fast as he could. Barry, who is a big man, as tall as Gary, said that he had been the one to pound on Gary's chest as Steve tried to breathe air into his lungs. "I think I might have broken a rib or two," he said apologetically.

Everything had happened quickly, and then time seemed to stand still. There had been no warning that Gary was in trouble, said Barry. The day had begun on a typically jocular note. As the group got their gear ready to depart, Barry had been struck by how cool Gary looked with his new color-coordinated helmet, paddle and life jacket.

"He was so finely arrayed I had to tease him a little," said Barry. He asked Gary, "Did your wife pick those out for you?"

"No, I did it myself," Gary replied, a little miffed.

I could picture the two big men climbing into their tiny boats, trading barbs and jokes as they eased into the rhythm of the river. After they had paddled a bit, Barry asked Gary to show off what he had learned over the summer, and he was impressed by Gary's control over his boat. "He was lookin' good," said Barry in his deep Cajun-country accent. "I was amazed by how much progress he had made." He gave Gary a big thumbs-up.

The men talked about a lot of different things as they made that seemingly endless road trip to the put-in point on the Cahabon. Barry said that at first Gary seemed more concerned about me than about his own ability to navigate the river.

"But you could see a switch in him. Then he was saying, 'Carol can take care of herself.' He stopped worrying about you."

But that didn't mean that Gary stopped thinking about me, Barry insisted. The morning after the group awoke at their campground in Tikal, everyone in the group except Gary got up to watch the sunrise from the tallest pyramid, Temple IV. As Barry told it, Gary said to his buddies, 'I'm gonna sleep in because I want to wait and watch the sunrise with Carol when she gets here.'"

Barry reminded me that it was he who had sold Gary his red Super Hero, which had been a big improvement over his previous kayak.

"Gary's last words on this earth bear out how appreciative and considerate a man he was," said Barry." He told me, 'Thank you so much, Barry, for selling me your boat.'"

Gary seemed to be maneuvering the new boat with ease. When the group came to a demanding set of rapids earlier in their journey, Barry watched Gary handle them easily. He wasn't even alarmed moments later when he saw Gary's boat and then his paddle come floating by.

"I just went after the boat. That's how little worried I was," he said.

Even after he saw Steve and Ben pull Gary ashore, he felt at first that Gary would survive. "Steve was heroic," he said. "I'm a first responder myself, and I've seen a lot of people be brought back. We can usually revive people. But not this time. Gary's spirit was already on the way back to you."

After they were sure beyond a doubt that Gary could not be revived, the men decided they would try to carry his body up through the jungle, using his kayak as a stretcher. Ben had gone ahead on the river to the takeout point to catch a bus to the closest town in order to get help. Meanwhile, two local men from a nearby Q'eqchi village arrived, after hearing all the commotion, and volunteered to help. The almost nonexistent trail up the slope was too narrow and the overhanging branches too low for the Americans to deal with, so the shorter Guatemalans hefted the boat, one at the front, the other at the back. But the jungle proved too dense, the boat too unwieldy and Gary's body too heavy for the small, wiry men.

I imagine the scene as something out of Werner Herzog's surreal movie *Fitzcarraldo*, with its quixotic, agonizing portage of a full-sized steamboat across a steep, muddy hill from one Peruvian jungle river to another, all in order to build an opera house. The movie was one of Gary's favorites, with its combination of river rapids and opera. As Barry described the chaotic scene along the Cahabon, I could almost hear the aria from *La Boheme* from the *Fitzcarraldo* soundtrack, followed by an anthem from Springsteen's "The River."

There must have something of the desperation of wartime in an alien land in those moments in the impenetrable jungle—a sudden death, the river rushing by and no apparent way out. Gary had told me about the universal rule in the military that soldiers never desert their fallen comrades, and his kayaking buddies felt a similar determination. When it was clear that trekking up through the jungle would not work, the decision was made to go back to the river and send Gary's body down the rapids to the point where the group had originally planned to disembark. The ambulance from the closest town with a hospital would meet them there. They placed him in his boat, sitting upright, and Barry guided the boat downriver.

"Gary finished the trip in style," said Barry. As another friend observed later, "He went out like a Viking."

As I envisioned Gary on his last journey in his red Super Hero, with its bright Mexican, Guatemalan and U.S. flags affixed on the prow, another image came to me, this one from our first trip to Portugal, when I had been transfixed by a small sculpture of the Virgin Mary reclining in a boat on her way to heaven. It was very like the Portuguese, with their proud history of pioneering navigation, to embrace the notion that the Virgin arrived in heaven on a boat. The sculpture was titled *Boa Viagem*, the Good Journey, and I kept the image as a screensaver on my computer to remind me of a graceful way to go out of this world.

But for us mere mortals, is there actually a good way to leave this world? If we had our druthers, how would we choose to make an exit? Certainly not in a hospital room, I thought, nor on a highway. Despite the trauma of what happened, Barry was still captivated by the beauty of the river, surrounded by the brilliantly green jungle canyon, where Gary died.

"It was the most beautiful place to die," he said.

Later, Ben Kvanli gave me a photo he had taken a year or two earlier of a nearby place in the river, with a rainbow arching over it. On the front, he inscribed, "Gary's love is eternal." And on the back, he wrote, "Gary's final takeout."

I'm not sure that it really gave me much comfort at the time, but Barry told me something that many of Gary's male friends would echo in the days and months to come. At least Gary died doing what he loved, Barry declared.

"He was a happy man when he went," he said.

Such a clichéd male way of looking at, I thought to myself. But it did remind me of Gary's rapt description of a trip he and Barry took with Ben to Mexico a year earlier, before Gary had really mastered the art of kayaking and was going more on sheer bravado than experience. They rode the fast-moving river through a narrow canyon, one by one, at such breakneck speed that fighting the current would have been futile. It was like a rite of passage that didn't allow reaction time but rather surrender to the river.

So on the Cahabon that fateful day, was it a random, unforeseen boulder looming in the current that had taken my husband from me and changed the course of our lives? Was it the hidden undertow that I had feared? I will never know for sure. But for his companions, the river was never the enemy. Gary's death has not shaken Barry from his passion for rivers, nor from his love of adventure. Having lived for many years on the margins of safety in Africa, he was not inclined to make his own life more secure because of a friend's death on a wild river.

"If it had been me," he told me, "I would have loved to go the way he did. It was a good way to go. The last thing I'd want is to wither away in some old folks' home or be revived and be half brain dead."

Barry paused for a moment. "And Gary wouldn't have wanted you to pull back either. He'd want you to go on with your life 'full bore.'"

Chapter 5

Walking in the Dark

That short December day, however, as darkness descended, all I knew was that Gary was gone and that our life together was wiped out as completely as though a tornado had touched down and left nothing in its path but shards and splinters. I felt utterly and completely alone, the shell-shocked survivor who emerges from the storm shelter to find a bare foundation where a happy home and the shared furnishings of a life had stood.

The word widow hadn't yet crossed my mind, and I would resist the label unrelentingly as I tried to come to terms with what had happened. No, I would not be a widow. Widowhood meant invisibility, a walking shadow that leaves no footprints. It meant the paint-smudged imprint of a hand on a temple wall before the peer-pressure leap onto the flaming barge. It meant the captain's wife pacing the confines of the widow's walk atop the saltbox house, gazing at the empty horizon for the sail that will never arrive. It meant the fifth wheel, the odd woman out, the new pariah left off the invitation list for the dinner party, the walking wounded too scary for polite company. It meant a sundering: once half a couple, part of a whole, now the torn remainder.

For all my resistance, though, I had become a woman in black. I had joined the ancient and universal sisterhood of women who have lost their men, some slowly and agonizingly to illness, some quickly and unexpectedly, to bullets, bombs, car and plane crashes, earthquakes, avalanches, rough seas. The messengers arrive in different ways with the news: the phone call at an odd hour, the men in uniform walking solemnly to the front door, the doctor wearily removing his mask as he emerges from the operating room. At that point, though, I had no reliable messenger. I didn't even know where Gary's body was or how he had died. It was as though he had gone missing in action, vanished without a trace. He might as well have died on the moon or been lost in space.

And so that night I began my journey, my unplanned, unwanted and uncharted descent into the world of grief, despair and loss, where all the old rules of reality are suspended, where the old world ends and where a strange and unfamiliar new life begins, with ashes, at ground zero. Had I been Orpheus, I would willingly have begun searching the underworld for my beloved, as darkness had quickly become my familiar element. Who wouldn't go to hell and back to retrieve a lost love? Surely there could be no demons or dragons worse than quiet suffering.

I could imagine Orpheus's dilemma. He has won Eurydice's freedom with a vow not to turn and look back. He must take it on faith that she is following behind him until they both cross the threshold from Hades into the upper world. But how could the grieving bard with the golden lyre not yield to the temptation to glance back, just for a moment, to make certain Eurydice is really there as he begins his ascent back to the light? He is, after all, a man of music, of the senses. He could hardly have heard her footsteps, the soundless echoes of a shade. A moment's loss of faith, and his loved one is gone. Again.

Did he keep looking back, I wondered, even after he knew that Eurydice had slipped back into the darkness? Which loss was harder—the first, which involved fate, or the second, which hinged on a flaw in his character? That is, if doubt can be considered a flaw.

As for me, in those first hours and days, I engaged in the usual makeshift personal rituals of loss. I made an altar on the chest of drawers beside our bed that gradually became crowded with photos and mementos of our life together. I had learned from the whimsical and celebratory Day of the Dead altars I had seen in Mexico that even the oddest and humblest possessions can stir memories and bring consolation. I paired Gary's suave RayBans with the glitter-speckled shades he had worn as part of the Elvis costume he had created for a Mardi Gras party. I burned candles and wrote little messages of gratitude I placed in a silver cup on the altar.

Thank you for cooking for me. Thank you for being so patient and helpful when I was having computer problems. Thank you for your passion for justice. Thank you for buying me the beautiful Pineda Covelin scarf and the rock-star jacket by Manuel. Thank you for loving me so well. Thank you for all the music.

I wore Gary's shirts with sleeves rolled up, and still do. I talked to him, particularly when I was taking the dogs for a walk, and still do. But I can't recall even a moment in the awful days and nights following his death when a single instant of hope, faith or delusion led me to expect that any kind of prayers, promises, sacrificial offerings or magical thinking, as Joan Didion called it with such bleak irony, would bring Gary back to life.

The magical thinking, as Didion implies, comes not only from the bereaved, but from those who would attempt to analyze or understand it from the outside, even from those who want to console. There are no shortcuts, no clear answers, no reliable maps, no timetables. For Christians, the formal rituals of grieving cease following the funerals, the wakes, the graveside prayers. I envied my Jewish friends the tradition of sitting shiva, with its weeklong gatherings and ceremonial rending of a garment.

I found myself wondering what it would be like to hire professional mourners, like the moirologists of the Greek Islands, or the Gaelic keeners eventually silenced by the Vatican, to weep and wail and stand in for me at times so that I could grieve in silence or take a break from the pain. A chorus of keeners would loudly lament my loss and praise Gary to the heavens. The moirologists would sing of the loneliness of the living left behind and wonder how the sun could even venture out to shine on such a dark and lamentable scene as a world without Gary.

The reason I love opera so much, and Puccini in particular, is that the great arias magnify the deepest human emotions—grief, rage, love, hate—and project them onto the stage with enormous, sometimes overwhelming, power. Like a Walter Mitty of opera, I had always wanted to be able to sing just one aria from *Madame Butterfly* or *La Bohème*—belting out modest Butterfly's anguish or the consumptive Mimi's longing with monumental passion. And now, of all times, I coveted the voice of Maria Callas so that I could ring out my grief to the rafters. But I was not on a stage. I was in a world without an operatic script or libretto that would do justice to the full measure of sorrow and loss that we feel as ordinary human beings and want to howl out to the cosmos, whether we are big stuff or small potatoes.

My progress through the alien land of grief would not follow the familiar sequence of stages that grief pioneer Elizabeth Kubler-Ross had initially described—from denial, anger, bargaining, and depression to acceptance. In later life she clarified that grief is different for everyone and that we all find our own strategies for survival. Denial, she wrote, is simply a way of coping.

"Denial," she said, "helps us to pace our feelings of grief. There is a grace in denial. It is nature's way of letting in only as much as we can handle."

But I had given up the luxury of denial in the time it took for the Guatemalan woman I had called out of the blue to answer a tremulous *si*.

I was not a good griever. I began to detest all the hackneyed and unexamined words and knee-jerk concepts usually associated with grieving. I particularly hated the word closure. I hoped desperately I would never find "closure," which sounded to me like signing the papers on a financial transaction. Life foreclosed on. Case closed. I was grateful that no one told me that Gary, who had never been religious, was now in a "better place." Those who told me knowingly that time would heal my wounds may have been well meaning and partially right, but it wasn't helpful at a moment when a seemingly limitless path of grieving stretched out in front of me.

I had no way of foreseeing then that my grief and loss would open the portals to a different kind of consolation. But I found, as I suspect many bereaved women do, that I had been preparing unknowingly for much of my life to deal with the loss of that which I held most dear.

Chapter 6

In the Company of Comforters

Friends, I learned right away, would be the first responders. According to Gary's Guatemalan-issued death certificate, with its embossed national seal, which I finally received days later, he died at 3:36 pm on that December afternoon that was like no other. And though it seemed an eternity, hardly an hour passed after that "official" time of death before friends began arriving at my house, bringing food and drink and companionship to fill the silence. Somehow they knew.

After making more calls to Guatemala and to Art Chapman, as I began the complicated process to retrieve Gary's body, I called my parents to let them know the barest details of what had happened—simply that Gary had died on a river in Guatemala. I then called our close friends Pete and Kathryn Lewis, who live in California but who happened to be in Austin because their daughter Laura was having a baby. Laura was in the middle of a difficult labor when I reached them at the hospital and didn't give birth until nearly midnight. Only later were we able to remark on the sequence of death and new life that seemed so closely entwined.

I called Marcia Ball, to let her know why I wouldn't be joining her for dinner. But I couldn't bring myself to call the many other friends who should be notified. I wasn't ready yet to share with others what had happened, in part because I still didn't really know what had happened to Gary. I didn't even know where he was. That is, where his body was. Was the body Gary inhabited now emptied of his spirit, his soul, his essence? That I didn't know. But I needed to start somewhere.

I sent a terse Facebook message to Ben Kvanli. "I need to know what's going on. Where is Gary's body?"

No answer. How absurd to be using Facebook to locate my dead husband's body. But I didn't know what else to do. I later learned that Gary's body had been taken by ambulance to the town of Coban and placed in the local hospital morgue. But at the moment, I didn't have a clue. Despite my reticence, though, word spread quickly, and I was soon surrounded in my house by a growing company of comforters. The phone began ringing nonstop.

I told friends who called not to come, as I looked around my disheveled house, embarrassed by the clutter even in my near deranged state. But a small crowd made the half-hour drive out to my neighborhood, which I sometimes refer to as East Jesus because of the reluctance of my town friends to brave the hills and curving roads at night. Marcia brought the savory gumbo that Gordon had made for their dinner party, but I was unable to eat a single bite. It would be months before I was able to actually taste food. It was only much later that I could joke about the effectiveness of the grief diet, as my jeans got looser and looser.

As I look back to that evening, I think I must have had that thousand-mile stare, the expression of far-off, dazed detachment that Gary told me he had seen among his buddies in Vietnam. Grief had sent me into an altered state. I was not in shock, at least not in the usual ways I've heard it described. It was more as though my psyche had performed a kind of triage, leaving some parts functioning and others put in temporary storage.

For much of the time to come, I would be living with the partial deadening of a patient given an inadequate shot of novocaine. I was numb, with some craziness around the edges, and with the constant awareness of the world of pain below the surface. I developed what I now think of as a form of grief-induced ADD. It would be months before I could actually read a book of any consequence, and I still haven't been able to watch a television show from beginning to end.

But death brings with it a load of duties, whether you are prepared or not. Gary left a big hole in the world for many people other than me. I knew dimly that first night that I needed to rouse myself for a succession of tasks that I knew nothing about but would have to learn very quickly. I owed it to Gary and to his wide circle of friends, students and colleagues to get myself together enough to begin the formal process of mourning.

So what do you do when the love of your life dies suddenly in the middle of a jungle? Always the list-maker, I began to make a to-do list of things I could never have imagined having to do. Number one: Get Gary's body back.

Chapter 7

A Network of Grief

Death may bring a powerful sense of isolation to the bereaved, but it's no respecter of privacy. As I was hunkering down in my grief that night, wanting nothing but wound-licking solitude, word of Gary's death had continued to spread, and I was getting emails of condolence from around the world. News of Gary's death had gone viral, as he might have expressed it in one of his online newspaper columns. Already there were tweets and Facebook posts expressing shock and sorrow.

Gary had commented frequently about the ways social media like Twitter and Facebook were changing the way we live, and he would have been intrigued by the way the Internet was facilitating an instantaneous and shared form of grieving. Just two months earlier, he had rented a bus and driven his freshman students to a local theater to see the movie *The Social Network*, about the founding of Facebook. He told me that he wanted to get his students to think about whether a virtual online network could actually become a genuine community, a means of changing the world.

Gary felt passionately that technology should always be in the service of the public interest. He had been the first director of Computer Professionals for Social Responsibility, a group devoted to that ideal, and he had continued over the years to create networks of interest groups and activists. And now the many networks he had helped to foster were vibrating with his loss.

I don't think Gary had considered the possibility of a network of grief. But I do think he would have relished knowing that I would be so comforted by the emails, by the Facebook and blog posts and by the widely scattered online reminiscences from his friends, students and colleagues. In my initial stage of shock, I didn't need or even want to be face-to-face with these folks to feel their genuine grief and their appreciation of Gary. In retrospect, such an outpouring in the flesh would probably have been overwhelming.

One of our friends, the writer Lawrence Wright, started an email list that grew day by day to keep our friends posted of progress in getting Gary's body back. The list kept growing, and it became a means for me to let everyone know about the many different ways that Gary's life would be honored. Our friend Grant Thomas and I eventually joked about the ever-expanding "electronic tribe of Gary." I treasured those early emails, some dashed off quickly, others carefully composed, as much as I did the cards and letters that filled my mailbox for the next days and weeks.

The growing collection of online accolades lauded Gary as a renaissance man, a visionary who could foresee technology's impact on society, an inspiring teacher, a kind, thoughtful and steadfast friend, the smartest and yet humblest man in the room, a leader of courage and conscience. A colleague at the LBJ School expressed his appreciation in somewhat convoluted but sincere academese: "Gary had a quiet but effective way of figuring out where right and wrong might be entangled with the nuts and bolts, and economics, of new technology, and communicating this in an intellectually solid and morally persuasive way."

One of Gary's students declared that he was so multi-faceted that "he was like the personification of a geometric paradox not even Escher could render."

The email that would linger longest in my heart, however, was from our gay French Algerian friend Zoubir, a devout Muslim of Tuareg descent whom we had last seen at New Year's in New Orleans.

Bonjour, Carol.

I was told of the sad happening to your darling husband. I wanted to let you know how sorry I'm feeling for you and I'm keeping you in my prayers.

Your husband is now in heaven beside god and the beautiful angels. He is in peace and safe. He will be watching over you and always love you. He will always be by you. He has never left for ever.

His time was called and I'm happy to know he has closed his eyes doing something that was close to his heart and made him happy by touching the spirit of the earth who is water. Water of mother the earth is a wonderful cleansing for the soul.

Remember his laugh and all the joy you both shared. They will help you.

Zoubir and I once had a long conversation about the nature of orbs, the strange phenomena that had begun showing up in low-light photos taken by compact digital cameras with built-in flash. Some theorists have explained the orbs as simply the result of the flash decreasing the angle of light reflection to the lens, thus increasing the camera's ability to capture the light reflected off normally sub-visible particles such as dust. Others consider the orbs to be a manifestation of spirits from another dimension. Zoubir, who adhered to the latter explanation, attached a photograph he had taken in his garden at night that showed what appear to be shimmering translucent balls of light suspended in the air.

"*These are orbs from my garden,*" he wrote, "*spirits going from one dimension to another. When we die we never really died, we just keep traveling to our next life.*"

Gary would probably have scoffed at Zoubir's orbs, as he had in so many of our conversations about the notion of angels and the possibility of life after death. But I know he wouldn't have scoffed at the idea of remembering the laughter and joy in our lives. Perhaps in part because he didn't believe in heaven, he had been all the more determined to live his version of the good life, which incorporated the Italian notion of *il buon vivere*, savoring the pleasures life has to offer, with a commitment to extending those pleasures and privileges to the many rather than the few, and to ensuring that technology was used as a means of serving human-determined ends.

Gary was a gadget-loving techie, but he was also what he would have called a neo-humanist, a phrase he liked that was used by Italian poet Salvatore Quasimodo in his acceptance speech when he received the Nobel Prize for Literature in 1959. Elsewhere, Quasimodo had written, "Culture has always repulsed the recurrent threat of barbarism, even the latter was heavily armed and seething with confused ideologies."

Gary and I became aficionados of the "Slow Food" movement, which began in Italy in opposition to a McDonald's that opened in Rome's magnificent Piazza di Spagna and had grown to encompass such things as Slow Cities. We were delighted when a Slow Food chapter, or *convivia*, as the gatherings are known in Italy, opened in Austin, and advocated such local specialties as barbecue.

Gary wrote an essay about technology and the "good life," in which he described the Slow movement as a "struggle for the soul of life and for the preservation of life's most basic pleasures amidst a global trend pointing to increased competition, consumerism, stress, and 'hurriedness'."

Hurriedness, however, with all its stresses and demands, was already there at my house. Early in the evening, as the online bulletins and shock-laden emails were already spreading, one of my friends who came to the house, an editor at the *Austin American-Statesman*, told me gently that there would be an article about

Gary in the next day's paper and that it would be posted online in a few hours. Would I be willing to talk to the reporter who was preparing the article?

It was a reversal of roles I could never have imagined. I had met countless deadlines in the past under extreme circumstances, calling in stories from remote places and summarizing complicated events in a matter of half an hour. But how could I possible sum up Gary's life in 500 words or less?

I thought about the many times I had interviewed those who had been suddenly stricken by terrible events—evacuees from Katrina who had left family members behind in the flood or who had watched an elderly relative die of a heart attack; friends and relatives of those who died in the Columbia space shuttle disaster; survivors of the final days at the Branch Davidian compound near Waco. I marveled now at their willingness to talk about their losses. Maybe because everything was still so raw and fresh for me, and so unexamined, I was far less willing and able to cooperate with an inquiring reporter than those shell-shocked survivors I had interviewed.

I could hardly muster the bare facts. As for how Gary died, I said that I thought he must have suffered a heart attack, even though no one knew for sure at that time, and my wild surmise, which found its way into all of Gary's obits, would prove to be wrong. The next day my friend Ruth Pennebaker took on the task of writing Gary's obituary for the *Austin American-Statesman*. She did a far better job than I could have done. And it was our friend Pete Lewis who wrote the most moving remembrance of Gary a few days after his death.

In thinking about Gary's life, Pete quoted Henry Thoreau: "I went to the woods because I wished to live deliberately, to front only the essential facts of life, and see if I could not learn what it had to teach, and not, when I came to die, discover that I had not lived." Similarly, Pete observed, "Gary went to the river because he lived deliberately. He learned what life had to teach, and he became a great teacher."

Thoreau also observed that in contrast to living deliberately, "most men lead lives of quiet desperation." Gary's close friend Grant Thomas reminded me of that quote when he came by to talk one evening shortly after Gary died. As we thought about all the good times Gary and I and he and his wife Margot had enjoyed together, and about the way Gary loved to share his passions, from good wine and opera and Apple computers to kayaking, Grant concluded that Gary had lived a life of "quiet exuberance."

Chapter 8

CPR of the Soul

By midnight, everyone had gone, and all was quiet. I registered numbly that my friends were leaving, and I was relieved to be alone to let my grief take its course. But at that stage, what I felt more than the presence of grief was the sudden and complete absence of meaning. Without Gary, nothing mattered, and I couldn't imagine that anything would ever matter again. It was Gary who had always known how to pull me out of bad moods, anxiety or gloom, handing me the perfect book, selecting the wildest rock 'n' roll song or most sublime opera aria to play on the stereo, sending me the funniest email, pouring me a glass of wine as the best antidote to whatever ailed me.

We dealt with disasters together. On the morning of 9/11, Gary called me from his car on the way to UT, telling me to turn on the television. As I did so, I saw the image of the second plane plunging into the tower, and I told Gary, "It's the end of the world. Come home." Through our tears, we decided to go to New York to volunteer at Nino's, a restaurant adjacent to Ground Zero that had survived the devastation and was serving emergency workers.

While we were there, we met a group of former drug addicts from a rehab ranch in Texas who had driven a truck laden with frozen meat and a big barbecue smoker to the site to cook brisket and chicken for the workers. Their Texas flag, which they had hoisted over the barbecue cooker, had gotten tattered and smoke-stained, so Gary and I searched the garment district until we found a big Texas flag to replace it. I still have the picture of Gary and me posing with one of the cooks, with the brand new flag flying next to the ruins of the twin towers.

Now it was just me, and disaster had hit home. I was in my own Ground Zero. I could remember clearly the desperate messages left on fences and walls near the Twin Towers that I had cried over, the weathered photos of missing loved ones that bespoke despair, the names written in chalk beside the firehouses. But I had never really known in my own heart such complete silence, such utter darkness, such profound emptiness. So this is how it feels to be at the bottom of the ocean. Now I know. My world had gone blank.

I was still sitting in Gary's usual chair at the end of the dining table, next to the fireplace. I hadn't budged for hours, even to bid my guests goodbye. I hadn't taken the dogs for their customary bedtime walk, as Gary and I had done together for so many years. I hadn't taken a shower, brushed my teeth, or done any of my usual nightly routines. I simply couldn't move. A few days earlier I had plugged in the Christmas lights that outlined the window, and I didn't think to unplug them. For the next few days, I would hardly stir from this vantage point that allowed me to see out the window to spot anyone who might be arriving. And it would also allow someone arriving at night to see me seated there, my silhouette outlined against the light.

I now think I might have been reenacting a scene of comforting if illusory domesticity from the otherwise forgettable film *Marley and Me* that had touched a strong chord in Gary. The exhausted husband, played by Owen Wilson, arrives home in the evening and looks through the living room window to see his wife smiling as she plays with the dog that had given them so much trouble. For the moment, all is well. The window frames an iconic but fleeting image of home and happiness.

The Christmas lights, though, probably evoked another remembered movie scenario. Gary had told me years earlier about a scene of familial comfort from Ingmar Bergman's *Fanny and Alexander* that had affected him deeply. In that scene, the children are caught up in a festive Christmas celebration that belies the sorrows and conflict later to come. I think Gary linked that scene and what followed to a terrible loss that he experienced as a child. His mother died in an automobile accident when he was two and a half, and he had endured a difficult childhood and stormy adolescence with a strict stepmother with whom he was always at odds. They had since reconciled, but the scars had remained.

I wondered if Gary considered our marriage as harmonious as Bergman's softly lit Christmas scenario that he treasured. I know he wanted it to be. He told me over and over, in multiple ways, that he loved being married to me. He would inscribe his carefully selected Valentine's Day, anniversary and birthday cards with pledges that he would love me forever. He might have been described as "uxorious," a husband who doted excessively on his wife, though I sometimes felt that he loved his vision of me rather than the often troublesome reality.

"My main job in life," he told me the month before he died, "is to make you happy." I wished now that I had heard what must have been a certain frustration in those words. I was not always a happy camper, particularly when I was dissatisfied with my work. The world of journalism was crumbling, and I was struggling, not always successfully, to reinvent myself. He had an impossible job, then, if it was my happiness that hung in the balance. I sensed that he often felt I wasn't living up to my "potential," whatever that may have been. He would tell me on occasion that an article I was working on was "beneath my talents" and that I spent too much time laboring over a piece for a minor publication. "Get in gear," he had said more than once, with a certain military impetus in his voice.

Gary, I would have gotten in gear, had I known which way to go.

Already I was feeling guilty that Gary had done more than his share of the heavy lifting in our marriage, and I had no chance of changing the balance. He cherished our modest little house, which had undergone several home-improvement upgrades after we bought it. He took a fanatical interest in creating warm and subtle lighting to make it as inviting as possible. He was much more of a homebody than I was. He even picked out color-coordinated rugs for us from websites he discovered. He made quite the picture of the ideal husband, the domesticated warrior coming home with a bag of groceries he had picked out to cook dinner for us. At times, I wondered if things were just too perfect, whether I deserved Gary. Who could have imagined a husband like this?

Guilty or not, I always relished the moment he came through the front door, the recycled bags from the HEB grocery swinging against his leg. Our dogs Zip and Molly would go to the door moments before he arrived, their Gary-sensing radar far more accurate than mine. And no matter what I was doing or working on at the moment, I felt my heart flutter every time he came home to me, for the 16 years we were married.

And so, that terrible night, as the light from the computer screen dimmed, I was sitting in the semi-darkness, simply unable to acknowledge that Gary would never come through that door again. And that was when I heard a sound just outside the door. I thought at first that one of my friends had forgotten something and had come back to retrieve it. Was there someone knocking on the door? But there were no other noises, no slamming of car doors or motors running, no voices. No lights were visible from my chair at the dining table.

The sound at the door was not like anything I had heard before. It wasn't a knock or a tap. It was as though something—or someone—had pressed gently but insistently against the door. It felt as though a sudden gust of wind had shaken the door, or as I realized later, as though something feathered had brushed its wings against it. I also heard a sound that was something like a moan, something unearthly and muffled, like a sound coming through a tunnel.

Already, his spirit was on its way to you.

Our dog Molly had gone to the door, her tail wagging, with the expectant look she always had when Gary came home from work. With strangers, she would be barking ferociously. But there she sat, her ears perked, looking up at the door, waiting. And then she stood up, looking intently at something through the window panes framed in the top half of the door. I ran to the door, flung it open and stepped outside. "Gary!" I shouted. I couldn't see anything but the empty moonlit path.

Gary's body was resting somewhere in the Guatemalan highlands. That much I knew. But some part of him, no more tangible than the wind, had found a way home to me.

That night I slept on Gary's side of the bed, still dressed in the clothes I had been wearing that day. I tried to sink into the imagined outline of his body on the mattress. That way, I thought, I wouldn't keep reaching for him. For the few minutes I was able to sleep, I dreamed that he made sweet, tender, but almost frantic love to me. And I awoke in the early morning to something else that alerted my senses. It was an aroma of wetness that I associated with swimming in rivers, of the muddy/dank way bathing suits smell when they've been left out too long before being hung up to dry. I wondered crazily if someone had brought wet clothes into the room from the washing machine. And then I realized that this would be the way a clothed body would smell after it had been pulled from the river. The odor of dampness was there for only a moment before it was gone.

He has never left for ever.

I got out of bed, still dressed from the day before, and took the dogs for a brief walk, putting one foot shakily in front of the other. I must have looked like a drunk trying to prove her sobriety. I didn't get far, but the dogs did their business. As we came back to the front walkway, the sun was warming my back, and it created a pattern of shadows on the walkway from the leaves that were waving in the breeze. I looked down, and the shadows were pulsating in the shape of beating hearts. I thought I heard a whisper as the shadows throbbed. "I love you, I love you, I love you," I heard them say.

I came inside and breathed on one of the windowpanes in the door, then drew the outline of a heart in the fogged-up glass. Inside the heart, I wrote Gary + Carol, like a kid carving initials on a tree. For days, I could breathe on the glass and still see the outline of the heart and our names. It was as though our love would survive as long as I had breath.

Taking my now accustomed seat in Gary's chair at the dining table, I was in a kind of trance, dazed, still clinging to the whispered evidence of love that I realized would now endure in a different form. And what happened next is difficult to describe because I was so overwhelmed and a little frightened. I found my head falling back and my mouth falling open. My breathing slowed and almost stopped as I felt a powerful inrushing of breath from some other source into my body. I felt that I could hardly hold so much breath, that I was too small and frail a vessel for so much life force.

Later it would occur to me that I must have looked something like Bernini's St. Theresa in Ecstasy, an extraordinary sculpture I had seen several years earlier in Rome. Bernini's enraptured saint has fallen back with her mouth open in such ecstasy of surrender that some of Bernini's prim contemporaries condemned the work as too sensual. Though I was far from a saint or mystic, I think that what I felt may have been at least something like what St. Theresa had described as being filled with the spirit of the divine. Inspiration, in its archaic form, meant to breathe life into. Theresa, who knew that she might not believed, described her experience of yielding to the divine as being pierced by an arrow that was also a "caressing of love so sweet" that she prayed to God "to make him experience it who may think I am lying."

For me, however, it wasn't divine inspiration or religious ecstasy that I had experienced, but what I came to think of as an infusion of Gary's essence, a kind of CPR of the soul that was meant to bring me back to life. It wasn't until much later that I thought of the very different scene of his friends' futile efforts to breathe life back into his body.

Was this something supernatural? Had I merely imagined it? I didn't ask those questions at the time because, like so many out-of-the-ordinary things to follow, it was simply something that happened and that I experienced as real. The skeptic in me was observing but not judging. I knew Gary himself would have been skeptical, had someone described the scene to him.

As I began to breathe more normally, I still felt broken. But I also felt weirdly strong and capable, as though I had taken on some of Gary's strengths and capabilities. The only analogy I could come up with was Popeye gulping a can of spinach and watching his spindly arms start to bulge. For a time I became calm, patient and, as I was to discover in coming days, surprisingly good at figuring out how to get things done on computers—all qualities that were Gary's and not mine. I became a fearless public speaker, despite my previous fear and loathing of speaking in public. And though those strengths wouldn't last, they took me through the next difficult weeks and months, when I would find myself doing things I didn't know how to do or that I would have struggled with before Gary's death.

I felt that the best part of me had died along with Gary, and that my brain had been permanently altered by grief. I wasn't all there. But I sometimes felt stronger than I ever had before. However deluded that momentary sense of strength may have been, it helped to compensate for the times when I simply couldn't do some of the most basic things I used to be able to do. I found it nearly impossible to compose more than a sentence or two, to read more than a page of a book, to cook anything but a microwave dinner or to eat more than a bite of food of any kind. The sporadic bursts of strength and strange aptitudes helped to compensate for the bouts of paralyzing fear and hopelessness that made me want to crawl into a cave and just give it up.

Chapter 9

The Hawk, the Meteors and the Wren

I spent the rest of the day after Gary's death seated at my now customary place at the dining table, getting up only to greet newly arrived guests. I was on the phone intermittently to Guatemala, negotiating with Roberto Valiente of Funerales Reforma, the funeral director in Guatemala City who had been recommended by David Chang, the American consul. Roberto, whose English was invariably glib and upbeat, assured me that he would take care of getting Gary's body to Guatemala City from the morgue at the small hospital in the regional capital of Copan.

Gary's remains would be embalmed in Guatemala City, but there were various formalities that had to be carried out before his body could be flown back to the United States, including the wiring of a considerable amount of money, a sum that was to keep rising day by day. Steve Smith had remained in Guatemala, vowing to stay there until Gary's body was on its way home. Ben Kvanli had left to take Barry Day to the airport in Cancun and to pick up the group that was scheduled to continue the kayaking trip, the segment that I was to have joined.

My parents had driven up from their home in Lake Jackson, near the Gulf Coast, as had my sister Ellen, who had come up separately because she would have to drive back to Lake Jackson later that day to take care of her children. My parents decided to stay at their cabin in the Hill Country that night. Ellen told me later that during the drive up to Austin, a red-tailed hawk had appeared suddenly and swooped down towards her car, lightly bumping the windshield, then headed back towards my parents' car. It brushed the windshield with its wings before flying off, apparently unharmed. It was the most dramatic appearance so far of the hawks and other ad hoc emissaries, as I came to think of them, that would continue to appear on my journey.

"Hawks mate for life," Ellen later wrote me in an email. "Gary will love you forever."

He has never left for ever.

Had I enlisted my friends, family and hapless feathered recruits from the animal world in my semi-deranged view of a natural world that responded to my grief and had something to say about what had happened to me?

This was not the first unusual appearance of hawks in my life. Ellen and I had talked before about the phenomena of animal totems, as I began exploring our Native American heritage in preparation for a book I never got around to writing. Though my father seemed determined to ignore his Choctaw ancestry, I felt that I had inherited a powerful connection to nature through him. Even before I began learning some of the Choctaw stories about animal guides, I had concluded that the hawk might be my guardian animal, as the beautiful raptors had begun appearing at significant times in my life.

I remembered in particular one afternoon, as I sat on a back-yard bench agonizing over whether to leave a job that I had grown to detest but depended on for health insurance. I looked up to see a large red-tailed hawk perched on a branch a few feet away. He simply sat there gazing at me for a long while, and I remember feeling a sense of comfort that if I should decide to wing it and leave the job, I'd have a safe landing. And so I did, though not giving any credit at the time to the hawk, in part because I wasn't sure whether the hawk had really had anything to say to me, and in part because there was no way to fit a helpful hawk into my conversations with Gary.

Gary hadn't put much credence in my forays into my Native American heritage, and it had actually been a point of considerable difference between us. I had begun attending a series of annual dialogues in New Mexico between physicists and Native American scientists and elders, in which I found a meaningful way to look at a world that included both the leading edge of particle physics and Native American wisdom. It was a worldview in which I felt at home. For a while, I tried to find various ways to explain to Gary why I felt so deeply connected to the natural world. I was always trying to find some shred of scientific evidence to back up my inklings and intuitions.

Eventually I gave up when I realized that Gary felt uneasy, even vaguely threatened, when I talked about things that couldn't be explained in a completely rational way. He told me once it was because it was something we couldn't share. But now, here were these insistent hawks that just kept coming, as though they were trying to deliver a message. Would Gary have shrugged them off? Probably. Could I shrug them off? And if they had something to say, would I hear it? Would I know what it all meant?

By late morning that day a succession of friends and neighbors began arriving, and my house was soon full of food and orchids. The two co-pastors of Central Presbyterian Church came by, as did a number of Gary's colleagues from the LBJ School. The school had already set up an online site for Gary's students, friends and admirers to leave condolences. Seated next to my parents, who were dressed in their Sunday best, was the firebrand economist Jamie Galbraith, who had arrived with a gift of special Chinese tea. He confided that Gary had been the key person for evaluating policy and getting things done at the LBJ School, something that I'm not sure Gary fully appreciated when he was alive.

The crowded living room had fallen silent for only a moment when my elderly neighbor Elizabeth Sanchez burst through the front door, breathless, wearing a housecoat and slippers. In her hurry, Elizabeth, who was nearing 90, had even forgotten to put in her teeth, she said, but she wanted to get here as quickly as she could. Gary and I had greeted her for countless mornings on walks through the neighborhood with our dogs, when she would be bustling around her yard tending to her latest rescue animals. She had told us a few weeks earlier that she had finally whittled down her collection of dogs to a noisy chihuahua and a small, shivering dachshund.

Most of that day remains in a kind of haze of hugs and tears. A little after sunset, everyone had gone home. The phone had finally stopped ringing for a while when I got a call from my father, who had arrived at the family cabin and gone for a walk on the gravel road to the dramatic point where the hilly spines of the Devil's Backbone formation come into view. He said that during the walk he was reminded of a similar moonlit night many years earlier when Gary and I came for a visit to the cabin. He had seen something unusual then that he wanted to tell me about now.

It was Gary's first time to meet my parents. We had been living in Boston then, and I had just gone through a painful divorce, not knowing how my parents would greet the new man in my life. That date marked a spectacular night of the shooting stars, when the annual Perseid meteor shower delivered about 350 meteors per hour, more than three times the normal number. My dad and Gary retrieved reclining chaise lounges from the porch and placed them in the middle of the road just down from the cabin, where they could watch the celestial show without having to crane their necks. I remember watching them from the front porch of the cabin, as they talked companionably and pointed out things to each other in the glowing sky, knowing that they would be good friends from then on.

"We saw a pair of meteors cross the sky together, side by side, like they were joined by an invisible bond," said my dad. His voice cracked as he described it. "I've never seen anything like it. And as I remember it now, those meteors were you and Gary going through life together."

Knowing my father, I wasn't surprised that the cosmos had revealed something that night so long ago about the nature of love, something that Gary's death and a walk in the dark had prompted him to remember. But it wasn't until weeks after Gary's death that my sister told me what happened when she arrived home in Lake Jackson after the long drive from Austin. As she prepared to leave my house, I had impulsively handed her Gary's favorite leather bomber jacket to give to her son Chase, for whom Gary had become a would-be mentor.

Gary had tried, without great success, to get Chase interested in kayaking, but he hadn't given up. He felt it was a way to bond with his young nephew, who was obsessed at the time with video games. When Ellen entered her home, carrying the jacket, she found a wren flying around inside, something that had never happened before. The bird darted from room to room, then into Chase's bedroom, where it landed on Chase's pillow. It perched for a few moments. When she opened the front door, it flew back out into the night. She wondered what significance a wren might have and discovered after an online search that wren feathers had been used by some Native American tribes as a charm against drowning.

Chapter 10

The Age of Miracles

E arly the next morning I was back on the phone to Guatemala, already tired and discouraged. Two friends had volunteered gallantly to deal with wiring the money to retrieve Gary's body, and the funeral home in Austin I had chosen, Weed-Corley-Fish, would help to negotiate with Funerales Reforma to iron out the details. I had an appointment later that day with one of their representatives to discuss arrangements in Austin once Gary's remains arrived. As it became evident, however, that things could drag on indefinitely, Bob Hutchings, Dean of the LBJ School, had also begun communicating with Roberto Valiente in his calm but forceful diplomatic way. But I still had no idea when Gary's body would be home.

I set down my iPhone. I was still unfamiliar with it and a little in awe of it, as I had just gotten it a couple of months earlier. Gary had loaded it with apps and music, but I hadn't done anything with it other than make phone calls and laboriously send text messages with lots of silly mistakes. I was always a step or two behind the latest applications and upgrades that Gary had insisted on with all our computers, and I had never used the iTunes mode to access the songs and albums Gary had loaded for me.

He had been making music collections for me ever since we first met, when I was off in New Orleans in 1992, working on a book while he was in Boston, where we both lived at the time. We were just getting to know each other, and he had sent me tapes of his favorite songs with annotated comments worthy of album jackets and recollections of times he had actually seen the artists perform live.

"Marvin Gaye's 'What's Goin' On,'" he wrote, "is more than just a casual addition. I have listened to it several times recently and my opinion has been reaffirmed that it's one of the greatest albums ever. Maybe even the best pop-soul recording of all time. I remember when it was released in 1972 and it was such an incredible breakthrough it left me speechless. It has it all—the themes: race, war, poverty, even the environment. I listen to it and I miss Marvin, the genius, the soul king, the drug-addled sex maniac, the explosive voice of 'Hitchhike' or the cream-smooth voice of 'Grapevine.' But 'What's Goin' On' is the masterpiece that a million artists and singers would die to have done. So listen to it again in the Reagan-Bush America and remember this was recorded 20 years ago. Amazing. Marvin, I miss you. God sang with your voice."

Over the years, Gary would burn music CDs to give our friends for birthdays and special occasions, and he was famous for his carefully composed party tapes. I was especially fond of one collection he had put together just before the 2004 election. I remember blasting John Fogerty's "Fortunate Son," the first cut on the CD, while driving back from Houston after poll-watching on election day, before the results were in and hopes were still high that the Bush-Cheney era was over. "It ain't me," I shouted out, rolling down my window. "It ain't me. I ain't no millionaire's son. I ain't no fortunate one."

Gary always seemed to know just the right song for the moment. He thought of music as a way to celebrate or commiserate, to connect people and to celebrate life. He loved music more than anyone I had ever known, and he also loved the very latest technology for listening to it and sharing it. He had tried to convince me that I was missing out on all the ways the iPhone could be used, and I had responded with my usual passive resistance to his enthusiasm for the nifty little gadget.

And so my sadly under-used iPhone was lying there on the dining table, unplugged, beside my computer, when it suddenly made a jolting noise as though it had just been plugged in. I looked down, and it had switched out of telephone mode. I looked closer. The phone had switched to the iTunes music mode and had apparently chosen a song on its own.

It was "The Age of Miracles," a song by Mary Chapin Carpenter. On the small iPhone screen was the cover image of the album of the same name. It portrays a woman behind the wheel of a convertible, looking carefree, her hair blowing in the wind, and a packed bag in the seat beside her. She seems to be leaving behind a columned white house behind a picket fence and heading somewhere into the future.

In that moment of stunned surprise, I thought, My God, she looks more than a little like me. But my feelings of astonishment and wonder died quickly, chastened by grief. "I'll never be that woman," I said to myself dully. I couldn't imagine myself ever heading so brightly into the future, into a new life, leaving the old one behind. For one thing, I had never really liked convertibles.

Before I could filter my thoughts, I wondered why Gary had chosen this song for me, a song about the possibility of miracles, when he had told me so vehemently that there was no such thing. Just a month or two before he died, we had talked one night about the possibility of miracles, and I reminded him that he had already been the beneficiary of one, when he had survived that terrible accident on Bee Cave Road that should have killed him. Another University of Texas professor, in fact, had died in a crash at that same spot just weeks later. I reminded Gary of yet another incident of unlikely survival a few years earlier, when our dog Zip was hit by a truck.

We had just returned from Italy, and Gary had taken Zip out for a walk and had let him off the leash, only to watch in horror as he darted into the path of a red Dodge Ram that came zooming around the corner. The driver slammed on the brakes, stopping with a front wheel on top of Zip. Gary had frantically waved the driver to back up, and he hurried home carrying Zip's limp body, certain that he was dead. By the time he set Zip down on the floor, the little dog started wagging his tail. We drove him to the veterinary emergency room in town, and after examining him, the vet said that his only injury was a dislocated hip.

My theory for why Zip survived had to do with a visit we had made to Assisi during our trip to Italy. I wanted to pay homage to Saint Francis, whom I revered for his love of animals, and Gary was willing to go along, mostly, I think, because of the beautiful Giotto frescoes that adorn the 13th-century Basilica de San Francesco. If art was involved, I could usually get Gary to suspend his aversion to anything religious.

We climbed down into the crypt beneath the lower section of the church and both lit candles. I was surprised that Gary joined me, but in retrospect I concluded that he had been willing to light a candle in honor of St. Francis because we had just enjoyed one of the best meals of our lives at La Boca del Lupo in the town of Gubbio, which was filled with images of St. Francis alongside the wolf he was said to have befriended. It could have been those candles, I told Gary, that had saved Zip.

Gary was not willing, however, to acknowledge that miracles might be possible, and I felt frustrated, as I often did when we had discussions about anything pertaining to spirituality. I had grown increasingly frustrated about his inability to see my point of view, however "out there" he thought it might be. I had a Ph.D., damn it. I wasn't an idiot. "Those events don't fit into your picture of the world," I said. "You don't have a place to put them. So maybe you could put them away in some compartment. And just keep collecting things that don't fit and put them into that compartment of the odd and inexplicable. And maybe someday your picture of the world will shift."

I was aware I wasn't making my case very well. I knew that I should be able to hold up my side of the rational vs. mystical point of view, but Gary was a brilliant debater, and I wasn't quite sure that my own picture of the world, though it was full of hawks with possible messages, would actually accommodate a dog being saved by St. Francis. Nevertheless I pressed on stubbornly, as we began talking about whether human beings were still evolving, or whether we were stuck in a rut and doomed to keep fighting wars and using up the earth's resources until we did ourselves in.

Gary said that he didn't think human nature was ultimately capable of basic change or transformation, but that it was important to keep fighting the good fight anyhow. My position was that it was possible for humans to learn and change our ways. I felt that connecting deeply with the natural world not only brought a feeling of belonging in the universe, but it was also a necessary step in coping with a world that was heating up and running out of clean water to drink. If we don't evolve, I said, we'll die. I remember telling him that I just wanted to be able to climb up the mountain and look over to the other side, grandiosely evoking Moses and Martin Luther King.

"I want to live long enough to see whether we'll get there," I said.

He looked at me with a touch of impatience, shaking his head in familiar skepticism. We clearly differed.

And now here was this song, "The Age of Miracles," which seemed a bittersweet coda to that discussion. I knew I wasn't strong enough emotionally to actually listen to the song, much as I wanted to. I feared that I would fall apart and not be able to put myself back together. So I looked up the lyrics and sat there, mystified.

In the first verses of the song, Carpenter conjures up familiar images of doom—Greenland melting and the West on fire—and asks whether we, as humans, will "get up that hill." But by the last verse, she evokes an image of affirmation, of monks in Burma walking barefoot in the rain in protest so that the world could bear witness. The chorus changes subtly from question to answer.

"It seems we're just standing still," she repeats, then shifts.

But one day we'll ride up that hill
in the age of miracles.
There's one on the way.

Was she suggesting that miracles are possible?

In an interview after the album came out, Carpenter admitted, "I didn't mean it in the religious sense. I'm allergic to that language... In the context of the song lyric, I'm saying that if you're lucky enough to believe that miracles exist, then they come—because you make your own luck, your own beauty, your own joy. You can try to pull it from other sources, see it in the world, but, really, it starts with you."

So she was begging the question. We make our own miracles, she was suggesting, with a little help—from the inspiration we draw from the courage of others and from the wondrous resilience of the natural world. Okay, good. Of course. Maybe Gary would have agreed, with a little arm-twisting. He loved Mary Chapin Carpenter.

For me, immersed in grief and desolation, with no hope for the future, the sudden appearance of this particular song on this particular device with this particular message at this particular time seemed to ask the question about miracles and then answer it in a way that Gary, who loved useful and elegant technology, like iPhones, could have framed it. And sent it, somehow.

Maybe I had been right about the question of miracles, it seemed to say. That is, if I kept my eyes open and my hopes up. And didn't get too carried away. It wasn't Steve Jobs who sent me that song. Obviously. Had some random algorithm conjured it up out of the ether? What were the odds? Gary had already shown with the seductive tapes he sent me in New Orleans that he knew how to love me from afar. So....

That evening, Ruth Pennebaker called to discuss details of Gary's obituary, which she was finishing up, and she said casually, "I had a kind of a dream. Well, it wasn't exactly a dream. It was more like something I saw as I was dozing off."

This isn't like Ruth, I thought immediately. Her sharp wit is often directed at anything that smacks of wacky spirituality.

"I saw Gary," she said. "He was dressed in white and driving a white convertible. He was bathed in white light and driving right alongside you. You were driving a convertible too. I'm not sure if you could see him, but there he was, right beside you."

Chapter 11

The Cloud of Unknowing

The next morning, as I was trudging along during the daily walk down to the lake with the dogs, a habit I was trying with some difficulty to maintain, I looked up to see Mike the Treat Man, as Gary and I called him. Mike, who is originally from Boston, carries treats in his pockets that he tosses to dogs he encounters on his walks in the neighborhood. Zip and Molly had already spotted him, and were dragging me in his direction. Mike, who can be a bit taciturn, beamed brightly when he saw me and opened his arms wide as he came towards us, his jacket flapping. He enveloped me in a huge hug.

"What can you say?" he muttered, as I tried to keep my composure.

He held my shoulders and looked me in the eye. "Don't get isolated," he said sternly, then ambled on.

"I'll do my best," I said, realizing even then that Mike's abbreviated advice was right on the mark. Three of my neighbors, as it happened, had died alone in their houses during the past year, all three heavy drinkers, one of them aged only 50, and I had sworn that would never happen to me.

As I arrived home, the phone was ringing, and I almost didn't answer. But it was my mother, whom I had told about my otherworldly experience at the front door the night of Gary's death. I didn't know what she'd make of it, as she is deeply religious but steers away from things that are at all "woo-woo." She asked matter-of-factly if Gary had come by yet to see me this morning.

"No," I said, puzzled and a little alarmed.

"Well, he wants to tell you something," she said. "He wanted me to tell you that he had a wonderful time on the trip to Guatemala and that he is thankful that you let him go on the trip."

Before I could even begin to process this news, my friends began to arrive two-by-two and then singly. When Sarah Bird, the novelist, arrived along with the designer Nancy Mims, they had hardly gotten through the door when Sarah declared, "You wouldn't believe the hawk we just saw. It was amazing."

A while later, Jennifer Vickers and Carol Burton came up the walk with the smell of freshly baked pumpkin bread wafting from Carol's shopping bag. The bread smelled good, and I wished that I could eat, but my body was still refusing food. I was sitting at my usual spot at the dining table, and they joined me at the table. My sessions with friends were beginning to take on a kind of séance configuration, I thought ruefully.

I explained to them that I seemed to be operating out of only one side of my brain, the right side, which processes such subjective things as music, emotions, images and intuition, while the objective left side, which categorizes and analyzes, seemed to have shut down.

"So it's like *Stroke of Insight*," said Jennifer.

She had just watched a TED speech by Jill Bolte Taylor, the neuroscientist who wrote a memoir about her injuries and recovery from a massive stroke in the left hemisphere of her brain. Taylor had ultimately regarded her stroke as a kind of revelation and, astonishingly, as a blessing. When the cells in the left hemisphere her brain lost function, they lost the capacity to inhibit the cells in the right hemisphere, and she shifted into what she described as an unfiltered consciousness of the present moment. She was in "La-la land," which sounded remarkably like my own present state, though the euphoria of the eternal present that she described had only come to me in brief glimpses, and it was always tinged with pain.

If I were living in right-brained La-la land, the land of unfiltered perceptions and impulses, that could explain the ADD, the inability to read or write, and the embarrassing impulse to blurt out

I love you indiscriminately to people I hardly knew. I had none of the usual social defenses or filters.

"You're permeable," my friend Sarah Bird had observed. "I was like that when I was pregnant."

I was so permeable, I thought, I must have been almost transparent, like Caspar the Ghost. Oddly, though, people seemed to be responding to me in kind. My right-brained impulsiveness and openness seemed to spark right-brained responses in friends and strangers alike.

I wondered if my right-brained aberration might be something more, perhaps even a hitherto unrecognized survival mechanism for grief. And perhaps something even more than that. Shifting to a different side of the brain might allow the bereaved a recognition of ultimate reality that would impede us in ordinary life. The notion that as humans we might all experience a grief-induced stroke of insight when confronted with death was a more satisfying explanation for what was happening to me than a concept like "denial."

"You know," said Jennifer, "Somehow, thinking about Gary lifts me up in a cloud of joy."

I looked at her, startled. I was reminded not only of the soul-stirring gospel quartet, The Mighty Clouds of Joy, but also of "The Cloud of Unknowing," the anonymous work of Christian mysticism written in the 14th century that became the spiritual guide to contemplative prayer in the late Middle Ages—and more recently to the contemporary practice known as centering prayer. The author urges supplicants to abandon all preconceived notions and beliefs or "knowledge" about God and to surrender the mind to the realm of "unknowingness":

"For He can well be loved, but he cannot be thought. By love he can be grasped and held, but by thought, neither grasped nor held."

I had been practicing centering prayer for several years, though I had yet to experience what the anonymous author described as the "cloud of forgetting" that leads to a spiritual union between the heart of the individual and the divine.

"Struggle to pierce that darkness above you," he had urged, "and beat on that thick cloud of unknowing with a sharp dart of longing love, and do not give up, whatever happens."

How ironic, I thought bitterly, if it would take lop-sided, right-brained grief to get me there.

Chapter 12

The Thin Places

My last visitor that day was my new friend Elizabeth, a writer whom I had met only a few months earlier, but with whom I had bonded instantly. Elizabeth, who is mostly of Irish descent, but with some Cherokee blood in the mix, shared with me not only the experience of leaving academia to become a writer, but also the influence of Native American ancestors. And now we shared the experience of suddenly losing our husbands. Elizabeth, who is a tall, graceful woman who exudes the pioneer strength of her hills-and-hollers Tennessee forebears, would become my mentor in grief, and she was as steadfast and true as a lighthouse in a storm.

She arrived bringing three important gifts. Her first gift that day was a Celtic knot, a rope that was woven into an intricate pattern that had no discernible end or beginning. Known as the eternity or love knot, she explained, the knot represents the union of two souls by interweaving two individual strands into unbroken loops that intertwine and are inseparable from each other. The knot also symbolizes the never-ending cycle of life, she said, with its interwoven pattern that has no beginning or end. The knot quickly found a central spot on my makeshift bedroom altar.

Her second gift was a list of the practical issues and obstacles I would be encountering as a widow. After her first husband died many years earlier of a heart attack while out jogging, she had learned the hard way that dealing with legal and financial complications comes at a time when women are least able to cope. My situation was going to be particularly complicated, she said, because Gary had not left a will. She warned me, prophetically, that insurance companies, which are so happy to accept premiums, are notoriously reluctant to pay off when the policy comes due. I would cling hard to that list over the next weeks and months when I felt I was about to succumb to bureaucratic cruelty and bungling.

The third and most important gift was one that was less tangible but which would actually be more lasting. When I described my bewilderment and wonder at some of the inexplicable things that had been happening after Gary's death, she nodded knowingly.

"Oh, yes. You have been in the thin places."

I had never heard the term, which had been first used by early pagan Celts and later by Christians to describe locales where the distance between heaven and earth, between the visible and invisible worlds, seems to "thin" or disappear. In the "thin places," according to the old wisdom, there is the lifting of a veil, and one can catch a glimpse of a transcendent reality.

Some places, I thought, must be thinner than others. My chair at the dining table had improbably become a thin place. I imagined, however, that the spot on the Cahabon where Gary died must have been one of the thinnest of places. As Pete Lewis wrote, "He was there one minute, as full of life as any man can be, and gone the next. It was a beautiful stretch of river, his fellow kayakers said, the kind of place that seems almost sacred in its beauty and peacefulness. A few minutes earlier, they said, Gary was as happy as they had ever seen him. Heart attack? More likely, he just found himself in a place that was so close to heaven on earth that he just paddled on through."

Chapter 13

The Solstice

O n the overcast morning of December 21st, I was going over my newly annotated to-do list. *Notify social security. Fill out insurance forms. Hire lawyer. Decide on cremation vs. burial. Plan memorial service. Choose speakers, songs and musicians for service. Figure out how to get into Gary's password-blocked computer, which has all his emails and photos and which UT wants back. Tell UT to whistle Dixie about computer? Figure out how to print photos for display for memorial service. Clean out Gary's office at UT. Sell Apple stock to get money to reimburse friends for wiring money to Guatemala. Just keep going. Don't give up.*

I was dreading the solstice for a number of reasons. For one thing, it was the shortest and therefore the darkest day of the year. And this year the solstice coincided with the night of a full lunar eclipse, the first time this had happened since the year 1638. If things had gone as planned, I was to have been with Gary, gazing at the disappearing moon from the top of the pyramid at Tikal. Instead, his body was lying in a mortuary in Guatemala City, and the clouds were gathering in the Texas sky.

Steeped in gloom, I walked out onto the back deck to call Billie, our big Maine coon cat, when I noticed something red on the withered vine entwined on the lattice above a planter box that had been neglected since the first freeze back in November. It was a small Roma tomato that had ripened, unnoticed, on the shriveled brown vine. I had no idea how it had found nourishment from a seemingly dead vine. Several unseasonable freezes had long since killed all the other annual plants in the box and in my small garden. I plucked the bright red tomato and placed it on the bedroom altar that was getting more crowded by the day. Anomaly, I thought. Probably a better word for now than miracle.

When I went inside to check my email, I saw that there was a message from the ever-cheerful Roberto Valiente of Funerales Reforma. He had sent me an email with the tag "Itynerary," as though Gary were going on a guided tour. "So the remains are gonna arrive the 23th at 12:45 hours let me know if you have a doubt!" Gary's body would be loaded on a plane to Atlanta the next day, and it would remain there overnight to be loaded the following day onto a flight to Austin. The body, with all the paperwork I had been waiting for, including his official death certificate, would be met at the airport by a hearse from Weed-Corley-Fish. A kindly spokesman for the Austin funeral home told me that the bereaved don't usually go to the airport when remains arrive from abroad, and I wasn't sure whether I was up to greeting Gary's body coming home in a box.

Meanwhile, I decided I could at least face the moon and the stars on my own after dark. What was the worst that could happen? There would be no witnesses if I fell to pieces. Even after the sun went down, the temperature remained unusually balmy for a winter's night. I brought out a rickety chaise longue onto the back deck so that I could just lie there and look up at the sky, trying not to think too much about the night Gary and my dad watched the shooting stars. I just lay there, a totally inert and passive receptacle for any heavenly action that might come my way.

And there it was, the elusive moon, so big and luminous that it seemed closer to the earth than usual. I never thought I'd see the moon as beautiful as it was the night Gary and I saw the Alhambra by moonlight so many years ago and cried from the sublime beauty of it all. But this moon was a reddish-tinted stunner. My friends who live downtown told me later that they hadn't been able to see a thing because of the clouds, but out in the hills of East Jesus, at least from my vantage point, the heavens were more accommodating. The clouds were there, but every few minutes, they would part briefly. And each time they would part, a bigger portion of the moon would be gone, until it vanished from sight.

I finally fell asleep in the darkness. It was so good to sleep for once, and I let myself go. But when I woke again, the interfering, infernal clouds had parted, and there it was again, the moon whole again, craters and all. It looked a bit pale, though, from its experience of being eaten by the sun. So this is the way it's going to be, from now on, I thought. Long days and nights of dark, drab despair with moments of radiance breaking through the clouds. I don't think I actually felt comforted by this cosmic show of disappearance and return, which felt far too celestial to touch my wounded earthbound heart. But I did feel a kind of grudging acknowledgment of its beauty and inevitability. Yes, the light comes back. The cosmos gives us at least that much certainty. Something the ancients knew how to commemorate.

Before Gary's death, I thought of the solstice in a blithely poetic way, as a symbol of ending and renewal. As the pivotal point in the year, when darkness reaches its zenith and the light begins to return, it was central to mysteries of death and rebirth in many religions and cultures, including Christianity. In early November, I composed a meditation and prayer based on three Bible verses chosen by my church as readings for Advent, the season observed as a time of expectant waiting and preparation for the celebration of the nativity of Jesus at Christmas. In retrospect, what I wrote for the church bulletin seemed to foreshadow what was to come.

The verses: Psalm 124, Genesis 8:1-19, Romans 6:1-11

The leaves have fallen, and nights are getting colder. During advent, as we approach the darkest time of the year, when the earth tilts so willfully away from the sun, how can we be sure that the light that seems to diminish every day will return? How can we be sure that we will find our way out of our darkest hours?

We are reminded in Psalm 124 of other times of darkness, when the people of Israel were facing the prospect of utter defeat, which the psalmist likens to being drowned in a flood or torn apart by monstrous fangs. But in this Song of Ascents, the Israelites are rescued from that dire fate, and they escape deathly entrapment, like a bird from a snare. They fly away from defeat on wings of divine deliverance.

This recurring theme of hope and divine intervention harkens back to the eighth chapter of Genesis, in which a weary Noah contemplates the floodwaters that have covered his world. In that story, it is the wings of a dove that bring hope of an end to inundation and a return to the rhythms of the seasons. The dove that Noah sends out returns from its second flight with an olive branch, a sign that not just Noah and his family, but that all creatures, including the lowliest of the creeping things that make up the bounty of creation, will find a place in this new world.

And so it is in the sixth chapter of Romans, we are reminded that we, too, are promised a way out of death and a way into a new life. In Christ, the dove has returned with hope. The defeats and the shortcomings that can feel like floodwaters drowning us in despair will recede. The birth of Christ promises the return of light: not merely sunlight, but son-light.

Prayer:

Help us to remember in our darkest hours, when we feel overwhelmed with despair and a flood of bad news, that you have always provided us with a place of safety and shown us a way out. Dear Lord, help us to hold on to hope like the dove with the olive branch. Even when the world is at its darkest, your light will always be with us.

Chapter 14

A Hero's Homecoming

The morning after the solstice I received an email from Pete Lewis saying that he and a few other of Gary's male friends wanted to be at the airport when Gary's remains arrived the next day. "It's a guy thing," he said. He asked if I would mind and if I wanted to join them. "I guess it's like choosing the pallbearers," he said. Airport security needed to have names and IDs before allowing anyone on the tarmac. I said I did want to join them, and I asked Pete's wife Kathryn to join me. With Grant Thomas, Gary's paddling buddy Don Hudson, and our friends Jack Nokes and Amon Burton, that made seven of us.

The following morning, as I was going through some of Gary's things, I came across his well-worn green beret, one of the few remnants he had kept of his life in the military. He had stuffed it unceremoniously in a box with his stethoscope from his days as a Special Forces medic. It had been almost 35 years since he was released from duty from active duty, back in 1976, but I felt a strong impulse to bring the beret to the airport. Possibly, I was sensing some elliptical connection between his military service and the fact that he was coming home in the way that fallen soldiers come home. One thing the military does well is ritual, I thought, though Gary wouldn't be getting a salute with Taps, glinting medals and rifles firing into the air.

His experience in the army set Gary apart from most of his colleagues in academia, in part because it kept him from getting involved in the petty disputes and silly turf wars that seemed a mockery of the battlefield. And it gave him a unique perspective on technology. He had written an award-winning book called *Computers in Battle* that questioned the wisdom and effectiveness of high-technology weapons that lacked the human element, and he fought hard to defeat the Strategic Defense Initiative, known as Star Wars, that had so enthralled Ronald Reagan.

Most people who knew Gary, however, didn't even realize he had been in the military, though people he met who had been in the army could spot a fellow ex-soldier right away. He got along instantly with the retired multi-star generals as well as the soldiers on leave from the Iraqi war who came through the LBJ School.

I got an email from C.P. "Papa" Smith, one of Gary's students, a just-retired Green Beret who punctuated his message with epithets of grief and frustration that Gary had died. I called him on the telephone to follow up, and his grief was still pouring out.

"His life was too f---king short," he said angrily. "I want him around! It really pisses me off!"

Gary encouraged him to go to business school, said Smith, and had written the letter of recommendation that he was convinced got him accepted. When he would start having doubts or worries, he would stop by Gary's office.

"I can see him now pushing back from his desk and taking his glasses off. 'So what's up' he would ask."

I said I could picture that scene too.

"All losses are personal," replied Smith. "But this is a loss for the community."

Lodis Rhodes, Gary's closest friend at the LBJ School, and with whom Gary had worked on issues of the "digital divide" between the prosperous and poor in Austin, told me that their shared experience in the military had helped to strengthen the bond between them.

"Very rarely did we even talk about the military," he said, "but the notion of camaraderie, not based on bullshit, that's the most intimate kind of relationship between friends. You ask yourself

'Who is it that I would want guarding my back'? Gary would be the one I would trust ultimately. I wouldn't have to say a word."

Gary, whose quiet confidence belied the stereotypical image of the macho Green Beret, described his training in Special Forces as an exercise in learning leadership and strategic thinking, and he had changed the way I looked at the military. He was slow to anger and utterly cool in a crisis. His medical training had come in handy several times when I had been hurt or injured, and he had known what to do with a minimum of stress.

After I developed a blood clot following a boating accident, he deftly and gently administered daily shots in my thigh for a week, which kept me from having to stay in the hospital. Once, when I asked him the best strategy for self defense, should I be attacked, he showed me couple of simple moves to go for the attacker's eyes, throat or knees. But the most important thing in hand-to-hand combat, he said, was to land as many blows as quickly as possible. It was good advice, I thought, for a number of endeavors.

Gary hadn't talked to me much about the dark side of his military life, though I knew there were experiences that still haunted him. But he told entertaining stories about basic training and some of his more unusual comrades in Special Forces, including a short, rotund, redneck jokester named Gentry who turned out to be the most admired man in his unit, the one you'd want on your team. Gary got in trouble early on when he threw a former gang member's ghetto-blaster out the window when the guy refused to turn it down. He had to stay in the brig for protection from the gang-banger's buddies for a couple of days. But the real conflicts, he said, weren't about race, but about whom you could trust. His best friend at the time had been a black recruit from the Bronx, the coolest man on the base, whose only ambition once he got out of the army was to own a hot dog stand in Central Park.

Gary particularly enjoyed talking about a black sergeant who gave him a rough time in boot camp but then recognized his potential leadership qualities and made him the head of his unit. Gary

did a great imitation of the irascible drill sergeant getting in his
face. The sergeant, he said, not only transformed his views on racial
equality but changed his life.

The Iraq War had disturbed Gary deeply, and it brought up some
buried feelings about the Vietnam War. One of the first casualties from Austin was the son of a janitor at the LBJ School whom
Gary knew, and it sent him into a quiet rage. I remember both of us
looking at each other in sad acknowledgment, at the edge of hopeless
tears, when we first heard John Fogerty's fierce "Déjà vu All Over
Again," which evokes the horror of watching history repeat itself.

Day by day we count the dead and dying
Ship the bodies home while the networks all keep score.

He came home one evening, more upset than I had ever seen him,
after meeting with a group of retired generals whom he described as
almost paralyzed with anger and despair over the folly of going into
Iraq with inadequate justification and with inadequate armor for the
soldiers. There were tears shed at the meeting, he said.

As the war dragged on, Gary felt strongly that the American
public, and in particular, his freshman students, had little appreciation of the ordeal their contemporaries in the military were
enduring. He had been disturbed by how little the students seemed
to value their own privileges in going to college while others their
age were risking their lives half a world away. He was frustrated that
they seemed so blasé about getting an education and found it hard
to even stay awake during class.

One day he decided to show them a much-reproduced photograph taken of soldiers crouching behind a fortification during a
firefight in Afghanistan. One of the soldiers, who had been roused
from sleep to take up his firearm without enough time to don his
fatigues, was still wearing the polka dot boxer shorts he had slept in.

Gary saw the poignancy in that photo immediately, and he was
hoping that his students would get it. My own craven thought was
that the students would probably be calling their parents to com-
plain that Gary was advocating gays in the military and there would

be trouble at the Tower (the university administration building). When the puzzled students chuckled at the spectacle of the polka dot shorts, Gary explained that the soldier had already been in more than a dozen firefights during the week before the photograph was taken. And that he had lost good buddies in his unit that week. And that he was only a year older than they were. Nineteen.

As I look back, I think I must have been clinging to that green beret more for my own sake than for Gary's. I was terrified of going to the airport, and it was a tangible part of Gary and his courage to hold on to. When Pete and Kath Lewis arrived to pick me up, I was still trying to pull myself together. Moments earlier, as I was taking the dogs out for a quick walk, a drab green helicopter, which I recognized as a Blackhawk, thanks to Gary's tutelage, appeared overhead and swooped down low, almost seeming to buzz the road in front of us.

Whenever Gary heard one of these portentous-sounding aircraft flying overhead, he would look up and scan the sky almost involuntarily, though it was actually the durable UH-1 Huey, which became the symbol of the Vietnam War, that he knew so well. The hypnotic sound of the rotors seemed to call up long buried responses, reminding me of a retired racehorse coming smartly to attention upon hearing the call to post. I had learned that automatic reflex from him, I thought, as I waved to the unseen pilot.

I put on something black to wear, although I don't remember specifics. I had begun keeping another of my infernal lists. This one was titled "Things I Could Never Have Imagined Doing." At the top of the list was: "Watching my husband arrive home in the cargo hold of a plane."

When we arrived at the airport and joined our other friends, we were met by two high-ranking security guards, who told us to follow them. I thought I was functioning well enough, that I could do this, but suddenly I couldn't walk. I couldn't breathe. In his little book *A Grief Observed*, C.S. Lewis talks about the similarity of grief to fear, with the fluttering of the stomach and the inability to catch one's breath. I started gasping like a fish stranded out of water, as though I were suddenly thrust into an element that wouldn't sustain life.

With Grant on one side and Pete on the other, I let the men carry my weight until I could walk again. Fortunately, instead of going through the scanner and other indignities of the usual security checks, we followed the guards through a series of hallways on the lower level of the airport to a waiting room that opened onto the tarmac. The room was empty except for a lone black soldier in fatigues who was sitting quietly, as though he had all the time in the world to wait.

That soldier has the face of an angel, I thought. He looked like a young Denzel Washington. I could see the stripes on his fatigues, so I knew he was a sergeant. And I suddenly felt that he was waiting there for Gary. And for me. I was still too shaken up to speak properly, so I asked Jack Nokes if he would ask the soldier to join us on the tarmac when Gary's plane arrived. Jack spoke to him, and I could see the sergeant nodding gravely. Of course.

The guards came over and told us that the plane was about to arrive. We stood up, and the sergeant joined us as we began to walk out to the tarmac. I walked over to him and said, "I thought you'd understand." And he shook my hand, then embraced me.

We civilians were puzzled when we saw two water trucks positioning themselves on either side of the runway a couple of hundred yards in front of us. The sergeant knew, however, what was going on and nodded.

"The city of Austin requested that your husband be welcomed home as a hero," said one of the guards.

"The water cannons on those trucks will be shooting water over the plane when it taxis in," he said.

I wasn't familiar with this ritual, but learned that it is used when fallen soldiers are brought home and, more rarely, when other local heroes, such as sports stars, are welcomed home in triumph after a victory. We were all stunned.

"Too bad it's so overcast," said one of the guards, as the plane landed and began taxiing our way.

The cannons began creating an arc of water for the plane to pass under. But as the nose of the plane reached the arc, the clouds parted just enough for a ray of sunlight to fall on the plane. For an instant, as the plane passed beneath the arc, there was a rainbow shimmering just above it.

"Well, looks like God approves," said one of the guards.

"Austin has welcomed Gary back into its arms," said Jack Nokes.

Gary was being welcomed back as a very different kind of warrior. He had taken the motto of the Green Berets—*De Oppresso Liber*, To Free the Oppressed—as a kind of calling for conducting his life after leaving the military. It was though he had been tapped to fight the ongoing battles, local and global, to ensure that technology was being used in a way that benefited ordinary people and that no one was being left behind in the sweeping digital revolution that was changing the world. At times, that call to duty was a burden that weighed heavily on his shoulders.

In a speech he had given in the middle of the Iraq War in honor of the great Texas free-speech advocate John Henry Faulk, Gary had quoted Faulk's lawyer Louis Nizer, who had said at Faulk's memorial, "When God examines us, he doesn't look for medals or honorary degrees He looks for scars. Scars suffered in doing some good for your fellow man."

I wondered what the passengers were thinking as their aircraft received a baptism. I could see people seated by the windows on our side peering out curiously. Later, I learned that the Delta pilot announced to the passengers that the plane was stopping short of the gate "because we have a very special person on board. We have a hero on this plane, and we're bringing him home."

The plane paused on the runway, and the cargo door opened. The van from Weed-Corley-Fish that had been idling nearby moved closer. Obeying yet another impulse, I handed the green beret to the young sergeant and asked him if he would place it on the box holding Gary's body.

Just before the box was loaded into the van, everyone paused. The sergeant walked over to the edge of the wooden box and saluted. He slowly and gently placed the beret on the box, then pivoted and walked over to us. We were standing in a line next to the box. He greeted each one of us with a solemn handshake, and when he came to me, he stopped and enveloped me in a warm embrace that felt for a brief moment like safe harbor.

I looked down and noticed for the first time the nameplate on the pocket of his fatigues. "Dorsey." No one else in the group knew then why I nearly collapsed again.

Dorsey. It brought back the night just two weeks before Gary left for Guatemala, when we were watching a documentary on PBS about the history of gospel music. At one point, the narrator had begun to introduce a song, saying many people considered it the greatest gospel song ever written.

Before he could name the song and composer, I had piped up, "It's 'Precious Lord,' by Thomas Dorsey."

Dorsey had written it in 1930 upon the deaths of his wife and son in childbirth. It was the favorite gospel song of Martin Luther King, Jr., who asked that it be sung at the rally he led the night before his assassination.

When asked how he had written the song, Dorsey said that he had been in complete despair, blaming himself for not being present when his wife and child died. But something happened, he said, and he felt at peace.

"I felt as though I could reach out and touch God," he said.

Dorsey found himself playing a melody, and the words to the most famous gospel song of all "just seemed to fall in place."

Precious Lord, take my hand,
Lead me on, let me stand.
I am tired, I am weak, I am worn.

Through the storm, through the night,
Lead me on to the light.

As we walked out from the airport, it began to rain.

"Well, it took Gary coming home to end the drought," said Grant Thomas.

That night, as I pondered the lone soldier at the airport, I couldn't help but think of him as some kind of angel who had been summoned for duty.

"The soldier was pitch perfect," Jack Nokes had remarked.

He obviously wasn't an angel in the usual sense, and he would probably have been uncomfortable with the word. But I began to think of him as a "necessary angel," in the words of Wallace Stevens, who had used the term in one of his poems and again as the title of a book of essays.

In "Angel Surrounded by Paysans," Stevens talks about an ephemeral presence, a glimmer seen almost out of the corner of the eye, that is earthly rather than heavenly:

I am the angel of reality, Seen for the moment standing in the door.

I have neither ashen wing nor wear of ore And live without a tepid aureole,

Or stars that follow me, not to attend. But, of my being and its knowing, part.

I am one of you and being one of you is being and knowing what I am and know.

Yet I am the necessary angel of earth, Since, in my sight, you see the earth again...

I wrote my doctoral dissertation decades earlier on Stevens' poetry, and I found myself thinking about him again, finding his work relevant to me now in a way I could never have anticipated. For Stevens, reality was elusive because our imaginations are constantly shaping the way we see the world. Stevens felt that we are driven by what he called a "rage for order," a deep hunger for harmony and meaning that has become all the more compelling as certainty about God and the divine has diminished. Because we approach reality with such a fractured understanding, we piece together parts of the world to make it seem coherent and imaginatively satisfying. We even invent what Stevens called "useful fictions" to make sense of what we experience.

And so I reached out to the pitch-perfect soldier who had appeared like a glimmer at the edge of the unfinished picture at the airport, pointing to possible consolations. Was his presence there more than a poetic coincidence? How could I calculate the odds of encountering, at the most painful time in my life, a black sergeant with the face of an angel who bore the name of the composer who had sought and found healing from wounds that felt so close to mine? *Lead me on to the light.*

And I saw the earth again, not as it was, but as it was becoming. For the moment, the pieces of my world settled into a picture that merged fragments of Gary's life with fragments of my own. Military ritual and a drill sergeant as redeemer came together with my yearning for the light and solace that glimmer in gospel music.

Chapter 15

Not Frigging Mardi Gras

The funeral director at Weed-Corley-Fish set aside a room for a "viewing" on the next day, Christmas Eve. As the folks there didn't know what to expect when the box carrying Gary's body arrived, they said they would let me know what they found when they opened the box. I said that in any case, I didn't want an open coffin. I had no desire to see Gary's body lying in a coffin, cold and inert, without his animating spirit. The last time I saw him, he was striding off into a new adventure, and that was how I wanted to remember him.

I opened the envelope of papers that arrived along with the coffin, which included the death certificate issued by Guatemalan authorities and a signed and sealed "Report of an American Citizen Abroad" issued by the U.S. State Department. Although I had assumed that Gary died of a heart attack, the Guatemalan doctor who examined his body found water in his lungs, which meant that he had drowned. On both official documents, the cause of death was listed as drowning. In Spanish, the term is the more graphic phrase *Asfixia por Sumersión*, or as asphyxiation by submersion. Place of death (*fallecimiento*) was listed as the bank (*orilla*) of the Rio Cahabon, in the village (*Aldea*) of Chiocx, Languin, Alta Verapaz, Guatemala. So far from home.

The director from Weed-Corley-Fish called, saying that Gary was "viewable." He said that the embalmers in Guatemala had put quite a bit of makeup on him, and that the coffin that they chose was actually American-made, though it was not a model Weed-Corley-Fish ever used.

"It's not frigging Mardi Gras," I snapped, though I found it oddly comforting that the Guatemalan undertakers had taken so much care to make Gary "presentable," as though he would be going on stage before his final journey.

I appreciated the director's candor and regretted my outburst, but I hadn't changed my mind. I repeated, more politely, that I didn't want an open coffin.

As Ruth Pennebaker put it, "Gary was a beautiful man, and we don't need to see him looking like Chita Rivera."

I asked a small group of friends to gather at 10 am, and I requested that chairs be placed in a semi-circle in front of the coffin, which turned out to be a rather garish metallic green, with silver cherubs perched on the corners.

"It's like a hotrod fade," said Jill Nokes, touching the metallic finish, making everyone in the room laugh and relax.

I felt that it was strange having the coffin there, almost like an altar, when at no time did I feel that Gary was actually present inside it. His spirit, as Ben Kvanli told me later, was "unleashed" the minute he died on the river. The coffin, like the body itself, was merely an empty shell.

Gary's spirit was already on his way back to you.

It would have been more fitting, I thought, to have a kayak in place of the coffin, or perhaps a small boat like the cherub-bedecked vessel in which the Madonna makes her final Good Journey to heaven. Or better still, one of the ethereal life boats created by sculptor Patricia Renick, who had been the beloved partner of Gary's aunt Laura, a renowned art educator.

Pat had created boats that seemed to float in mid-air in order to depict various stages and states of mind in her life. Laura described the boats as a ghostly flotilla that seems to be drawn together by an unknown current. Just three years earlier, at Laura's request, Gary and I had taken a small envelope containing some of Pat's ashes to scatter into the rapids of Barton Creek at a beautiful point called Sculpture Falls, where the water has carved the creek bottom into undulating curves.

I had decided, after consulting with Gary's father, that Gary's body would be cremated, and I had vague thoughts of where I would scatter his ashes with the help of friends and family. I thought of all the rivers he had known and loved and of all the currents that would carry parts of him out to various seas to become part of the great blue oceansphere that bathes the earth. He would be everywhere. And nowhere.

I was already beginning to plan a memorial service to take place at Central Presbyterian Church in two weeks, and I was thinking of this little gathering as more of a Choctaw Funeral Cry, a holdover from the old tribal ways I had learned about. A Cry was not actually a lamentation, but rather the Choctaw equivalent of an Irish wake, with a celebration of the life of the departed with stories and songs and laughter as well as tears. If I had been able, I would have sung the beautiful Choctaw Meditation on Death, first sung by the Choctaw on the Trail of Tears, and which remains a part of the Choctaw hymnal.

The Choctaw believe that two shadows are released after we pass on. One, the *shilup*, the inner shadow, moves on to the afterworld and takes its place with the ancestors, while the outer shadow, the *shilombish*, lingers to carry out any unfinished missions. I rather liked the idea of a bifurcated soul—the notion that Gary's spirit could move on, unencumbered, to a higher plane, not having to remain here to deal with unfinished business, including my own pain and sorrow, but that I could still connect with his "shadow," a part of him that could be reached and loved.

Steve Smith, the doctor who tried so valiantly to save Gary, made it to the gathering after traveling back to his home in Corpus Christi from Guatemala. He brought me a little ceramic angel he had gotten in Guatemala City, and he also brought gifts relating to chocolate. He told us the story of starting the journey on the Rio

Cahabon the day after visiting Tikal and climbing the pyramid. They had stayed in an eco-hostel adjacent to a cacao plantation, and they began the day by eating chocolate bars known as "chocolate heaven" sold by local vendors. As they plied the river, Gary had a big grin on his face, and he had been the happiest Steve had ever seen him on the water. And then later, as he worked on Gary on the bank of the river, he noticed that they were positioned under a cacao tree.

"We started the day with chocolate heaven," he said, "and Gary died under a cacao tree."

As it happens, chocolate comes from the beans of the tropical *Theobroma cacao* tree, which thrives in Guatemala. The tree's scientific name is derived from a combination of the Greek word *theobroma*, meaning "food of the gods," and the Mayan word cacao, which means "god food." The Mayans were the first chocolate aficionados, and they used it in ceremonies and placed it in burial tombs as offerings. The cacao tree, which appears prominently in Popul Voh, the sacred Mayan text, was incorporated into their mythology as the place where immortal ball-playing twin gods begin their successful battle against the gods of death.

From a Mayan perspective, then, after Gary visited the pyramid dedicated to the King of Chocolate, he began his last day on earth with the food of the gods and ended it under a tree that played a role in creation. Perhaps it would be the beginning of another myth, of a great warrior who arrived in the land of the Maya in a boat and who was captured and sacrificed under a cocoa tree, but whose immortal spirit lives on to fight other battles.

Grant Thomas talked about a happier time on the river, when he and Gary and Don Hudson had run a stretch of the upper Guadalupe. Don and Grant packed sandwiches and beer for lunch, while Gary planned a more elaborate picnic. He had found plastic wineglasses with take-apart stems and packed them along with a good bottle of cabernet with a screwtop, a hefty portion of prosciutto and a selection of cheeses, all of which he was ready to share. And so they all partook of a bit of the good life on the river. Grant said that he and Don felt like bums by comparison.

Elizabeth's husband Jerele also brought a story that I hadn't heard. He and Gary had only met recently before Gary died, but they hit it off immediately. While I was out of town, he recalled, he and Gary got together, just for a glass of wine, and they were still talking after four hours. Gary told him about some of his frustrations with teaching an apparently unresponsive freshman class. At one point, Gary told the class, "This isn't working. Let's talk about what you want to know." He had them go to the board and write about what they wanted to get from the class. At the end of the semester, he asked them to write about what they liked or didn't like about the class. Some were not entirely positive.

"These kids didn't realize they had been taught by Socrates," said Jerele. "Gary just couldn't understand how a young person could be blasé about the opportunity to learn and be part of the great chain of knowledge."

Jill Nokes brought a poem to read by the Irish poet John O'Donohue. She had chosen "Beannacht," which means blessing in Gaelic, and which uses the image of a currach, an Irish canoe from olden times made of canvas stretched over a wooden frame, as a vessel led safely home across a dark ocean by a path of yellow moonlight. The poet asks:

May the nourishment of the earth be yours,
may the clarity of light be yours,
may the fluency of the ocean be yours,
may the protection of the ancestors be yours.
And so may a slow
wind work these words
of love around you....

Elizabeth also brought a poem, "The Telephone," by Robert Frost. I had told her about the "messages" in music I had gotten from my iPhone after Gary's death, and she found that Frost had conveyed a similar idea, but with an absent or departed loved one speaking through a flower.

> *When I was just as far as I could walk*
> *From here today,*
> *There was an hour*
> *All still*
> *When leaning with my head against a flower*
> *I heard you talk.*

It was an apt choice, since the word telephone is derived from Greek words meaning "voice from afar." Frost's flower was undoubtedly a daffodil, with its cup and stem resembling an old-fashioned upright candlestick telephone that rested its mouthpiece atop a stand. Frost was deftly merging the natural world and technology to suggest the ability to communicate with the unseen by listening closely.

I told the group that I wasn't sure that Gary would speak to me through a flower, but that he might have spoken to me through the young soldier at the airport. The sergeant who helped me bring Gary's body back home was a "necessary angel," I said. He wasn't the perfect angel and maybe not even the best possible angel, but he was a necessary angel. He was the one at hand, the one who was present.

In the Biblical book of Hebrews, the faithful are told, "Be not forgetful to entertain strangers: for thereby some have entertained angels unawares." In the original Greek, the word angel in that scripture was *aggelos*, meaning messenger. It seems clear that the reference is to people, not angelic beings.

"All of you," I said, "have been necessary angels, helping me find my way and to see the world again." I mentioned that the soldier's name was Dorsey, the namesake of the composer of "Precious Lord."

Jerele, as it turned out, knew the words to "Precious Lord" by heart, and he began to sing in a beautiful tenor.

When the darkness appears and the night draws near
And the day is past and gone
At the river I stand
Guide my feet, hold my hand

We all clasped hands and joined in, all my necessary angels in a makeshift chorus, singing as best they could.

Part II

Into the Mystery

One cannot step twice into the same river, nor can one grasp any mortal substance in a stable condition, but it scatters and again gathers; it forms and dissolves, and approaches and departs.

— Heraclitus

Chapter 16

The Spot, the Spider, the Owl and the Deer

For the next weeks, as I thought about the day Gary died, I wondered why something so momentous and so terrible could happen so suddenly, without warning. Even a tornado is presaged by a change in pressure, by ominous cloud formations, by a strange green tint in the air. Before a tsunami, the water retreats before making its assault on the land. Until Art's phone call, though, it had seemed a day like any other day. Had I missed a warning, like the oblivious tourists on the beach about to be inundated?

When I look back beyond that day, combing my memory for possible omens and presentiments, I realize that the days, weeks and months preceding Gary's death had not been ordinary. It had not been a season like any other. There was something different, even peculiar about that autumn, as leaves turned brown early in the season in my semi-rural neighborhood that hugs Lake Austin at the edge of the Hill Country. It wasn't just the drought and the stubborn heat that lingered late into November even as the days grew shorter. There was something else.

I can't really say that I saw it all coming in some way, that I felt even an inkling that the love of my life was going to perish in a remote jungle, thousands of miles from home. I was blind-sided by Gary's death. What I recall from that hot, dry autumn is not a dark, heavy feeling of dread or impending loss, but rather an uneasy sense that things weren't as usual. There was something in the wind, and if I were an animal, my ears would have been pricking; I would have been sniffing the air. Something was coming. I would have rounded up the cubs and nuzzled them into the lair. But I simply didn't know what to make of the oddities and anomalies that began showing up around our house as we made plans for the kayaking trip.

First, there was the strange growth that appeared on the skin above Gary's heart. It was purple, asymmetrical and nasty-looking, and I urged Gary to see a dermatologist to get it checked out. One of my former classmates at Rice, the screenwriter Warren Skaaron, had died of a melanoma that first appeared over his heart. Gary had hemmed and hawed and finally went for an appointment about two weeks before he left for Guatemala. The doctor agreed that the growth was suspicious, and Gary reluctantly had it biopsied the following week.

When the results came in, Gary told me casually that the growth had been cancerous, but that it had all been removed. Not a problem, he said. It wasn't until a couple of days before he left for Guatemala that he inadvertently referred to his "melanoma." He apparently wasn't going to tell me that the growth was far more serious than he wanted to admit, but it had slipped out. He tried to be reassuring, using his ultra-calm medic mode, saying again that it had all been removed, and I was not to worry.

One night, however, in the middle of a conversation, he blurted out, "I don't know if you could handle it." I didn't know what the "it" was, and he wouldn't elaborate. But I think now that he must have feared what could happen if the melanoma spread. The remark stung, and I was close to tears. He obviously felt penitent for his outburst and promised he'd go to church with me on the Sunday of my choice when we returned from Guatemala. Which threw me for a loop. Gary never went to church, ever. I thought it must be his way of making peace.

A few days after he died, a letter from his dermatologist arrived, saying that he had been trying urgently to get in touch with Gary by phone. Not knowing that Gary had died, he explained in the letter that a review of the biopsy had shown that the melanoma was more serious than they had thought and that further surgery would be required. In retrospect, I have often wondered if Gary had somehow spared both of us a long, agonizing ordeal with a dangerous cancer. "Maybe he bailed," one of my friends speculated. But I didn't believe that and still don't. I think Gary fought like hell on that wild river to live.

For other ominous signs, I had to look no further than my Facebook page, where I had unknowingly left a trail of strange images and portents. In mid-September, I noticed that a large garden spider had set up camp on the deck behind our house, building a web that stretched from a window ledge to an overhanging eave. One day, she captured a large green grasshopper, even bigger than she was, and she began wrapping him up to devour later. It was a gruesome spectacle, but I had to admire her tenacity, particularly when I noticed that she had spun an egg sack, which meant that she was storing up food for her children.

I posted a picture on Facebook of the spider and her outsized prey, writing flippantly that Spider Man had nothing on Spider Woman. In the world of spiders, I said, it's Spider Woman who pulls the strings.

I knew that garden spiders, also known as writing spiders, are nonpoisonous and essentially benign, despite their fearsome appearance. Her web had a distinctive silken zigzag, known as the stabilimentum, in the center, and she would lurk there, hanging head-down, waiting for prey. She would vibrate the web, using the stabilimentum for leverage, whenever I walked by, as though to make sure I noticed her. Or perhaps to make sure I didn't walk into the web and ruin all her handiwork. It was like watching a weaver shaking out her silken carpet. I would greet her every morning as I walked across the deck to my office in a separate building, and she would vibrate the web in response, as though waving hello. The zigzag stabilimentum looked like some kind of hieroglyphic, I thought.

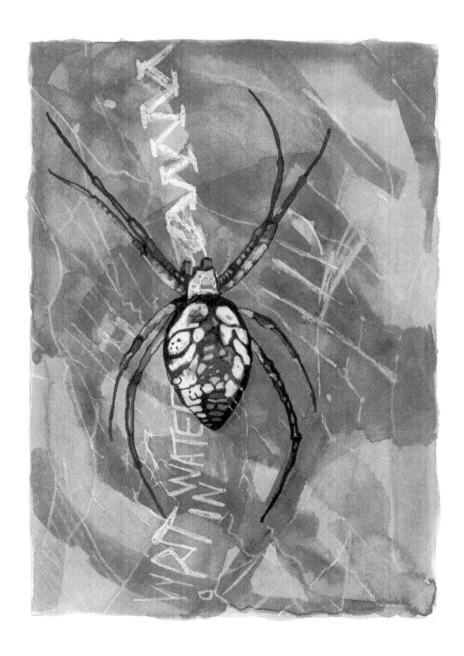

Was my writing spider like E. B. White's Charlotte, spinning cryptic words to bring notice to the world of the specialness of a friend in danger? Or was she more like Spider Woman in Native American stories, for whom the world is the interconnected creation she has spun? Or was she Penelope, weaving patiently, waiting for Ulysses to return? Was there a message in the warp and weft? Or was she just an opportunistic spider that had found a good place to catch grasshoppers?

In retrospect, I think I must have absorbed some kind of subliminal message from my resident spider related to connecting, perhaps a prompting to strengthen my own web as winter approached. On Facebook, I had begun connecting with old high school friends as well as friends from my days in Boston as an editor at the *Boston Phoenix*. That autumn, I felt an urge to strengthen those old ties. I attended my first high school reunion in decades and traveled to Boston for a reunion of Phoenix friends that culminated in a commemorative softball game. I made a side trip to a farm in Lincoln near Walden Pond, where I had ridden my retired Arabian racehorse along dirt trails through the woods and across fields, through changing seasons, until both of our backs decreed it was enough. It was as though I were gathering up pieces of the past to weave into my frail web to give it more heft and weight, my own zigzag stabilimentum.

At the end of September I began hearing the distinctive call of a barred owl in the distance. I had never heard one in our neighborhood before, and I asked Gary to come out in the yard with me one night to listen to it. The owl was too distant to photograph, so I found a picture from a nature site to post on Facebook. I was familiar with barred owls from my time living in Vermont, and I could actually do a pretty good imitation: *Who cooks for you? Who cooks for you?* The question is followed by a downward trill that requires a kind of melodramatic vocal quiver to reproduce. The first time I heard that plaintive call I was so spooked I thought it was a prankster in the neighborhood trying to scare me.

I did know that in the oral traditions of many Native American people, the owl is a harbinger of death. In Choctaw stories, an *opa* perched in a barn or on trees near the house foreboded death among near relatives. But at the time, I was simply fascinated that we had a new and unusual resident in the neighborhood. One night, when I heard the owl calling, I went out on the deck with a flashlight, and when the light fell on the spider's web, she began to vibrate it. The silvery zigzag seemed to shimmer in the moonlight with some enigmatic meaning.

If these odd appearances were intended somehow to raise alarms, I still wasn't getting it. I simply wasn't in that frame of mind. To say that nature was actually signaling me in some way would have been to engage in that most dreaded of poetic follies: the pathetic fallacy. Clouds, of course, can't be angry, nor can the wind be cruel. Nor, then, should nature be able to be exceptionally kind, except in children's books. What's more, if there were such a thing as divine or perhaps supra-natural providence, why would it favor one being over another? In retrospect, however, nature was somehow bending in an unusual way that autumn. From a Native American point of view, the sacred web of creation, in which we are bound together, may well engage us in a reciprocal relationship, in which its creatures can become guides to help awaken us to our connectedness.

The spider could hardly have spelled out in her enigmatic web what was going to happen. But her appearance did stir something in my awareness. At the very least, she engaged my imagination and became part of my story. It was a story that seemed to be unfolding on its own, written by something outside myself, and by something outside the spider. It was as though the invisible filaments of connection in my life were becoming visible.

If I had been a writer of fiction, I would have left out the appearances of the spider and the owl as too implausible.

But in mid-November, the story went from implausible to bizarre. I saw a tiny newborn deer in our backyard, which wasn't unusual in itself, given the large population of deer in the neighbor-

hood. Because it was in the evening, I thought what I was seeing must be a trick of the light. The deer was solid black, from ears to hooves. The deer population in our neighborhood was growing, and this was the second fawn to be born behind our house.

The next day, I saw the deer again, and it was indeed black. I had never heard of a black deer, so I did some research and discovered that black deer, known as melanistic deer, are even more rare than albino deer. I wondered if she were like a white buffalo, which was sacred to a number of tribes. I posted a picture of the fawn, which I decided must be a female, saying, "Hope she's a good luck charm."

She may have been more like a black swan, however, like the one Gary and I saw on Lake Austin one morning three years earlier. The swan was alone, and she was calling plaintively as she swam upstream. As it happened, we had just been reading philosopher Nassim Nicholas Taleb's provocative book titled *The Black Swan: The Impact of the Highly Improbable*, which is about the illusion of certainty that comes from predictable events. For Taleb, the world is actually most changed by "black swan events," by which he means unique, unpredictable outcomes of accidents and luck.

Later that day Gary had told his dear friend Elspeth Rostow, who was still teaching at the LBJ School in her 90th year, about the swan we had seen and what a strong impression it had left on us. And just two days later, Elspeth died suddenly. In his grief, Gary recalled the rare and improbable swan and connected the appearance of the swan with losing Elspeth. He wrote a letter to several of our friends, saying that when we heard the news that Elspeth had passed away, "we knew that the black swan had been an omen that we didn't recognize—except that I was given the opportunity to tell Elspeth about it, just before her death."

Gary wrote that he "immediately thought about the richness of the image: grace, rarity, a regal quality, and of course the portent of the color. The black swan on the lake was alone, as swans usually are not; I'm not a believer in omens or signs, but this was one that could not be ignored. In retrospect, it seems both eerie and perfectly natural at the same time."

Having discovered what the black swan means to philosophers, he was even more struck by the coincidence, for Elspeth "was a 'black swan' among us. If routine interactions with other human beings were to understandably lead you to the certainty that people are vain, selfish, ungenerous creatures, then Elspeth was the 'black swan' who disproved that by her very existence. She was highly improbable, and to have known her was pure luck."

On December seventh, a week before Gary's death, I posted another picture of the black deer on Facebook, asking for suggestions of what to name her. I had already decided, however, to call her Issa, which is the Choctaw word for deer. When I saw her standing in a vacant lot near our house, along with several other does and fawns, I called out to her. "Issa." And she walked towards me expectantly. A doe, clearly not her mother, nudged the black fawn roughly, and I wondered if Issa was being bullied because of her color.

That same week, I noticed that the spider had disappeared. Her usually tidy web had been getting ragged, and she had gotten noticeably thinner. One morning, she was gone. I gathered that she must have died. At least her babies are still there, I thought, looking at the brown paper-like egg sack that was hanging next to the tattered web. One morning, however, I saw that the babies must have hatched because tiny garden spiders were now arrayed on the remains of the web. When I looked closer, the wee things started vibrating the strands of web that they were clinging to. They were indescribably endearing in their bravado. I felt sad, though, knowing that they had hatched too soon and wouldn't survive the winter.

The night before Gary left for Guatemala, I heard the owl again. This time, however, it was not in the distance. It sounded very close. It hooted, *Who cooks for you, who cooks for you*, the rhetorical question without an answer. I went out on the deck, and the owl hooted again. And now I could see it, perched on a branch above the deck, clearly visible. It was a big owl, and it was looking directly at me in the moonlight. Who cooks for you? It asked insistently. Well, Gary cooks for me, I could have answered. He cooks for me nearly every night.

A few days after Gary's death, I realized that I hadn't seen Issa the black deer, and I asked neighbors if they had seen her. One neighbor said she must have been hit by a car because he saw her body lying beside the road.

Eerie and yet entirely natural.

Chapter 17

Christmas Roses

As the days went by after Gary's death, I hardly registered that Christmas was approaching. I couldn't bring myself to send Christmas cards with cheery greetings signed only by myself. Gary's father said Gary's Christmas gift, the new Keurig coffee maker that we had picked out the week before he left for Guatemala, arrived the day after he died. *Merry Christmas from Carol and Gary.* My heart was heavy as I walked with the dogs around our customary route through the neighborhood.

One afternoon, I walked past my elderly neighbor Elizabeth's house as she was tending to her yappy little dogs. She came out to give Molly and Zip her usual lavish affection and praise and decided for the first time to accompany me for a few blocks. She wanted to tell me a story about her trip the previous day to buy dog food at WalMart.

A mother had been dragging a sobbing, shrieking child past the Salvation Army Santa, and Elizabeth said she had been tempted to shove the child into the big iron kettle. She had leaned over and whispered into the child's ear that Santa was going to bypass her house this year if she didn't shape up. The child had immediately stopped crying, she said, and the mother had given her a grateful thumbs up.

Elizabeth was getting a little out of breath, so we walked back to her house, and I gave her a hug. She had made me laugh for the first time since Gary died.

Following the Christmas Eve gathering for Gary at Weed-Cor-ley-Fish, I headed for my parents' home in Lake Jackson. It would be my first Christmas there without Gary since we had first gotten together. I was taking along the presents I had bought for them before Gary's death, and I was also taking along a measure of anger that was weighing heavily on my spirits. Now that the ordeal of getting Gary's body back to Austin was over, I was beginning to deal with the onslaught of practical problems that come with any death, and particularly with a death abroad in a developing country.

I panicked when realized that I had no idea what had happened to the possessions Gary had taken to Guatemala. His body had arrived in Austin without his wedding ring, and I was seized by frantic fantasies about someone stealing his credit cards, his iPhone, his camera. I later learned from Steve Smith that Ben Kvanli had Gary's things and would bring them back to Texas after completing the second part of the kayaking expedition, as originally planned.

Ben had already posted a photo on Facebook of a scene from the Rio Dulce, where Gary and I would have been, too, if all had gone as planned, and he talked about the blissful experience of swimming with manatees. I was already upset that I had to find out on my own what had happened on the Rio Cahabon, and I was stunned that after Gary's death Ben had moved on to the second part of his expedition, leaving Steve Smith to deal with Guatemalan bureaucracy while he and the next group of kayakers plied the sweet Rio Dulce and swam with manatees. How could the world go on without Gary?

Gary had told me that Ben was not only physically brave, but also a person of strong religious faith. I wondered, however, if his faith as well as his considerable physical prowess may have made him overconfident that he could deal with any setbacks on the trip. I held him completely blameless for Gary's death, but I felt that he had fallen short of his responsibilities to me, the grieving and over-wrought survivor, in the aftermath. I gathered from his email mes-sages, once we began communicating, that he felt that my urgent desire to have Gary's body returned to Austin was somehow excessive. He even suggested that Gary's remains be buried in Guatemala. Which to me, in my altered state, was like letting the Mayans keep their high-value captive. It didn't occur to me that Ben was speaking from his deep love of Guatemala, which to him was like home.

I talked over my anger with my mother after I arrived in Lake Jackson, and I wondered how I could ever let it go. I kept running through that terrible death-day scenario, replaying my desperate question, *Está muerte?*, and then the stabbing answer, *Sí*. I realized that I was not in a rational state, but I knew that anger would prevent me from healing. It didn't occur to me at that point to question whether Ben, too, might have suffered deeply from what happened or whether he, too, would be in need of healing. It didn't occur to me that Ben had done his best in a traumatic situation. And that, in fact, on that afternoon like no other, he had been very much the hero that Gary had thought him to be.

As my mother and I were talking, my iPhone made one of the unexpected electronic beeps that were now becoming familiar. I picked it up to find on the screen a cryptic message, "Nothing to undo." It was a prompt from the system, I supposed, though I had no idea what it was prompting me to not "undo." I later learned that the "undo" message can pop up when the iPhone is shaken, and that it was considered a "bug" in the system. But I also took it as a message that I couldn't "undo" what had happened in Guatemala, and that my anger was pointless and misdirected.

A few minutes later, as I was talking about my dilemma with my sister Ellen, the iPhone zapped into action again. This time, as we were talking, we heard the sound of rushing water and tropical birds. The sounds were identical to what Gary would have heard on the Cahabon, and we were both a little freaked out until I realized that for some reason, iTunes had turned itself on, and the selection that it was playing was called "Angelic Forest," from an album called Spirit of Healing. Because of its serene tropical river sounds,

I had sometimes used this selection for background when I was per-
forming reiki healing on Gary to try to soothe his tinnitus.

"Don't poison the waters," I thought.

This was a clear message, no matter what its source. I knew that
Gary would not have wanted me to blame Ben or anyone else for
what had happened. I was using blame like a blowtorch, and I was
going to leave scars if I weren't careful. I needed to forgive Ben,
and in so doing, I could begin to forgive myself for the catalogue of
shortcomings that kept running through my mind like a litany. *Why
did I…Why didn't I…How could I*….And then perhaps I could even
forgive Gary for dying.

The litany diminished as I began to think about the music for
Gary's memorial service. I was touched that my niece Maddie had
volunteered to sing at the service. Only 14, she possessed a sweet,
pure soprano voice, and she had already won prizes in talent con-
tests. We went through a list of possible songs and settled on Sara
McLachlan's "Angel." With Ellen's help we were able to buy sheet
music online and download and print it. My dad sat down at the
piano and began to run through the opening bars. Maddie was suddenly shy, and so I began to sing, and she joined me. As we sang the
chorus, my voice cracked, and she went on alone.

In the arms of the angel
Fly away from here

Later that evening, as I lay down on the bed in the room where
I had spent so many nights as a restless teenager, dreaming of my
elusive prince charming, I was drifting off toward the bottom of the
ocean when I heard my dad at the piano again. My parents are both
gifted pianists, though my mother had not been able to play since
her eyesight had begun to fail. My dad, though, still played when
the spirit moved him. Now he was playing a jazzy version of Carol
of the Bells on the old Baldwin Acusonic, which resonated with
memories. My mother had learned to play on it while growing up
on a farm in East Texas, and I had first started practicing on it as

a kid before realizing my talents were better suited to other instruments, like the oboe.

I let the music wash over me, and I felt a wave of gratitude, filtering up through my grief, that I had grown up in this loving, musical family that could enfold me like a shivering child wrapped in a comforting blanket. Just a year ago, my father had undergone an operation for colon cancer, and it had been touch and go. I think this was the first time that I realized that gratitude had a heft that might eventually outweigh or at least counterbalance my grief.

As I was preparing to leave for Austin the next afternoon, my mother pointed to the bowl of white roses on the dining table that I had hardly noticed. I had told her about the "miracle" tomato that had ripened after Gary's death, and she said she had another "sign" to add to my list of anomalies. The roses, she said, were from her garden, and they had bloomed on Christmas Eve, the first time they had ever bloomed so late in the season.

"Even though our world changed and your world changed," she said, "this is a sign that God is still in control. He sends the Comforter, the Holy Spirit, to be with us when we ask. The roses are a sign, like a dove or any living thing that will grow with us."

He has never left for ever.

Reluctantly, I gathered up my presents and headed back to Austin, still unused to driving Gary's SUV, which was so much heavier and steadier than my little Subaru WRX. I was having a hard time focusing on the road as I drove through the swampy coastal plain north of Lake Jackson, with its huge moss-draped oaks and palmetto undergrowth. I had gone only about 20 miles when I saw something at the side of the road that made me slam on the brakes, causing Zip and Molly, who had been standing up in the back of the vehicle, to lose their footing. It was a large brown and white bird, clearly dead. I had shot past it, and I backed up carefully until I was next to it. It was an owl, lying on its back, its wings outspread. I parked the car on the shoulder and got out to get a closer look.

As I had suspected, it was a barred owl. Though I had never seen one up close like this, it was a double of the owl I had seen on the deck behind my house before Gary died. The decorative "bars" for which the *Strix varia* (varied stripes) gets its name were unmistakable. Its fluffy white breast was marked with horizontal brown bars, while on its lower underside, the bars were vertical. Its black eyes were partially closed, and its gold-tinged talons were curled as though trying to clutch an invisible prey.

The owl had died on the road, surrounded by a lush, green habitat of swampy bottomland forest, the familiar habitat in which I had grown up. As I knelt down beside the bird, overcome by its beauty, and by the coincidence of its timely appearance, an elderly man in a cowboy hat, driving a maroon pickup truck, stopped and rolled down his window.

"Need some help?" he asked.

Ordinarily, I would have just waved him on with a cursory "thanks but no thanks." But he had a kindly face, and I found myself telling him about Gary's death and the owl I had seen on the deck. He said that he had lost his younger brother suddenly and that he understood something of how I must feel. He got out of the truck and knelt down next to me beside the bird.

"He's beautiful, isn't he," he said.

"I'd like to have a feather from this bird," I said. "Do you think it would mind if I took one?"

The old man pondered a moment.

"No, I don't think he'd mind," he said gravely, as if he got questions like this all the time.

He introduced himself as the Reverend Richard Smith and explained that he was the minister at the little Assemblies of God church just down the road. I can't remember the sequence of events at that point, but the next thing I knew, the Reverend Smith was holding my hand and praying for me. Ordinarily, I might have been concerned about an Assemblies of God prayer, since I knew from experience that those folks are wont to start speaking in tongues.

And they can go on forever. But the Reverend Smith kept his prayer brief and to the point.

"Lord, we ask that you lift the burden of grief from this woman's shoulders in the way that you lifted the grief from my shoulders when my little brother died."

I asked the reverend if he would help me take one of the bird's feathers. He went to his pickup truck and returned with a hunting knife. He knelt and quickly cut a feather from the bird's outstretched wing and handed it to me.

I carried the feather back to the SUV and placed it in my purse. I waved goodbye to my necessary angel of the day and started up the motor. And for the first time since Gary died, I felt some of the heaviness of my grief begin to lift.

On wings of divine deliverance.

Chapter 18

The Hawk on the Water

The emails between Ben and me had gotten far more cordial, and he sent a message to let me know when he would be arriving in San Marcos after his long drive from Guatemala, through Mexico and across south Texas. Our mutual friend Don Hudson agreed to drive me down to Ben's establishment in San Marcos in his truck so that I could pick up Gary's possessions and my kayak. I planned to give Gary's kayak and kayaking gear to Ben for use with the disabled veterans he was working with and to give him my blessing as well. I felt that I needed to connect with Ben in a meaningful way, as Gary's body was to be cremated the next day, and I knew that Gary would have wanted peace for both of us.

We drove down to San Marcos in the dark, and I wasn't sure what to expect. As we pulled up to the rambling old house that served as headquarters for Ben's kayaking ventures, we could see his trailer parked at the back of the building, still loaded with kayaks. A wiry, bearded man walked towards us, and Don didn't recognize him at first. He hadn't seen Ben with a beard, and Ben's beard was threaded with gray that made him look older than his 36 years. He looked haggard, bereft and utterly weary. He told us that his beloved long-time partner, with whom he had shared a life focused on a passion for rivers, had decided to leave, and he had arrived to an empty house and a life that had changed quickly almost as much as mine had. Later, Ben would tell me that he felt that in some way he had died in the river along with Gary and had had to rebuild his life, much as I had.

I embraced Ben like a brother, knowing that we were entwined forever, as he had said in one of his emails, because of what had happened on the Rio Cahabon. And I knew that Gary would have relished the idea of Iraqi war veterans learning from Ben how to negotiate the rapids of the San Marcos in his Jackson All-Star. I thought of the phrase "peace like a river" as we wept together.

We were all too exhausted to do much talking, and we just sat together quietly for a while until grief subsided from waves to ripples. Ben handed me Gary's duffel bags and a smaller backpack that held his waterproof digital camera and iPhone. The batteries on both had run down, so I would have to wait to look at the last photos Gary had taken before he died. The moment I got home, I placed the camera battery in its charger so that I would be able to see Gary's photos first thing in the morning. The sturdy camera had come through the journey apparently undamaged, and I was hoping the photos would be retrievable.

Waking up before dawn, I turned on the now charged-up camera and saw that Gary had taken only about two dozen photos of his trip before it had all ended so abruptly. I clicked through the scenes of waiting on the road and of the border stop that had delayed their journey. There was a scene clearly taken from the top of the pyramid at Tikal and one of the eco hostel where they had launched their kayaks on the Cahabon.

The next-to-last photo, obviously taken by one of his companions, showed Gary sitting in his bright red Jackson All-Star, sporting his red and black jacket, black life jacket and black helmet. He looked fashionably attired in his color-coordinated gear, and I thought it was no wonder that Barry Day had ribbed him about it. And then there was the last photo, this one clearly taken from his kayak while on the river, not long before he died. It was Gary's last postcard before leaving this world, and it was a doozy, as my mother would say.

At first I wasn't sure what I was seeing, so I enlarged the photo on my computer and printed it out on good photo paper. Gary had pointed the camera directly ahead, and I could see Barry Day's kayak in the distance. There was steep jungle on either side of the smooth-flowing water. The Rio Cahabon was a beautiful river, just as Barry had described it.

On the horizon was what appeared to be a white light glowing in the distance, as though Gary were heading toward the mouth of a bright tunnel. I knew the light couldn't be coming from the sun because although they had been heading west, it had been too early in the day for the sun to be so low on the western horizon. Directly in front of him, hovering just above the water, was what appeared to be a translucent brown smudge. As I looked closer, I was stunned to realize that the smudge was in the unmistakable shape of a hawk. It was as though a phantom hawk were leading Gary toward the white light.

Eerie and yet entirely natural.

Native Americans would call this transparent bird a spirit hawk. I thought, of course, about all the hawks that had made appearances after his death, and I had to wonder if Gary, who had been so wary of my Native American connection, had found a guardian animal guide to help him on his transition out of this life.

Yes, it could all have been a trick of the light. But I kept staring at the outline of the hawk, which had now become a part of my story. For many Native American people, the hawk is the messenger that brings portents of change, reminding people to wake up and be aware. From what I had learned, the person guided by the hawk is said to bring visions of the future, though such visionaries are often ahead of their time. "Hawk people" are often not honored or recognized for their work until after they crossed over, though their work is said to live on and touch the lives of people around the world. The hawk person was given the special task of holding the energy of what could be, of the potential changes waiting to be envisioned and imparted.

If ever there were a hawk person of that description, it was Gary, the visionary who was so often ahead of the wave. And so I clung to that last image of Gary heading toward the light, guided by the phantom hawk, as I awaited the telephone call from Weed-Corley-Fish that the cremation of his body was about to take place. I had decided, as most of the bereaved do, that I would not want to witness the casket going into the crematory. I wanted my own way of letting go of Gary's body, ashes to ashes, dust to dust.

After the phone call, I sat down in front of my makeshift altar and turned on the stereo full-blast to play Mozart's *Ave Verum Corpus*, which translates as Hail True Body. The music was written as a setting for the sacrament of the eucharist, in which bread and wine are consecrated as the body and blood of Christ, and which is often referred to as a foretaste of death.

Eso nobis praegustatum in mortis examine. Be for us a foretaste in the test of death.

Mozart composed his majestic motet in D major, only 46 bars long, less than six months before he died. Gary had played it for me at times in the past when I was stressed out or troubled. The previous summer, he had chosen it when a friend held a birthday gathering and asked celebrants to choose their favorite piece of music and to explain their choices. Gary had said simply that he thought it was the most sublime piece of music ever written.

The music soars to heaven, from flesh into spirit, suggesting the possibility of eternal tranquility in freedom from the earthly body. In a bitter irony, I had often thought in the past that if I were dying, I would want the music to accompany my departure. And now, in my utter aloneness, I wished that I could have flown up and away with the music on the wings of the phantom hawk, into the light, along with Gary. *On wings of divine deliverance.*

A few moments later, as I lay on my bed, worn out from racking sobs, the phone rang. I decided to pick it up, as I never knew who would call.

"Congratulations," said a recorded voice. "You've won a new home security system."

Chapter 19

Ashes and Dragons

I told Gary a few weeks before he died that 2012 would be the year of the dragon, according to the Chinese zodiac, and that it should be a good year for him because he had been born in a dragon year. In China, the dragon is regarded as the most powerful of all the zodiac signs, and every Chinese parent hopes for a dragon child, a born leader. But the Chinese also believe that dragons are not well suited to growing old. The helpless feeling of youthful strength ebbing away is unbearable to them.

At least Gary would never suffer that fate, I thought, grasping at the flimsiest of consolations. As one of my friends told me, I'd never have to watch him grow old and infirm or wither away from sickness. At one point, Gary had told me he couldn't imagine himself as an old man puttering around Austin. If he was going to get old, he declared, he wanted to do it in Italy.

On the morning of New Year's Eve, I hadn't really thought about how I would spend the time that would mark an ending rather than a beginning of something new. I had looked forward to growing old with Gary, and the years of possible infirmity ahead hadn't daunted me. Nor had that damned melanoma. But now it was the end of my time with Gary, and there was absolutely nothing ahead of me that looked anything like a possible life.

I wasn't able to carry out much more than a stilted, zombie-like approximation of ordinary human actions. Must eat, must sleep, I told myself, though I wasn't doing much of either. Must brush teeth, take shower and change clothes. Not doing much of those either. I wasn't bothering about keeping up with appearances. Being around me was undoubtedly not particularly pleasing to the senses of my friends. I must have looked and smelled like a homeless person. But I did know, as I assumed the homeless person does, that I had to keep moving. Although I didn't want to think about it, there was still the matter of the ashes. Weed-Corley-Fish had called to say that Gary's cremated remains, or "cremains" as they are more crassly known, were ready to pick up.

To my mental list of "Things I Could Never Have Imagined Doing," I added, "Picking up my husband's ashes at a funeral home." I found it absurdly mundane that I would simply drive to the funeral home, which was just down the road from the gun shop where Gary and I had bought shotguns for our new hobby of sporting clays, and pick up his ashes. As though they were clothes from the dry cleaner's.

In my state of partially functioning semi-coma, I couldn't come up with a more solemn and ceremonial way to acquire the ashes, which had been stored in the simple urn I had chosen. This particular style of urn was designed, I was told, for those who want to scatter the ashes rather than keep them displayed on a mantle. I felt that there would be something creepy about keeping the ashes displayed at home in a decorative urn. Yes, those are my softball trophies, and there are the remains of my husband.

I wasn't sure at that point, in my state of vacillating lethargy and wired nuttiness, that I even wanted the ashes. I felt that Gary's spirit, his True Body, had already soared up and away from the remains of flesh and bones and the elements they were finally reduced to. Actually, the ashes in question were not precisely ashes. After cremation, only dry bone fragments remain, which are then pulverized by a machine called a Cremulator, a kind of super blender, to process the remains into a substance with a texture more like sand than ashes. The average weight of the remains of a male body that has been cremated and then pulverized, I learned, is 6 pounds. For women, the average is a mere 4 pounds. I imagined that Gary's ashes would weigh more than average, as he was tall and big-boned. And surely the remains of a significant life should weigh more than those of a wasted life, I thought.

Before I picked up the ashes, I had yet another task that would challenge my ability to keep functioning. The LBJ School informed me that they would need Gary's office to be cleared for his eventual replacement, and I had agreed to stop by his office to begin the process of disposing of his books and files and all the mementos he had placed on the shelves and hung on the walls. It was the first time I had been there since he died, and I had to sit down for a while in his swivel desk chair.

These possessions that remained from his life in teaching, I felt, held more of his spirit than his ashes. His books covered the range of his interests, from Galileo and Rousseau to the future of the Internet. On one shelf was a framed, glamored-up photo of me alongside silly little gifts I had given him over the years. We both loved funny wind-up toys, including walking cubes of sushi and cymbal-clacking chimps. In a desk drawer were his headphones, which he used much of the day, not so much because he wanted to listen to music, but because he was desperate to drown out the intrusive noise of his tinnitus. A seemingly endless renovation project at the LBJ School, with constant jackhammers, had made sitting in his office nearly unbearable.

As I sat in his chair, looking out the window toward the LBJ Library, thinking about Gary's great pride and joy in teaching, I got a call from the UT human resources office informing me that there was a "problem" with Gary's life insurance. Until I had gotten an email from UT, complete with forms to fill out, in the days following his death, I didn't even know that Gary had taken out a policy. He was the first to admit that he was financially challenged, and I had always done our taxes and investing. Finances had often been a sore point between us. But I was greatly relieved to know that I wouldn't have to rely solely on our savings and my freelance income as I tried to rebuild my life. In my darkest moments I had been imagining myself, as so many women do, whatever their accomplishments, as a potential bag lady with sagging stockings and cluttered shopping cart. The homeless person who has to keep moving to stay alive.

Now, however, I was facing the first of the many legal complications that I had dimly anticipated, but which I was hardly ready to deal with. The "problem" would mean having to hire a lawyer and eventually, absurdly, having to endure the insurance company's investigation into Gary's "manner of death," in which the company implied I might have played a role. Because Gary had died in a corrupt and violent place like Guatemala, I was told by an insurance representative, documents could be forged, people could be hired. Fraud was rampant. Maybe Gary wasn't even dead but had disappeared so that I could collect the insurance.

"Sure," I told my lawyer sarcastically, as the days and weeks dragged on, and my legal bill ticked higher. "I hired a scuba diver to wait underwater at that particular bend in the Cahabon to grab Gary's kayak and tump it over."

It would take the company months to determine that Gary had, in fact, died, and that he had not been murdered at my behest.

Oddly enough, I wasn't feeling depressed over the legal battle I was facing. I was angry. And even though I had no idea then how long the battle would drag on, I was still fuming as I drove to the funeral home. As friends had warned, insurance companies tend to be at their most corporate and uncaring when widows are at their most vulnerable and befuddled. It felt almost comical that I was being cast as a possible shady character when I could barely tie my shoes in the morning.

As I returned to my car with the urn, wrapped in a purple velvet drawstring cover, and placed it in the front seat next to me, my anger was as strong as my sadness. As with the shiny green casket that had arrived from Guatemala, I had no sense that the urn actually held anything of Gary's essence. Having Gary's ashes beside me in the passenger seat of his vehicle gave me no further pain, nor did the ashes give me any comfort. At that moment, ashes were just ashes. And I have to confess that for a very brief nanosecond, I had an impulse to throw the urn out the window. It wasn't about Gary; it was about what I was facing without him, and without the preparation or the resources I needed. I just wanted it to be over.

That evening, I was looking for some kind of ritual to mark the transition to the year that should have been Gary's as well as mine. Something other than the usual champagne and noisemakers. The prospect of sitting at home, watching the hours tick by, waiting for the ball to drop, seemed even more unbearable than watching other people get tipsy and sentimental and smoochy at midnight. The Church of Conscious Harmony, located just off the road where Gary had survived his terrible accident four years earlier, was holding a midnight service, and I decided at the last minute to go.

The service was to be a Taizé service, a meditative candle-lit ceremony based on the contemplative prayer tradition developed in the Taizé Community of France that was formed during World War II. The ecumenical monastic community gave shelter to war refugees, particularly Jews, and its ritual of repetitive songs, scriptures and silence has been gradually spreading to churches around the world.

Wearing a leather coat of Gary's, which swallowed me up like an oversized Batman cape, I took my place near the back of the church as the congregation chanted a simple litany, over and over, then meditated in silence.

You turn us back into dust
To your eyes a thousand years are like yesterday,
Come and gone, no more than a match in the night.
Make us know the shortness of our life
That we may gain wisdom of the heart.

Individual members of the congregation began filing up to the front of the church, where a large icon with an image of Jesus had been placed on the floor. I couldn't imagine joining them as each person knelt next to the icon and placed their hands on it and prayed silently. The pastor had invited all those present to come forward, if they felt so moved, to lay down their sorrows and their burdens on the icon. My sorrows, I thought, would simply be too heavy. Didn't Jesus have enough to bear without the dark weight of my grief on his shoulders? In the most vivid depictions of the crucifixion, he seems to be bearing the weight of the world's shortcomings.

"Why hast thou forsaken me?" he cries to heaven, echoing all of those who have suffered and felt forsaken by providence.

And yet I found myself walking forward and joining the community of the sorrowful and the heavy-laden. When it came my turn, I knelt and placed my hands on the painted wood and let the tears flow. In my anguish, it was as though my tears were joining all the tears that had ever been shed, flowing like a river, washing over hills and valleys, over the deserving and the undeserving, over the wounded and the whole, over the fortunate and the afflicted, over the living and the departed, until they merged into the great ocean of human suffering. As my tears finally stopped, I felt that my grief had been divided up into hundreds of tiny parcels, which I might possibly give away, day by day, until my heart was light again.

Until then, however, I had to find a way to keep going. As I left the church, which is set on a hilltop, I found myself standing on the edge of a steep drop-off. Looking out into the darkness, I wondered briefly what it would be like to just sail off the edge, into the night. It wasn't like the temptation of Christ, where Satan offers Jesus the world if he'll take the chance and jump. For me, the temptation was just to find quick oblivion. No earthly reward. But the impulse to sail away into the night lasted only an instant. That was not my fate, at least not a fate I would choose willingly. And never again did I feel as strong an impulse to end it all, in dramatic fashion or otherwise. The next morning, I felt as though a few little parcels of grief had been taken away while I slept.

Chapter 20

The Many Languages of Love

I woke up on the morning of Gary's memorial service thinking about rivers. A river had taken Gary away from me, but I bore it no grudge. How could I hate a river? Or even stop loving a river? Rivers signified onrushing time, time that you can never stop or recapture, except in memory. The real lesson of Orpheus and Lot's wife, both punished so brutally for looking back, is that looking back is futile because what you're looking for is no longer there.

I wanted desperately to hold on to the moment on the Cahabon when Gary rolled the first time and came up triumphartly, his friends cheering him on. If only I could stop the river there, at that moment. Stop time, stop change. Impose a fixed pattern on this elusive world in flux that eventually carries away everything that we hold dear. Instead, I was poised on the edge of a waterfall, clutching at the current in vain, with each moment rushing by, falling over the edge and gone. I simply couldn't let go, even though I knew the clutching was in vain. All I could do was remember what I couldn't keep.

What I was remembering mostly that day was love. Not the smarmy kind, but the kind that cuts like diamonds into the soul. As I prepared my remarks for the service, I was thinking about the differences among the kinds of love I had known. With Gary, there was passionate and physically charged *eros*, the love of romance and intimacy, the love that binds. From friends and family had come altruistic, generous *caritas*, the good-hearted love of one's neighbor enshrined in the scriptures and explicated so beautifully by St. Paul in the Book of Corinthians, in the passage I had chosen as a reading for the memorial service. In moments of grace following Gary's death, I had experienced hints of *agape*, or the divine love at the top of the Platonic ladder. Boundless, mysterious, unmerited, unsought, inexplicable, mind-bending love that passeth all understanding.

To that essentially classical taxonomy of love, I had to add another order: that otherworldly and yet worldly kind of love that seemed to infuse the strangely intimate interactions I had been experiencing with creatures from the natural world. It was something like *biophilia*, or the bond with nature that biologist Edward O. Wilson describes as the connections human beings subconsciously seek with the rest of life. And that they perhaps seek with us, should we be open to it.

Eerie and yet entirely natural.

I had gotten an email the day before from Stan Stearns, one of Gary's oldest and best friends, who said that while he appreciated the impressive obituaries he had read in papers like the one in the *New York Times*, he felt that they expressed mostly the admiration that people felt for Gary and missed the deep affection for Gary that his friends felt for him. The obits had missed the love.

"Gary's friends loved him," he wrote. "They loved his generous spirit. They loved his compassion. They loved his sense of adventure. They loved his laugh—he laughed a lot. They loved his smile and the mischievous twinkle in his eyes. Gary engendered affection for himself in people like almost no one I have known."

Stan, who is a geologist, was currently living on the island of Bahrain in the Arabian Gulf region. He recalled an episode when Gary and I joined him and his family on an adventure trip into the uncharted dunes of the Singing Sands desert of Oman. We had stopped to camp on a remote, deserted beach on the Indian Ocean, and Gary had been stung by a huge stingray while wading in the water.

"He knew how terrible the pain would be," wrote Stan, "but that it would last only a limited time. Without complaining, he lay down on the sand and covered his face with a towel and suffered without making a sound."

Gary had told us, before going into near shock, that he wasn't going to die. But we weren't sure.

Stan continued, "My ten-year-old daughter Grace felt the affection for Gary that is common to those who knew him. She knelt down next to him, fanned his head with a towel and patted his hair while he suffered."

Stan and I had held hands and prayed. It was all we could do because we were a full day's drive away from help. I recalled, too, that Grace had traced a heart in the sand beside Gary and written his name in the middle of it.

"That expression of affection," said Stan, "is how all of Gary's friends felt about him. That expression of concern is how I feel for you as you suffer now."

Yes, Gary knew love in all its forms, though he had declared so often that he didn't believe in God or an afterlife.

And so I found myself thinking of a bittersweet irony as I walked up to the pulpit to talk about Gary to the packed gathering at Central Presbyterian. Gary bore the same name as a famous but rather sappy motivational speaker, and he would occasionally get phone calls asking, "Are you the Gary Chapman who wrote The Five Languages of Love?"

Well, of course, he wasn't. But he could have been the author of The Fifty Languages of Love, I told the gathering. Gary loved Austin, he loved the Hill Country, he loved teaching, he loved his students, he loved cooking, he loved art, he loved Italy, he loved Puccini operas, he love porcini mushrooms, he loved Slow Food, he loved Machiavelli's brilliant pragmatism, he loved the films of Kurosawa and Miyazaki, he loved my family, he loved our dogs, he loved Bruce Springsteen, he loved Mozart, he loved mystery novels, particularly ones set in Italy, he loved his iPhone. He loved rivers. He loved life. And he loved me.

Gary also loved building community and making deep and lasting connections. He did it so well during his life, and even now, I said, he was continuing to bring people together. Everyone present, I said, had already become honorary members of what Grant Thomas and I had already dubbed the "emerging tribe of Gary." I quoted my sister Ellen, who had told me, "Gary's into spiritual networking now." Even in leaving us, Gary had taken yet another step in connecting, I said. Beyond wireless, into higher technology. The tribe of Gary is global, I said, and it has no boundaries. Like the motto of the church where we were gathered, I said, the tribe of Gary is "deliberately diverse and fully inclusive."

I was grateful that my friend Jill had helped create a smooth-flowing liturgical structure for the service, as I could now become a member of the congregation, rather than a seemingly brave but deeply terrified protagonist in the drama. Huddled in a front pew, I was gripping my 83-year-old mother's hand as though I were five years old again.

I watched in grief-addled wonder as my 14-year-old niece Maddie sang "Angel" in her pure, ethereal voice. Our friend Marcia Ball, who was on tour and couldn't be with us, had recommended her talented friends Chris Gage and Christine Albert, known as Gage and Albert, to provide the music for the service. Maddie had taken only a few moments before the service to rehearse with Chris Gage, who would accompany her on the piano. She had never before sung with a professional musician, but she was pitch perfect. Just as the soldier at the airport had been.

As the congregation joined in the reading from the Book of Corinthians, I felt that St. Paul's great peroration on the power of love could have been written about Gary, who was the kindest, most patient, most tolerant, most peaceable, most humble, and most truth-seeking of men.

Love suffers long and is kind; love does not envy; love does not parade itself, is not puffed up;

does not behave rudely, does not seek its own, is not provoked, thinks no evil;

does not rejoice in iniquity, but rejoices in the truth....

These sublime scriptures, which are so often read at weddings, also help to explain why we are so utterly bereft when we lose our loved ones. Without Gary, I felt, nothing I did would have meaning.

Though I speak with the tongues of men and of angels, but have not love, I have become sounding brass or a clanging cymbal.

Paul was probably referring specifically to the practice of zenolalia, or speaking in tongues, one of the gifts of Pentecost described in the book of Acts. But Paul also seems to be suggesting that without the divine compass of love, even the most extraordinary talents and the most inspired oratory are rendered empty and meaningless. Did that mean that the loveless and forlorn should be silent?

Following the service, friends gathered in the church fellowship hall, where members of the women's circle that I belonged to prepared refreshments. Another friend had prepared the flowers, and still another had prepared a guestbook for those present to sign. My necessary angels had been busy.

I found myself looking for my neighbor Elizabeth, though I knew she wouldn't be there. The previous day, a next-door neighbor had dropped by her house, concerned that she hadn't seen Elizabeth bustling around the yard with her dogs. Elizabeth never locked her door, and so she walked into the small living room and found Elizabeth sitting in her favorite easy chair, seemingly asleep. But she didn't stir. She had passed away peacefully some hours earlier.

At the reception, I lost count of the friends who came over to tell me a special story about Gary. Our friend Daphne, who in her '80s still held a post at the LBJ School, wanted to tell me about the time she had been frustrated with her old computer, which kept crashing. Gary had told her to meet him at the local Apple store, where he had chosen two computers for her to try out. "No one else at the

LBJ School or anywhere else would have taken the time and trouble for an old computer phobe like me," she said.

There was even an old girlfriend of Gary's who hadn't seen him in decades, but who had traveled all the way from New York to say goodbye. I smiled sweetly at her, without a great deal of effort, and said that Gary would have been happy that she was there. A high school friend who hadn't seen Gary since their graduation night, and who had a fear of flying, had taken a train from Los Angeles all the way to Austin. And then there was Nancy Mims, who said she had seen a hawk zooming across the sky that morning with a small bird in its wake. "It was the strangest thing," she said.

On wings of divine deliverance.

As they sipped punch and reminisced, friends wandered over to a corner to watch a slide show with pictures of Gary and of our life together that one of my neighbors had prepared for me, using the photos I had gathered from various piles in our desk drawers: Gary going over a waterfall on the San Marcos River; Gary as a little boy in a cowboy hat riding in a wheeled rocketship his dad had made for him; Gary sitting at an alfresco table laden with antipasti beside Lake Garda; Gary gesturing to a monkey casually sitting on his head in Bali's Monkey Forest; Gary and I walking hand in hand in the mountains of the Garfagnana in northern Tuscany; Gary gesturing behind a lectern in a columned amphitheater as he spoke at a Chatauqua gathering; Gary at 20 looking incredibly skinny but proud in his army dress uniform.

At my request, my tech-savvy friend had inserted a background soundtrack of Marvin Gaye's "What's Going On," and I was happy to see folks discreetly swaying to the music. Marvin, like Gary, had known how to move people. I thought about the over-the-top note Gary had written about that song so long ago in New Orleans and amended it.

Amazing. Gary, I miss you. God spoke with your voice.

Chapter 21

Magic Mushrooms

Two days later, another gathering of the far-flung tribe of Gary convened in the ski-resort town of Andalo in the Italian Alps. Diego Latella, a computer scientist who lives in Pisa, had asked if I wanted to attend the winter session of ISODARCO, the International School on Disarmament and Research on Conflicts that Gary had been part of for nearly 20 years. Founded by two of Italy's most eminent physicists, ISODARCO held both summer and winter sessions in beautiful places, mostly in northern Italy. I had attended several meetings with Gary over the years, and those times had been among the happiest of our lives together. The organization was planning a memorial for Gary at Andalo, said Diego, and he was hoping I would be part of it.

Diego was one of Gary's closest friends, and he had been shocked to hear of Gary's death. He had sent me a simple email: "No!!!!!!!!!!!!!!!!" before expressing his grief more fully. Gary and I had spent holidays in the Garfagnana region north of Lucca with Diego and his wife Mieke, and they had stayed with us in Austin. I told Diego that I would be too busy planning Gary's memorial in Austin to travel to Andalo, which was a long bus ride into the mountains from the city of Trento, in the heart of the Dolomites. But the truth was that I wasn't sure I would ever be able to go back to Italy. I couldn't imagine being there without Gary, and the memories of our happiness there, I thought, would be too painful to bear. We agreed that I would write a reflection on what ISODARCO had meant to Gary to be read by Mieke at the memorial.

When I first met Gary, he told so many beguiling stories about his experiences at ISODARCO that I could hardly wait to join him on his next jaunt there. In the summer of 1998, the course was to be held in Candriai, yet another ski-resort village nestled in the Dolomiti. We wound our way up imposing Monte Bondone in a tiny rental car, and almost before we were unpacked, we found ourselves searching for porcini mushrooms with one of the Italian scientists who would be talking on the subject of "Technology Transfer," the theme of that season's session.

I had thought somehow that pigs were used to hunt porcini, as they did truffles, but humans, it seems, are the best porcini hunters. The amiable but exacting physicist taught us precisely where to look for the elusive *Boletus edulis*—only under a certain kind of tree. "Look first for the scouts," he said, pointing out a small stand of little white-capped mushrooms poking up from a bed of musty chestnut leaves. When I found my first porcini, whose hiding place was revealed by tell-tale white-capped scouts, it was like discovering gold.

Our treasures, however, had to be examined by the local "mushroom police" in order to make sure we didn't poison ourselves. We handed over our bounty to a school secretary, and I assumed that was that. But at dinner, we watched as our precious porcini emerged from the hotel kitchen in sliced and sautéed form on a platter big enough for everyone at the school to be served a delectable portion. It was as though they had multiplied like the loaves and the fishes.

It was then that I began to get a glimmering of the value of Slow Food and of the good life, or *il buon vivere*, that Gary had always told me was Italy's great gift to the world—that is, other than Machiavelli, Michelangelo, Galileo and Puccini. Along with technology, the ideals of Slow Food and conviviality should also be conveyed around the world. For Gary, technology was always a means toward bringing the good life to everyone.

The summer course held the next year in Rovereto brought more lessons about the importance of making strong human connections across borders and about what happens when those connections fail.

The subject that summer was "Computers, Networks and the Prospects for European and World Security."

One afternoon Gary and I visited the "Zona Sacra," atop one of the nearby mountain peaks, which commemorates the heavy loss of life there during World War I. We were moved to tears by the beautiful and enormous Maria Dolens, the "Bell of the Fallen," made from the bronze of melted cannons from the Great War. It tolls 100 times every evening at sundown to honor the dead of that terrible conflict and to ring forth a message of peace.

We visited the Sanctuary of Castel Dante, an ossuary dome housing the remains of more than 20,000 Italian, Czech, Austrian and Hungarian soldiers who died nearby in battle between 1915 and 1918, and then we followed the "peace trail" that winds south to the battlefields and trenches on mountain slopes where so much bloody fighting took place. We were astonished at how close the trenches dug by the two sides were to each other. Soldiers on one side could hear those on the other side talking, singing or coughing away their lives with the deadly influenza that took more lives than did the bullets.

The great highlight for Gary of ISODARCO came in 2002, when the summer course was held in the city of Trento. As usual, there were scientists and military experts present from around the world. That summer also marked Gary's 50th birthday, and the organizers held a birthday celebration for Gary at Masso Sasso, our favorite inn in the world, located on a mountainside overlooking the Adige Valley. The inn bore the official insignia of Slow Food, the iconic snail. Here we enjoyed Italian regional cooking at its best, with a hundred guests from around the world toasting Gary in multiple languages.

It was another scenario so perfect that I would have wanted to capture it on film so that we could savor those moments again and again. I didn't have even a single photo from that night, nor could I find one in Gary's pre-digital collection of snapshots. After Gary's death, I searched frantically for the leather-bound book that the eminent physicist Carlos Schaerf had presented to Gary that night, signed by all those present in various languages and alphabets.

I remember that we were seated under a grape arbor next to a jolly if acerbic Russian general, who amazed us by pointing to a spot in the Adige Valley where still another old battle had taken place, this one from the Napoleonic wars. It was here in this valley south of Rovereto, said the general, that the French had defeated the Austrians and their Russian allies, securing the Adige valley. That battle, he said, was commemorated on the Arc de Triomphe, with the name of the victorious French General Vaubois engraved at the base—a fact that we verified on our next trip to Paris. The French casualties had been light; the Austrians lost 6,000 men.

It was difficult to imagine such carnage and bloodshed in that verdant, vineyard-laden valley as we toasted each other with wine from that very valley and talked to each other over plates of lovingly prepared food that represented generations of tradition. The air was full of conviviality, of different languages and accents and points of view, all converging in this beautiful place. The possibility of mean- ingful connections across borders hovered over us like a sacral dove. Over dishes of perfectly prepared strawberry-infused semifreddo, world peace does not seem like a pipe dream.

In my reminiscence for Gary's memorial at ISODARCO, I quoted a phrase from the essay he had written about the good life, about his own hopes for a convivial world in the future, which I thought could have been inspired by that night, nourished by groups like ISODARCO and those willing to think in original ways about how to make a better life:

"It may only be over the course of many years that we come to recognize an emergent, new way of thinking, which is likely to take different but related forms all over the world. The common thread that may unite many disparate but like-minded efforts, from food activists to digital rights activists, is thinking about technology as malleable, as capable of serving human-determined ends, and as an essential component of 'il buon vivere,' the good life."

Chapter 22

A Sabbatical for Grief

Once Gary's memorial service at Central Presbyterian was over, I began to lapse back into the state of mind that I was beginning to think of as the Slough of Despond, the image of slogging despair I recalled from *Pilgrim's Progress*. I was sinking down into "This Miry Slough," as John Bunyan called it.

As the sinner is awakened about his lost condition, there ariseth in his soul many fears, and doubts, and discouraging apprehensions, which all of them get together, and settle in this place; and this is the reason of the badness of this ground.

Grief, the unwanted visitor, was settling in for a long, indefinite stay. It was not exactly loneliness that was enveloping me, but rather the overwhelming feeling of "aloneness," as Gary's aunt called her own feelings of grief after losing her beloved partner. The feeling was scary as hell, and it wasn't going away.

Aloneness, I thought, is the grudging and infinitely sad recognition that you are no longer part of a chosen plural life—"us", "ours" or "we"—but an involuntary singular one—"I," "me" or "mine." I had not yet, however, been able to give up the illusion of "us," "ours," or "we." I still hadn't changed the message on "our" landline answering service, so that those who phoned would hear Gary's cheerful, velvety voice telling callers they had reached the home of Gary Chapman and Carol Flake. On Facebook, I was still married to Gary Chapman. Online, at least, I was not a widow.

As I thought more about Bunyan's plodding but persistent pil-grim, I wondered if getting on the road might be a way of finding my way out of the Slough of Despond.

"This is your gap year," my friend Elizabeth said one day. "It's unwanted and unplanned, but it's still a gap year. A kind of invol-untary sabbatical."

Students and scholars use gap or sabbatical years to rediscover themselves, to travel to parts unknown, to explore ideas, to write without deadlines and distractions, to fulfill postponed dreams, to find their true purpose. A time out from the grind of ordinary life. My friend Sarah Bird had written a novel called *The Gap Year* about a mother and daughter whose lives part as the daughter comes of age and follows an unpredictable path to adulthood.

A gap year wasn't such a far-fetched notion, I admitted. I had already been hurled abruptly into a condition of disengagement from life as I had known it. So maybe this could also be a time to begin reinventing and reconstructing a life that had suddenly van-ished into thin air. I was in a kind of limbic, in-between stage of my life, with one life ended and another yet to be born. A new life that I couldn't begin to envision.

I could stay mired in limbo indefinitely if I weren't vigilant about trying to move on, to just keep walking, like the restless, homeless vagrant I sometimes saw in the mirror. But where? And how? In my periodically crazed state, I wasn't in any kind of shape to make sound decisions. I still had the feeling that I was talking to people from the bottom of a well. The most frequent and firm piece of advice I had heard about widowhood was not to make any important decisions for at least a year.

Travel, I thought, wouldn't involve permanence. With travel, you could make mistakes and still get back on track. I could always change course or come home. As I began to think about places I might want to go during my "gap" year, I realized, with Elizabeth's prompting, that this could also be a year of pilgrimage, and that my travel could be purposeful—not an attempt to outrun or walk away from my grief. In a sense, I had already begun my pilgrimage the day Gary died. And so what if I made a mistake? Grief was the dragon guarding the road, no matter which way I went or whether I stayed home.

I did have some misgivings, however. I had seen my share of pilgrims over the years, and many of them had been engaged in something that I thought of as groveling. I had seen barefoot grandmothers climbing up with bloodied knees towards miracle-promising icons, statues and relics around the world: up the rocky slope in Medugorje where Our Lady was said to have appeared to village children; up the padded lane to the marble Panayia Evangelistria church on the Greek island of Tinos with its jewel-encrusted icon of Mary, said to be the work of Saint Luke; up the stony road to La Parroquia de la Purisima Concepcion, with its floor of coffin lids, to touch the milagro-surrounded statue of St. Francis known as "Panchito," in the ghostly Mexican mining town of Real de Catorce.

I felt little kinship for the flagellators of the flesh who went searching for miracles on their knees. To mortify the flesh, it seemed to me, was to wish it dead—which made life not a gift but a dolorous burden. St. Francis was said to have asked pardon of his body, which he called Brother Ass, for the self-afflicted penances he had done. But I couldn't imagine that he would have wished such bodily suffering on those seeking his blessing or that he would have looked for scars and scabs on those who came to him for help as proof of faith. Nor could I imagine reaching a state of enlightenment by inching my way along the ground.

I much preferred the sort of story-telling camaraderie and the motley cast of characters that Chaucer described in Canterbury Tales, with the desire to go on pilgrimage as natural as virtue blooming like flowers in a spring rain after a drought.

Whan that aprill with his shoures soote
The droughte of march hath perced to the root
And bathed every veyn in swich licour

Of which vertu is the flour...
Thann longen folk to goon on pilgrimages.

One of my friends had followed the well-worn pilgrimage trail in Spain to Santiago de Compostela after the death of his wife, and he had trained for it for months. The characters he had encountered seemed as vivid and varied as those Chaucer had described. He had come back still grieving, aching and weary, but with a sense that the journey had put him on the road to recovery.

I wasn't thinking, however, of the usual hallowed landmarks or familiar trails for my own pilgrimage. Gary had no special connection to the places considered "sacred" destinations. He had gotten a bad headache and not much else while we were at Medugorje. The closest to reverence for a particular place I had ever seen in Gary was at the Alhambra, whose undeniable Moorish splendors he admired for their aesthetic rather than spiritual power. We had both shed tears over its beauty in the moonlight.

I had already learned that thin places aren't necessarily located far from home. And as I considered more seriously the prospect of making a pilgrimage of my own devising, I was thinking that I should visit the places that had held special significance for Gary or for our life together—and that I should also consider exploring unexpected places where I thought I might find healing. In other words, this would be an open-ended pilgrimage. The destinations, I thought, would reveal themselves as I went along.

Some destinations would simply be states of mind. Art historian Eleanor Munro had come close to describing my yearning in her lovely, meditative book about pilgrimage, *On Glory Roads*. Pilgrims, she said, "need to feel they are on a journey that rises out of the past while preserving its connections with it, in order to rise out of the way of hopeless death."

Pilgrimages, of course, cost money, even those made with backpacks or on hands and knees. As a new widow, I was in jeopardy of making the kind of financially disastrous mistakes that widows are famously prone to make. Every grieving widow, it seems, makes a crazed and wrong decision having to do with money. And going on a pilgrimage could be seen as an indulgence or extravagance I could ill afford. But I felt that my survival was at stake, and I needed to throw caution to the wind in order to make it through the next months. I sensed that this was a make-or-break time in my grief. Saving money for the long term didn't seem important when I wasn't sure there would be a long term.

Gary and I had been accumulating shares of Apple for many years, and we had bought most of our shares at an absurdly low price. Gary had always had great faith in Apple and Steve Jobs, and it had paid off in creating a nest egg that we thought would allow us to consider retiring in Italy, though in fact it would hardly have bought us even a tiny foothold in expensive Verona, the city Gary loved best. I had already sold some shares in order to bring Gary's body home. And so I decided to sell the remainder of the shares of Apple that had been part of the vanished dream of our life together in old age. I wasn't sure what Gary would have thought of that decision, but given that he was prone to extravagant gestures that we sometimes couldn't afford, I felt that he would have understood.

I regretted that Italy, which had brought us such joy in the past, was off limits for my pilgrimage. I couldn't imagine being there without him. My first destination, I decided, would be closer to home and just as close to my heart. I decided to go to New Orleans, the city that had always felt like my second home, and where my love affair with Gary had begun. I went to graduate school at Tulane during the 1970s and returned to the city during the early 1990s to write a book about Carnival. The ossified social structure of New Orleans had begun to unravel amid challenges to Carnival organizations' all-white membership policies and amid a crime wave that had swept across the city.

For all the masking that goes on in New Orleans, there is a commensurate unmasking, and during my time there I realized that I loved Gary, which meant putting a painful end to another relationship and venturing into a risky new life with the man I felt I had always been waiting for. Gary had joined me on a madcap Mardi Gras day that culminated my year of research into the city's arcane Carnival clubs and practices. We enjoyed that day so much that we continued to celebrate Carnival wherever we were living.

While we were renting an apartment in Somerville, Massachusetts, we created the expatriate Carnival Krewe of Barney, in honor of the disparaging nickname old residents of the city gave to newcomers, and held a parade of miniature floats. In Austin, Gary became famous for his outlandish Mardi Gras costumes. My favorite was his weird Elvis impersonation, with a foot-high pompadour he had created out of papier-mâché and boots that shed gold glitter when he danced. New Orleans seemed to bring out the wildly eccentric artist lurking inside his cool exterior.

Chapter 23

The Pelican and the Veteran

On the way to New Orleans, with Zip and Molly riding in the back of the SUV, I began to wonder if this improvised pilgrimage was a mistake and would simply be too painful, no matter where I went. Would all the places I visited be laced with such aching remembrance? My heart could hardly have been heavier as I circled Houston, passed Beaumont and approached the state line, where the landscape started getting swampier. I stopped at the welcome center just over the Louisiana border, where Gary and I had often stopped to break up the long drive.

The park sprawled along the edge of a coastal swamp, and I walked out among the cypresses and lily pads on a boardwalk. I hadn't been this way since before the Deepwater Horizon oil spill the previous summer had sullied the Gulf, and I was glad to see that there was no evidence here of the damage. A lone pelican circled and then landed so close by I could almost touch him. He perched there companionably as I took photos of him. As the state bird of Louisiana, the brown pelican seemed to represent the resilience of a place that had made comeback after comeback, despite hurricanes, corrupt politicians and slipshod oil drillers doing their best to sink it.

As I got back on the road, the dark, gathering clouds seemed to reflect my mood. But then I noticed a pattern in the clouds I had never seen before. They appeared to be stacked one upon another, with long, dark, parallel stripes marking their horizontal edges that looked like rungs on a ladder reaching up to the heavens. I thought of Jacob's Ladder, one of the most vivid images I retained from my

Sunday school Bible classes from long ago. In Jacob's dream, he sees angels ascending and descending the ladder, and he concludes that this must be the gate of heaven.

On impulse, I opened the glove compartment and retrieved some CDs that Gary had left there, and I put them into the CD player. I pressed the button to start the first CD in the carousel, Van Morrison's *Into the Mystic*, which seemed perfect for this stage of the journey. The player, however, jumped instead to another CD. Like my iPhone, it seemed to be driven by some mysterious DJ who was choosing songs from a cosmic playlist. It landed in the middle of Boz Scaggs' "Sierra," from his album *Fade into Light*, an ethereal lament about a departed love.

I had never been sure from the ambiguous lyrics whether the lost loved one has died or merely moved away into the mountains, where he has a "bird to give him warning." And now it seemed clear. After asking about "the one who said he loved you," the song admonishes, "Don't bother trying to find him way up in the icy air." And then comes the chorus, with the image of angels that "lay their clouds across his sky."

I continued driving toward the ladder in the clouds, and the distinctive rungs gradually vanished into the mist, as if the gate to heaven had closed.

And so it was that in the middle of the Louisiana swamp I found myself again in the realm of synchronicity, as Jung called those strange coincidences that can't be explained by ordinary means—events that happen together with no discernible connection or causality, but which hold the promise of connection in a context we are not yet able to see.

I arrived in New Orleans in a daze. Early the next morning, I headed from my friends' house in the French Quarter to the Moon Walk, the walkway by the Mississippi River named after Moon Landrieu, the city's beloved, pragmatic mayor who had recognized early on the importance of integrating the city's institutions.

Gary and I had begun our amazing Mardi Gras day 18 years earlier on the Moon Walk with the arrival by beer-keg-laden rowboat
of the motley Krewe of Stella. Probably the smallest of Mardi Gras
krewes, or clubs, this one consisted of a handful of already tipsy
young men whose mission was to clamber onshore and run down
the streets of the French Quarter yelling "Stella-a-a-a," in imitation
of Marlon Brando's histrionic agony in *A Streetcar Named Desire*.
A young man wearing a sheer white nightgown disembarked first,
followed by the bare-chested krewe captain sporting an unbuttoned
admiral's jacket, plumed hat and plaid boxer shorts. An even tipsier
onlooker pulled Gary's sleeve, pointing to the faux skipper. "He's
living it," he said. "He's living the dream." It was a scene that Gary
loved to recount for years afterward.

That day, we were laughing wildly as we ran farther down the
Moon Walk to catch the arrival of the paddlewheel riverboat *John
James Audubon*, which was bearing the King of the Krewe of Zulu
and his royal court, including Mr. Big Shot and the Witch Doctor,
all in retro blackface. It was a festive if surreal scene I recalled with
sadness 12 years later, in 2006, when I joined a jazz funeral and
parade held by Zulu during the first Carnival season following
Katrina. As krewe members marched lugubriously in their formal
gold-colored jackets past their boarded-up clubhouse, through
ruined neighborhoods where they had once lived, they mourned
the members they had lost during and after the flood. Some had
died of heart attacks after being evacuated and finding themselves
in unknown places, separated from their roots and their families.

The procession was joined by people who came out of seemingly
vacant houses, some women still in curlers and slippers, to walk
and dance in rhythm behind the jazz band, their numbers swelling
with the growing collection of followers and mourners known as
the second line. I recalled the inevitable turning point in the parade,
the one that comes with every jazz funeral. At a signal from the
parasol-toting parade marshal and a shift in rhythm from the band,

the dirgeful mourning turned into celebration, and the second line came to soul-stirring life, dancing with the joy of being alive.

I had felt that pivotal moment, marking a shift in music and mood from sorrow to joy, many times in New Orleans, along with the opposite pivotal moment, around midnight, when the wantonness of Mardi Gras shifts into the sobriety of Ash Wednesday. "From lust to lust, ashes to ashes," as one friend called it. I had always marveled at that ability to shift from celebration to penance and back again. Now, however, I didn't know if I would ever be able to make that pivot myself, from sorrow to joy. But at least I knew what it felt like. I knew that it was possible.

This time, I made my way slowly down the Moon Walk, past ragged men snoozing on benches, looking up only to ask for a handout when people passed by. One of them, however, stood out by holding out a card attesting to his status as an army veteran. He was a slender, unshaven black man with short, grizzled gray hair. "I'm a veteran," he said, "and I can prove it." His eyes were red-rimmed and rheumy, and he had the look and smell of too many days and nights outdoors. But there was something about him that had made me stop for a moment. There was something a little more focused about him than the other men sprawled or hunched on the benches.

"My husband was a veteran too," I said, and for some reason I started telling him about losing Gary. I didn't have any money with me, but I told him I'd stop on my way back. I headed up the Moon Walk and over to a side street to an ATM. I walked back to where I had seen the veteran and handed him the money. "This is from Gary," I said and walked on.

The next morning, I walked up the Moon Walk again and saw the veteran seated on the same bench. But he looked different, somehow. When I got up closer, I saw that he had changed clothes. His eyes were clear, and he smiled at me in recognition. He took my hand and looked at me with infinite sweetness. In my defenseless permeability, I felt as though he were looking into my soul.

"Everything's gonna be all right," he said, echoing the words of Gary's and my favorite Bob Marley song, "No Woman No Cry." "Don't worry," he said. "You'll be all right," he said, nodding confidently. And I could feel another small bundle of grief lifted from my heart.

Chapter 24

Second Line at the Lake

As I drove back to Austin, thinking about jazz funerals, and about the first jazz funeral I had witnessed in New Orleans, I realized that much of my time there during my impressionable twenties had been a kind of rehearsal for grief and consolation. That celebration back in 1974 had been for Billie Pierce, who with her late husband Dede had been one of the great legends of New Orleans music. I followed the funeral procession as it pulsed past a housing project where I would never have ventured on my own. The band launched into the one of Billie's favorite songs, "Nobody Knows You When You're Down And Out," and I found myself dancing in rhythm with the other celebrants in the second line, who had crossed that ineffable turning point, from mourning to celebration.

I felt such an inexplicable surge of vicarious joy that I hardly knew what to make of it. I rocked, bobbed and bugalooed along with the crowd in some kind of contagious ecstasy. How could death lead to such jubilance? Looking back, I realize that what I experienced was an epiphany—a showing forth, a revelation of something behind the curtain. I had stumbled onto something, as my friend and mentor Walker Percy might have put it. I had unwittingly begun a search, one that losing Gary had deepened, widened, and sharpened. I suppose it was a search for glimmers, as I had grown to call them. Wrote Percy:

"The search is what anyone would undertake if he were not sunk in the everydayness of his own life. To become aware of the possibility of the search is to be onto something. Not to be onto something is to be in despair."

It was one of my creative writing students at Tulane, however, who taught me the most memorable lesson about the power of the second line. Dorris Bagur, a retired social worker in her fifties, had been the star of the fall writing workshop I taught in a continuing education program. She disappeared in mid-semester, without notice, and returned a month later with a batch of really good poems. She had written them in New England where she had gone to see the autumn leaves. And to learn how to die. Dorris had been diagnosed with inoperable cancer, and she was determined to go out in a burst of glory. With their last, glorious blaze of color before winter, the trees, she said, were throwing themselves a jazz funeral.

Dorris died a few months later, and as she had requested, her family and friends attended a jazz funeral in her honor, like the ones that had sent the great musicians of Preservation Hall to their rest. That day, the Olympic Brass Band led the second line, and the music and dancing were so infectious that strangers from along the way swelled their numbers.

When I first told Gary about how I much I loved the second line tradition, he said he thought it must be akin to the state of being that the anthropologist Victor Turner called *communitas*. This form of spontaneous community, as Turner described it in uncharacteristically exuberant prose, creates bonds between people that are "undifferentiated, egalitarian, direct, extant, nonrational, existential, I-Thou, spontaneous, immediate, concrete." So the second line, I thought, with its disjointed, ever-widening parade, defies the strict lines of the military marching band, just as it cuts through the boundaries between life and death, joy and sorrow, friend and stranger.

After Gary's death, it occurred to me I had been living in New Orleans, writing about poetry and learning about the consolations of music, at a time when Gary had been in the army learning how to be a sharpshooter and a medic—both scourge and minister, to echo Hamlet; someone who wounds and heals. He, too, had set out on a search, though in his case I think it must have been more like a quest to find his way in this world as a peaceful warrior. Gary was a man of action as well as vision and wouldn't have been satisfied with glimmers. I imagined that he had sought remedies for those earlier contradictions in his life in philosophy and music and later in teaching.

I had been thinking for a while that I wanted to honor Gary with a second line, and Marcia Ball had promised to play for a "peace, love and barbecue" picnic when she had a break in her touring schedule. Though I found it immensely painful to walk down to the park at the lake near our house, where Gary and I had walked our dogs every morning, the park seemed a perfect place for a celebration in honor of Gary. He had served as head of our local community association for a couple of years and managed to transform endless acrimonious meetings at the clubhouse by the lake into orderly get-togethers. He was popular in the neighborhood.

One of our neighbors, an army veteran who ran a Christian catering service, volunteered to provide the barbecue. Others promised to put up tents and bring the drinks. The musicians in the neighborhood were delighted at the thought of playing with Marcia Ball, and they set up the outdoor sound system. I bought paper parasols to distribute for an impromptu second line, though I wasn't sure what my neighbors would make of the tradition.

As it turned out, I needn't have worried. As Marcia and the pickup neighborhood band played into the afternoon on a bright, crisp March day, our friend Lodis Rhodes, who knows New Orleans well, picked up a parasol, and he and I started a second line from the playground swings down toward the boat dock. Gradually, everyone followed, paper parasols bobbing up and down. It was as sweet and as vivid an image of *communitas* as Gary could ever have wished. As Marcia pounded out "Oh Didn't He Ramble," we danced our way down to the water. Kerry, one of my neighbors, whose husband had committed suicide five years earlier, had brought rose petals in a bucket, and we all dug in and grabbed some. At a signal from Kerry, we wafted them out over the water. The wind scattered them, but the current gathered them up and swirled them into a design. "Hey, it's a comma," said Kerry. "That means it's not the end of the sentence, just a pause." And there was a glimmer.

Chapter 25

Imagined *Retablos*

My consolations were coming randomly, something like found objects that came floating down the river. But they did keep coming. I began making a list of the things that had consoled me, and the closeness of family and the kindness of friends made up much of the list. But some items on the list were hard to categorize. As I thought about them, their solidity seemed to waver and almost vanish on closer examination, like the demigod Cupid when doubting Psyche held up the lantern in the darkness. Even so, the feeling of being loved and fleetingly embraced by something intangible lingered.

In addition to second-lining neighbors and the homeless veteran on the Moonwalk, these inexplicable comforts on my list included: the mysterious brushing sound at the door; the shadows of leaves pulsating on the sidewalk like a beating heart; the smudged image of a hawk in a final photo; the lone soldier at the airport; a wooden icon taking on my sorrow; a dead owl offering up its body for inspection; songs popping up on my iPhone and CD player like messages from a cosmic playlist.

I hesitated to think in terms of miracles, and so my working term was "comforting anomalies." It's possible that I was in a state of almost constant pareidolia, in which I perceived meaningful images and patterns in apparently random phenomena. But I could also have titled my list "meaningful coincidences," as Jung did, or "serendipitous encounters." Or maybe "synchronicitous nudges." Anything but out-and-out miracles, which would have to pass muster by the Vatican or some such august body. I had no doubt that my "miracles" would fail scrutiny by the scientific method as well, as few of my experiences were repeatable or obeyed the laws of probability. How could I explain to my examiners why I should have been singled out for preferential treatment, for nature bending its rules on my behalf? I would have to then awkwardly admit that I suspected that Gary had somehow become my intercessor, my guardian angel, my guide in a reconfigured cosmos.

If these anomalies were moments of grace, which was the way I experienced them, they came unexpectedly—and undeservedly, as grace usually does, from what theologians have had to say on the subject. Grace that seems to fall from heaven is not earned, but given. None of my consolations resulted from anything I did myself, except the little post-it notes of gratitude I folded into the silver urn on my dresser. Even those, however, seemed to come unbidden, as I tried to capture my sweetest memories of Gary. Gratitude seemed a way to stop time long enough to savor those moments before regret set in that they were gone forever. I imagined a scale in which each ounce of gratitude would eventually balance every ounce of grief.

Maybe I should have been making *retablos* of thanks, as they do in Mexico, painting remembered scenes of healing or miraculous recovery and spelling out their gratitude in messages to the Virgin or the saint who interceded. I still have a *retablo* over my desk in which one Juan Ortiz thanks Our lady of the Lake for helping to find a lost cow that had been thought to have drowned in a flood. It's dated April 11, 1937. The *retablos* make visible, in bright colors and in precise detail, down to date and place, the working of grace on the earth. Combined with *milagros*, the tin miniatures of body parts that have been miraculously healed, they suggest the possibility of answered prayers—or at least to a way of communication between the human and something greater, even if the spelled-out yearnings and thankfulness come from a wounded or wishful heart, and the salvation from chance rather than from above.

When my wounded and wishful heart was finally healed, per-haps I could place a tin miniature of it on my altar. But if I were to paint a *retablo*, it would be addressed to Gary rather than to a distant saint. I would not, of course, paint a *retablo* depicting him in a kayak, proudly brandishing his paddle after defeating death, December 14, 2010. I couldn't thank him for not dying. But I could depict scenes of him in the kitchen making risotto; peering help-fully over my shoulder at my dysfunctional computer; dancing with me in his determinedly funky but unrhythmic way. I could thank him, down to the dates and places where he had intervened in my ordinary life to make it extraordinary. Even miraculous.

Chapter 26

The Night of the Spoons

D espite the moments of grace that parted the clouds, there were times when I felt as though I were drifting along the bottom of the ocean, like the diaphanous creatures that have evolved in the darkness without eyes. But more often, I felt that I had become a simple yes-or-no organism that instinctively moved toward light and tried to inch away from the darkness. I almost always said yes to my friends who tried to get me out of the house into some semblance of the life I had known before. In the spirit of the second line, I was always looking for the turn toward life.

One night Larry Wright, his wife Roberta and his daughter Caroline, an artist who also plays the cello, had organized a kind of hootenanny at his house. It was an annual event, but this time they had decided to make it a special tribute to Gary and me. Larry is a member of a band called WhoDo, made up of an unlikely group of musicians, including a West Texas rabbi, a psychology professor at UT, and a reporter for National Public Radio. Although Larry had won the Pulitzer prize three years earlier for his book *The Looming Tower: Al-Qaeda and the Road to 9/11*, I always suspected he was nearly as proud of playing the keyboards with a blues band. Larry had invited a number of local musicians to the gathering, including our mutual friend Marcia Ball, and he told me to bring along my spoons.

Among other things I thought I'd never do again was play the spoons, but I could hardly turn Larry down. I have a peculiar talent for playing the spoons, which I developed in New Orleans by imitating a street musician called Mr. Spoons. I had sung backup and played the spoons for a jug band there called the Bad Oyster Band, and I had occasionally joined WhoDo for a song or two over the years when they were playing in Austin.

Larry and Caroline selected songs that had a special significance, including Moon Mullican's country classic, "I'll Sail My Ship Alone," and the old familiar hymn "Just a Closer Walk with Thee." There was Bill Withers' "Lean on Me," which promised someone to lean on "if there is a load you have to bear, That you can't carry." And for a change of pace, they included Mose Allison's sardonic "Your Mind Is On Vacation," though I knew they didn't realize how apt the title was for my current state of mind.

Playing the spoons doesn't require a great deal of brainpower, nor does it require sharply focused concentration. In fact, the looser the better, I had found in New Orleans. So I played my spoons along on everything that night, including songs they didn't belong on, but everyone said that they added a special touch. I played without tears through John Prine's "Paradise," with its melancholy chorus, "When I die, let my ashes float down the Green River." And I played without pause through Dylan's anthem, "I Shall Be Released." I got an inkling, however, of how musicians are able to play when drunk, stoned or semi-deranged. I felt oddly numb that night, despite the music and the kindness, but I did feel some relief from the ever-present pain and emptiness.

And so when Larry sent an email asking me to be sure to bring my spoons to WhoDo's next gig at Jovita's, a club in South Austin, I said yes, of course. Jovita's turned out to be a front for a ring of drug-dealers who were caught and jailed the next year, but none of us had a clue then that Jovita's served anything but good, if slowly delivered, Tex-Mex food. I arrived alone that night and sat at a table at the back of the room, not sure if this was too soon. Two women with short steel-gray hair were seated at the table next to me. As the band launched into "Sixty Minute Man," with Larry on keyboards and vocal, I got my spoons out of my purse and started tapping them tentatively under the table, thinking I should warm up before I got on stage.

Before I could get a rhythm going, one of the women at the next table looked over at me disapprovingly. "Will you please stop that noise," she snapped, with the righteous, harrumphing indignation of Dana Carvey's church lady. It was as though I had giggled during the death scene of *Madame Butterfly*.

I was still reeling from the sting of disapproval when Larry beckoned me on stage to join in a rendition of "High Blood Pressure." The band then launched into Hank Williams' jouncy "Jambalaya," and I found myself smiling with unexpected joy, forgetting everything but the music. Still smiling as I walked back toward my table, I was startled to feel a hand reach out and grab me. It felt more like a claw than a hand, actually. I looked down, and a severe-looking woman who appeared to be in her early sixties was glaring at me. "I, too, am a widow," she said, in what sounded like a German accent, but which I realized later was a Texas accent laden with reproach. "My husband died five years ago," she said. "And I could never have done what you are doing," she spat out.

Chapter 27

The Call of the Whooping Crane

My old friend Andy Sansom, who grew up just down the street from me in Lake Jackson, and who went on to become head of the Texas Parks & Wildlife Department, felt that getting back to work would be a good way for me to reenter the mainstream of life. I had written frequently for *Texas Parks & Wildlife Magazine* in the past, and I always relished going into the wild in search of a story. Andy was now the head of an institute devoted to water conservation in Texas, and he mentioned to Louie Bond, the editor of *Texas Parks & Wildlife Magazine*, that he thought I might be ready to write for them again. Their special water issue was coming up, and I had written frequently over the years about Texas waters.

Growing up near the Gulf, I had roots on the Texas coast as well as in the inland bayou country that had once sustained sugar plantations. In Lake Jackson, I had never been far from water. The reclaimed swampland along murky Oyster Creek, with its prehistoric-looking alligator gars and primeval vegetation, had given me a special connection to slow-moving waterways. As a kid, I used to take out my father's rowboat and pretend I was plying the Amazon. I once caught a six-foot alligator gar, which far outweighed me, with my dad's fishing rod, and it scared me so much I cried as I reeled it in, its mouth gaping with razor-sharp teeth.

Long before Gary and I took up kayaking, I had rowed and canoed my way along a number of rivers and lakes. I still owned five kayaks, three of which were Gary's, though I didn't think I'd ever be able to take one out again, even on utterly calm Lake Austin near our house. It was one of those items on my mental list of things I thought I'd never do again.

Andy didn't seem to realize that grief not only shadowed many of the places and pastimes I loved, but it had also wiped out my ability to put together more than a sentence at a time. The prospect of organizing interviews and doing research had become as daunting to me as dancing a jig would be to someone in a wheelchair. I had a vague memory of being able to write, but I felt I had lost the necessary wiring to get up and do it. When Louie Bond called, however, I couldn't say no because it meant saying no to the possibility of recovering the power of words and to getting on with my life. I said I would be happy to do a story on the health of Texas bays, as long as I didn't have to get in a kayak.

I had been relying on lists, my old standby, to help me get through the days when I felt overwhelmed, and I figured I could use lists to help me remember how to write an article — a kind of written version of painting by the numbers. I had been talking to a "survivor relations advisor" at my bank, and she confided that she, too, had lost her husband suddenly, and that, she, too, had relied on lists.

"You'll be amazed at your ability to make lists," she said. "A list can walk you into the future, step by step. Just don't expect to do everything on your lists."

I told her that I was already placing post-it notes around the house like someone afraid of slipping into dementia.

Pulling an idea out of the air, I told Louie that I would like to use whooping cranes as the centerpiece of my story. I liked the prospect of going to Aransas Wildlife Refuge on the Coastal Bend, where the whoopers made their winter home. I had followed the roller-coaster story of the migratory whoopers over the years, and I knew their survival was in question. I had never actually seen one of the birds, although the refuge is not far down the coast from Lake Jackson, and it's close to Mustang Island, where Gary and I had made a trip a few years earlier that was memorable in unexpected ways.

I had been assigned to do a feature story on the island, and I decided that we'd start by exploring the new paddling trails that the Parks & Wildlife Department had mapped out through the marshes on the barrier island. The first day of the trip was a comical disaster, as we had arrived during a late fall storm. Mustang Island is so famous for its blustery winds that country singer Pat Green has a lyric about bravely standing out in the island's winds. That day, the wind was blowing so hard that despite desperate paddling, we made absolutely no progress on the canals that cut through the marshes.

We noticed so many ducks flying in V-formations overhead that the sky appeared to be emblazoned with chevrons. When we finally began to inch our way into the saltwater flats edging Corpus Christi Bay by using our paddles as punting poles, we heard gunshots coming from the vegetation along the shore. We then heard angry shouts from the camouflaged hunters, hidden in duck blinds, who had sent shotgun pellets whizzing over our heads. I had neglected to notice that I had scheduled our trip on the first day of duck hunting season.

This time, I scheduled my trip during the annual Whooping Crane Festival, when theoretically there would be no shooting, other than camera clicks. My plan was to spend the night near the beach at Port Aransas and take a boat the next morning along Corpus Christi Bay to areas of the wildlife refuge where the cranes had marked out their winter territory.

Late that afternoon, shortly after I arrived, I walked down to the beach from my hotel. The wind picked up, and the plunging waves attracted some surfers near the jetties. I watched the piping plovers skitter along the sand, marveling at their hardiness. Like the whoopers, each one of the birds is banded, signaling that they are both protected and endangered. And like the tall whoopers, the tiny plovers make the perilous migration every fall from Canada to the Gulf. They number more than the whoopers, and their critical habitat is more widespread, but at this stage of the game, their survival was just as precarious. I imagined a photo-shopped postcard with a whooping crane towering over a tiny plover, emblazoned with the motto: "Partners in survival."

As the wind whistled and the surf roared, it occurred to me that Gary and I should have tried spending time on the coast in order to relieve his tinnitus. For Gary, silence had been the enemy. If being on the river gave him a break, surely the pounding of the sea would have soothed the endless ringing that tormented him when all was silent.

I took off my shoes, rolled up my jeans and waded into the cold water. With the waves buffeting my legs, I started a conversation with Gary in my mind that continued when I got back to my hotel room and sat at my computer. I began to write to him, as though I were sending him an email, the way I always did when I was away on a trip, researching a story. The words came out awkwardly, and I felt like a high school student unable to translate my turbulent emotions into anything but trite and stilted language. It was as though I had been sent back to a remedial writing class. Nevertheless, sending my words into the ether felt something like meditative prayer, since I wasn't expecting an answer. I hadn't really been able to pray in the usual way after Gary died, as all my words aimed at heaven wound up being directed to Gary.

> *Dear Gary,*
>
> *I'm here in Port Aransas, wishing you were here so we could go for a walk on the beach together. I was thinking when I heard the roar of the surf that we could somehow have figured out what to do about your tinnitus.*
>
> *So what did you mean in that dream the other night when you told me I should put you on "yesterday's slide rack"? I've never heard of a slide rack. I googled it, and the only slide rack I could find was one where you hang things on and slide along a pole, like hangers on a clothes rack. So you were telling me I should slide you over to the edge of the closet, out of sight, where your shirts are still hanging, still starched and pressed from the cleaners?*
>
> *I can't do that.*

The next morning I joined the crowd of devoted binocular-wielding birders who had boarded the 75-foot S.S. Wharf Cat and marked out stations on the deck as the boat chugged across Aransas Bay. I felt that I was not completely on board, not really present in the way the birders were, the way I would have been before Gary died. Part of me was dragging along the bottom of the bay like a heavy anchor. But I braced myself against the rail and focused my binoculars on the marshy edge of the refuge, as two white blobs resolved themselves into a pair of huge birds feeding in a shallow pond.

One of the birds lifted its head in our direction, as though in acknowledgment of our approach. There was no mistaking the distinctive reddish-capped head, the prominent beak, the long, curving neck, the stilty blue-black legs.

Partly because my grief was a kind of veil, and partly because of the mist hovering over the marsh, I felt that we had come upon a pair of unicorns that had appeared out of a mythical age. Tears filled my eyes. There were so few of these luminous creatures. So few. And despite their heroic size, they were so fragile. A shortage of blue crabs just two years ago, brought on by drought and the resulting drop in water salinity, had led to a terrifying die-off of their numbers. I was feeling particularly vulnerable to any suggestion of mortality, and my joy in seeing the birds was overshadowed by a fear that they would disappear before my eyes.

A voice crackling over the loudspeaker broke the spell. "That's Old Lobstick," said George Archibald, founder of the international Crane Foundation, who was guiding the day's expedition. But his crisp, authoritative voice was laden with suppressed emotion. He had spotted an old friend, I thought. He loves these birds beyond measure.

I thought of the old gospel song, "His Eye is on the Sparrow," inspired by the words of Jesus in the Gospel of Matthew. Jesus grants an intrinsic value to birds and indicates that each one is not only valued, but counted: "Look at the birds of the air; they neither sow nor reap nor gather into barns, and yet your heavenly Father feeds them ... Are not two sparrows sold for a farthing: And one of them shall not fall on the ground without your Father."

The bird known as Old Lobstick, the grand patriarch of the Aransas flock, had been banded and numbered by concerned birders 32 years earlier. His nickname was derived from his nesting area in Canada, located in wetlands along Lobstick Creek, in the Northwest Territories. According to George Archibald, Old Lobstick was the oldest known whooping crane, surviving long after the average longevity of 23 years. Although cranes mate for life, they are known to take a new mate when a mate dies. Old Lobstick's longtime mate had disappeared along the way, and he had apparently found a younger mate. But the pair hadn't brought a chick along with them during the fall when they arrived at the refuge after their long migration from Canada.

I wondered if Old Lobstick had grieved for the loss of his old mate, whether images of her flashed in front of him as he waded in the marshes or followed the familiar skypaths from north to south. The courtship dance of the whooping crane is such a hypnotic ritual, I thought, perhaps the birds should also perform a dance upon the death of a mate.

Animals do mourn in their own way, I knew. Although they may or may not be aware of their own mortality, death does not leave them untouched. I could imagine elephants gathering solemnly around the body of a matriarch who has died, then returning to touch her bones with their trunks years later. Our dog Zip had gone into mourning after the death of our older dog Dave, refusing to eat. And he had shivered fearfully next to me in my bed for many nights after Gary's death.

Old Lobstick had been granted more than his fair measure of time. But his survival was entwined with factors beyond his own pluckiness and genetic grit. Something as seemingly insignificant as a small shift in salinity could spell the end not only of Old Lobstick, but of all the cranes who find refuge on the Texas coast every winter. During the drought of 2008, when nearly two dozen of his flock-mates died of starvation, Old Lobstick was observed to have trouble flying. But he had managed to survive, and he was still the first crane birders spotted when they neared the refuge.

I thought of Old Lobstick as a kind of outsized canary in the mine, a long-legged sentinel patrolling the edges of survival to gauge the state of the environment – and of human connectedness to the natural world. Counting cranes, it seemed to me, seemed to be a way of taking the measure of our souls.

Two years later, as I began sorting through the memories and notes from my pilgrimage, I was curious to find out how Old Lobstick was faring, and I learned that a crane feared to be Old Lobstick had been shot and killed in the vicinity of Miller, South Dakota, during the winter migration. Old Lobstick would have been 34 years old. Because Old Lobstick had long since lost his numbered band, the identification wasn't definitive. It was generally assumed, however, that Old Lobstick had perished. But Captain Tommy Moore, the skipper of the Black Skimmer, a whooping crane tour boat that anchored in Port Aransas, vowed that he had seen a very large crane in the territory that had been claimed by Old Lobstick, and he believed the old bird was still alive.

On wings of divine deliverance.

The whooping crane's murderer had not been caught. But I tried to imagine the man with the gun who saw the old bird standing in the cold Dakota marsh like a mirage, as rare a sight as a unicorn. His response to this vision of wild and startling splendor was to shoot it. I wondered if he had even paused for a moment of wonder before pulling the trigger. I simply couldn't comprehend the barbarity of killing something so beautiful and so rare. But in the Native American view, the increasingly distant human relationship to the natural world has become so distorted and fractured that for men like the crane killer, the only powerful connection to nature that remains is a gun.

Thinking back to Mary Chapin Carpenter's "Age of Miracles," and its suggestions of a possible future, I had begun to make yet another mental list, this one on whether humans would "get up that hill," as she had pondered. I felt that in some way, my own ability to get up the hill was tied in with a larger destiny. If I didn't have faith in the future or in my fellow humans, my own quest to climb out of my despair seemed quixotic and maybe futile. I needed to believe that the canary could survive the mine in order to believe that I could find my way out of the darkness.

Chapter 28

The Body Disconsolate

arner's, the company known for making corsets and then brassieres, introduced a black corselet in 1955 named after The Merry Widow, the 1905 operetta. The new "merry widow" design, which combined bra and girdle, featured demi-cups and a shorter girdle than earlier models. Its "support" wires were wrapped in black satin. The result was a paradox of velvet-and-satin-encased misery. Ironically, the design became a standard for bridal lingerie. Lana Turner was said to have declared at the time that the merry widow must have been designed by a man because a woman "would never do that to another woman."

"I could never have done what you are doing," the unmerry widow had said. And just what was it that I was doing, I wondered. So far, though I had leaned heavily on my friends, I had essentially been winging it on my own in dealing with my grief. I was walking around in a shell-shocked daze much of the time, and I was unbalanced, as I discovered when I tried unsuccessfully to resume my yoga practice. Even the simplest poses brought on severe vertigo and nausea.

My ADD had proved so extreme that I gave up reading anything other than Jack Reacher thrillers, which a friend had recommended. The last thing I wanted to read was something that would make me think or feel. I would read a paragraph or two of Reacher-in-action, taking out villains, every night when I went to bed and sometimes more in the wee hours when I couldn't sleep, which was most nights. With Reacher, Lee Child had created a character who was completely lacking in the "remorse gene," as he put it, which made his violent adventures ideal escape fiction for someone who was submerged in grief and second-guessing. I would always forget the story line from the previous night, but somehow it didn't matter, as Reacher, the unencumbered drifter, always seemed to be on the bus to someplace different.

Obviously, I wasn't normal or anything close to it. But I was pretty sure I wasn't crazy, though the disapproving widow clearly thought I must be out of my mind. The proof of at least partial sanity was that I had been able to write a decent piece about the plight of the whooping cranes, though the process had been agonizing, and it had taken far longer than it should. Nor was I depressed, in the usual sense. I had come up with my own diagnosis: I was simply shattered; I was in pieces. Focusing on the memorial events for Gary had kept me together enough to function. But now that the public rituals were over, I thought that before continuing on my pilgrimage, I should probably try the more conventional kind of consolations for the bereaved that were available in Austin.

I had gone to my doctor, who gave me prescriptions for Xanax for anxiety and Ambien to help me sleep. I stopped taking them after only a couple of nights, however, because I felt they were just masking the pain, and they upset my already dysfunctional digestive system. I had an overwhelming fear of getting sick because my body had taken such a heavy blow. I knew that trauma affects the body, and I felt that grief had taken root in every organ, every muscle, every cell. I was grief-ridden. I felt that somehow my mind had taken leave from my body, just to get away from the pain. My psyche was an evicted ghost hovering outside my body, trying to find a way in. It reminded me of a recurring dream I had about finding myself in the back seat of a car when there was no one in the driver's seat. I could never find my way to the steering wheel in time, and I would wake up with my heart pounding.

A friend had given me a gift certificate for a massage, and at even the lightest touch, tears poured down my face. I felt that grief was coming out of every pore. I hadn't been touched in a meaningful way since Gary died, and I had a fleeting moment of understanding why lonely men went to prostitutes in order to be touched.

I decided to consult a somatic psychotherapist, who specialized in mind-body connectedness. Laura, who had started a wellness center that housed yoga teachers, midwives, relationship coaches and acupuncturists, said that my symptoms were common to women who had suffered the loss of a husband or of a child. Grief is extraordinarily stressful on the body, she said, and because it lasts a long time, the body can remain in high-stress mode. Reducing stress, she said, was crucial. As we did exercises to gauge where I was storing my pain, it appeared that I was holding it primarily in my shoulders and in my solar plexus and stomach. As she led me in a relaxation exercise, I could feel how abnormally I had been carrying myself, like someone bent over in pain and carrying a weight on my shoulders.

Though some analysts in the past attempted to have grief categorized as a disease or disorder, it seemed to me that it was more like getting beaten up and having a limb removed. Healing of the bruises was possible, but the lost limb would continue to hurt indefinitely as though it was still there.

The body, some writers have said, is not really separate from mind, but rather acts as a "slow mind." The unconscious mind, in this view, speaks through the language of the body. And that was the language I was hearing in my pain. When I was finally able to start reading again, the writing I found most consoling came from a group of Buddhist women who wrote about coming to terms with suffering in physical as well as spiritual ways.

In a splendid collection of essays called *Being Bodies: Buddhist Women on the Paradox of Embodiment,* Joan Iten Sutherland wrote that healing was not the elimination of illness, but rather a falling in love with the poignancy of being alive. For illness, I substituted the word grief. In that same collection, Darlene Cohen had written of her spiritual practice of meditation that to practice mainly to get rid of your suffering rather than to express your life is "narrow."

By focusing on grief, I was shutting out everything else. I think what I feared most was getting lost in my suffering and being defined by it. And so I was clearly not an ideal candidate for a grief group, or at least for the one that I joined briefly, at Laura's recommendation. We gathered in a peaceful space, lined with cushions, the walls painted a soothing and peaceful green. I looked forward initially to hearing the stories other women had to tell. I particularly liked a feisty woman named Willa in her early 40s whose older husband had died while they were making love.

"It was the kind of classic heart attack known as the widow-maker," she said, with a wry smile, though no one laughed.

Willa's favorite book, she said, was *Widows Wear Stilettos*, which she said was about a group of younger widows who were determined not to be "old hags." I told her that I could imagine a companion title, *Widows Wear Cowboy Boots and Play the Spoons*. Willa asked if I had felt Gary's presence after his death, and I told her about "The Age of Miracles" popping up on my iPhone.

"Wow," she said. "Like intergalactic texting. You're lucky. My husband has been a lazy ghost. He hasn't called or written. Not even a dream."

We then heard from a university librarian who appeared to be in her fifties who had not been able to get on with her life after her husband passed away. She had not gotten beyond "going through the motions," she said. She wept uncontrollably as she told her story, and all of us shed sympathetic tears. But I felt a shiver of fear when she said that it had been more than five years since her husband's death. No one who is still new to grief wants to hear about mourning without end.

Another woman, well into her sixties, told about losing her mother many years earlier. As she related her story, the grief was punctuated with unacknowledged resentment over still unresolved disagreements. She kept talking and talking. And talking.

A broken record that kept skipping to the same sore spot. I kept looking around to judge whether it would be rude to leave.

My discomfort turned into an itchy, uncontrollable get-me-out-of-here urge when one of the group leaders, who was more than eight months pregnant and apparently about to pop, asked us to hum along with the crystal bowls that she was striking. Bong.....We were supposed to let go of this and that and tune into something or other as we hummed. I was so out of tune with the group that I had an impulse to laugh, but the impulse was too close to tears to indulge.

What was wrong with this picture? I asked myself. What I saw was a lovely, earnest young woman with a new life growing inside her and no storms on the horizon trying to counsel a group of frayed, falling-apart women beyond child-bearing age who had seen the worst and who were dealing with endings rather than beginnings.

I had a feeling I wouldn't be coming back. I knew that sharing grief with other women would be helpful to many widows. Isolation, as Mike the Treat Man had warned, was one of the worst side effects of grief. But I dreaded the notion of getting stuck in my story, as a therapist friend later put it. I already had a tendency to absorb other people's problems, and in my porous state, I didn't have the strength to maintain my boundaries.

I later learned that many researchers who studied the benefits of grief counseling, in which professionals or peers try to "facilitate" the grieving process, came up with rather discouraging results. Two quantitative reviews of the working-through-grief process found no significant gains from it, while a third found only modest positive effects. "Many bereaved individuals may need no particular advice or help," concluded one researcher. But I wondered if part of the problem in such studies may have been an assumption on the part of helpful peers or would-be counselors that grief is like a boil to be lanced — that it needs to be brought to the surface and purged, somehow.

My own view was that if "grief counseling" doesn't appear to have much of a positive effect, it's because there is no "cure" for

grief, that each of us who grieve may instinctively seek out our own paths back to the land of the living. I was not going to talk or weep my way out of grief; I was going to have to live my way out of it.

My friend Elizabeth, who checked in with me every day, became a grief group of one. She had suffered a very similar shock to mine, with her husband dying so suddenly, and she was candid about the mistakes she had made in the aftermath. Most importantly, she had come through her grief and made a new life, step by step. She remarried, and she radiated a contentment with her life that shone in front of me like the illumination of headlights on a dark road. It was Elizabeth who told me that for a good while I probably wouldn't be able to see farther down the road than the length of a flashlight beam.

Rather than focus on my pain, I wanted to do as the Buddhist women had advised, which was to focus on life. It was what Gary's Cajun friend Barry Day had told me that Gary would want for me — to go on with my life, full bore. But I knew I was far from ready. Rather than thumbing through books on grief, which I wasn't yet able to read, I began to skim through books on happiness. Happiness, so the experts said, could be a choice. And apparently it didn't hinge on money or twists of fate. Everyone, it seems, has a baseline of relative happiness, to which they return, even after great sorrows or great triumphs. But the notion of being born relatively gloomy or cheery seemed drearily deterministic to me. I preferred the outlook of positive psychologists, for whom happiness — or the lack of it — could also result from choices. I would dread a test to see if I were destined genetically for gloom.

My friend Emily, who had endured severe physical pain for many years, told me that at every fork in the road, where it was possible to choose, and at every juncture that required a positive or negative judgment, she tried to choose the positive alternative. She reminded me of the Choctaws who had talked about staying on the "bright path," their way of maintaining their identity in the midst of loss and displacement. The seemingly random designs on their embroidery and beadwork, with arrows pointing toward or away from the center, actually showed a pathway of choices.

Was I guilty of trying to escape or to deny my status as a widow? Widowhood was hardly a choice. It had happened to me as a twist of fate. But if there had been a pew in church reserved for widows, I'm not sure I would have wanted to be there. I would rather have been singing in the choir—that is, if I could sing—or maybe playing the spoons.

All I knew at the time was that I needed to resume my pilgrimage, to get back on the bright path. Three significant dates, which I dreaded, were approaching: Easter; my birthday; and the four-month anniversary of Gary's death. I had been warned that the four-month period would be far harder than I could imagine. And I knew that my birthday, which Gary always made a special occasion, would be difficult.

As I tried to envision a place where I would suffer least, I thought about the always irreverent writer Molly Ivins, who, in the late stages of her fatal illness, preferred not to talk about dying, but talked instead about going away to France. At her funeral, a friend declared that Molly had not died, but had gone to Paris—a euphemism that many of us had adopted subsequently when we lost someone dear.

And so it was that I decided to go to Paris, even though I could hear the unmerry widow's finger-wagging refrain, "I could never have done what you are doing." Although she had not been a necessary angel, she was perhaps a necessary scold to keep me questioning as I proceeded on my pilgrimage.

Part III

Slow Grief

A shared vision of the "good life" is never complete, but
is always adapting; it should be in harmony with the
human condition, which means that it encompasses
suffering, loss and conflict as well as pleasures, reverence
and common goals of improvement.

~ Gary Chapman

Chapter 29

Joyeux Pâques

I had a particular dread of my first Easter without Gary. It wasn't a holiday I wanted to experience alone, though I don't recall that Gary ever gave Easter a thought. Even as a child, I felt that the greeting "Happy Easter" had a peculiar ring to it. If I had known the word then, I would have called it an oxymoron, or a contradiction in terms. The story of the long, drawn-out, gruesome death of the son of God didn't quite fit with beribboned baskets, the big white bunny and the festive dyed eggs hidden in the grass.

Nor could I make the story fit with the new finery that I sported proudly at church every Easter Sunday. Yes, that's my Easter dress, my Easter hat, my Easter shoes, my Easter gloves, my Easter purse. And yes, Jesus died on the cross for my sins. So that I could be "saved." Saved for what? From what? Was I worth it? Were any of us worth it? Was my quiet Sunday School mate Luis B. worth it, who later came back from Vietnam to become a pioneer in domestic terrorism?

I remember one Easter photo in particular, where I am wearing a new pink linen dress, sewn by my grandmother on her ancient foot-powered Singer, and a skull-hugging white hat with a wisp of a veil. I am clasping my new white Easter purse and smiling proudly in that now faded photo, my eyes squinting in the bright sun. How could I reconcile that apparent pride in pink-and-white homemade sartorial splendor with the primordial agony entwined in the holiday?

The "happy" part of Easter had to do with the resurrection, I supposed at the time. So Jesus wasn't dead after all. What a turn-around. But if you've just learned that the Easter bunny isn't real, it becomes difficult to know what to believe. I was so haunted by what happened before the stone rolled away from the tomb, by the horrific images of the unimaginable suffering of Jesus on the cross, the nails hammered into hands and feet, the spear in the side, blood pouring from his wounds, that I couldn't get my mind around the idea that he had actually risen from the dead. Why wouldn't Thomas have doubted? And yet I often spoke to Jesus in my prayers. He was always on call, ready to listen. So he must have made it through somehow.

He has never left for ever.

Growing up as a Southern Baptist, I never quite understood why the ordeal of Jesus on the cross was referred to by the Catholics in town as the "passion" of Christ. Why would Jesus have been passionate about his suffering? It wasn't until later that I learned that the word "passion" actually derives from the Latin word for suffering: *passio.* Which implies that suffering is inseparable from passion. After all, suffering could hardly be dispassionate—or you wouldn't be suffering. As writer Pico Iyer once pointed out, in his acerbic but lyrical way, if you think about the etymology, the opposite of suffering is apathy. And so the passion of Christ, he wrote, is a "reminder, even a proof, that suffering is something that a few high souls embrace to try to lessen the pains of others."

Every Easter Sunday, our pastor, Brother Johnny Beard, would graphically describe for the congregation, trapped in unforgiving pews, shifting uncomfortably in their new pastel finery, the series of humiliations Jesus endured before dying on Golgotha, the place of the skull: the Roman guards gambling over his clothes, the placing the crown of thorns on his head, the vinegar held to his lips, the tacking on the cross of the label "King of the Jews" as a cruel mockery.

For a child, those vivid images of suffering and humiliation, with their bloody horror-movie details, seemed far more real than the resurrection. And I still found Easter more wrenching than spiritually uplifting. There was just too much darkness before the light, too much room for doubt. And now, with Gary gone like the fisher king, like Osiris, like all the dead heroes awaiting mystical rebirth with the blooms of spring, I wasn't sure how I could bear it. There would be no stone rolling away from the tomb, no good news to share.

The idea of spending Easter in Paris actually came to me when I saw festive images of store windows filled with huge, beautifully decorated chocolate eggs and the sculpted chocolate versions of the winged bells that had, according to tradition, flown back from Rome after being blessed by the pope. As they flew, they dropped eggs in gardens and rang out the joy of the resurrection, *Joyeux Pâques*.

I imagined that Parisians, with their Easter embellished by choc-olatiers, would not be haunted by gruesome images of Golgotha, despite the presence of so many masterfully painted crucifixion scenes—say, Bellini's, which is almost delicately beautiful—in the Louvre. I must have been hoping for some vicarious joy, that the City of Light would simply swallow me up in its rhythms and that its flavors would feed me through my skin, no matter how wretched and alone I was feeling.

I had no schedule or plan except to meet up at various points with Don, Gary's paddling buddy, and his wife Annie, who had become a good friend. Annie was working as a gofer for an experi-mental moviemaker who was shooting scenes in Paris, and they were staying at a hotel near mine. I settled into a tiny, cloister-like room in the Hotel Crystal, where Gary and I had stayed twice before. I loved its location, next to the fabled Café de Flore and across from the Église de St. Germain des Prés, the oldest church in Paris.

I arrived early in the day and headed out onto the Boulevard St. Germain, my memories vacillating wildly from my first time strolling on that stylish street when I was a wide-eyed and vulner-able twenty-two to the first time I had walked past the cafes and shop windows hand-in-hand with Gary, early in our relationship, with the same sense of wonder and discovery.

That first time, I had succumbed to a quick, forgettable and foolish affair with a *chasseur*, a hunter, as he called himself, and this time, I was with my true love. I had been so overcome with love and lust for Gary as we walked across the Pont Neuf that I stopped in the middle of the bridge and surprised him with a big, full-body hug and kiss. From love imagined to love found. And now lost.

Still thinking about that time when I was so carried away by love, I stopped at the Café Deux Magots, where Gary and I had often lingered over our coffees. I found myself sitting next to a pretty young American woman who was scribbling sporadically in what appeared to be a well-worn journal. Just like me when I was here in my 20s, I thought. Trying to take it all in and get it all down. In my still-permeable state, which often prompted me to talk to strangers, I asked her where she was from.

"I'm from Philadelphia, but I've been living here a couple of years," she said. "My husband has a job here, and I'm trying to figure out a life."

I wondered what that would be like, trying to make a new life in a dazzling city far from home. I was still feeling like an anchorless vagabond, uprooted from my old life in Austin, and I was more than mildly curious about what it would be like to live in Paris. I had no illusions about the glittering expatriate life, a la Hemingway and Fitzgerald. But Paris is seductive, and I was feeling that without Gary I had no real home. Why not Paris?

"So how do you like it here?" I asked.

She thought a moment, measuring her thoughts—deciding whether to be forthright, I felt.

"You know, the French are very hard on themselves," she said.

I was startled by the observation. That would not have been my take on the exquisitely styled French women I had been half-envying. They made it look effortless, maybe even genetic. Noticing my puzzled look, she continued.

"The sense of style comes at a cost. Everything has to be just so, whether it's food or clothing or conversation. The French are wound very tight. I think it's exhausting for them. I know it is for me."

She's right, I thought. The picture began rearranging itself as I continued down the boulevard, wondering how much preparation went into the perfectly draped scarves, the precisely correct hemlines, the dashing bangs cut just the right length, all put together in a seemingly casual way. It made me tired just thinking about it. I found myself feeling a little less envious and even a little homesick.

I arrived at the long lines wrapping around the Musée d'Orsay, surprised to see that a visiting exhibit of Pre-Raphaelite photographs, which were paired with congruent paintings, had actually arrived there from Austin's Ransom Center shortly before I had. The title had shifted en route, however, from the prosaic "The Pre-Raphaelite Lens" to the more melodramatic "Ballads of Love and Death," which someone must have thought was better suited to Paris. Although I had always rather liked the Pre-Raphaelites, with their delicately portentous stained-glass Gothic sensibility, this time I found them cloying and artificial, enmired in the Victorian sensibility they were trying to transcend: love and death in dreamy poses.

Clearly my ADD irritability was extending to art as well as writing. I speed-walked through the exhibit and found some relief in an exhibit on Manet, "the Man Who Invented Modernity," though I bristled, as I always had, at the nude model posing on the lawn like a large dessert for the gentlemen's picnic in *Le Déjeuner sur l'Herbe*. Manet's modernity went only so far, I thought.

I made my way back to the Église de St. Germain des Prés, which had already become as familiar to me as a local church. I had a bone to pick, so to speak, with René Descartes, whose funeral stone lies under the window of the second chapel. Descartes died in 1650 without resolving the great mind-body duality argument that has continued to plague us. I wanted to tell Descartes that he might have done the world a great service with his mathematics but that he had given us a setback with his disruptive notion of a mind-body dichotomy.

Admittedly, he had been right in certain circumstances. My mind was definitely on the outs with my body at the moment—the ghost hovering outside the machine, as Descartes debunker Gilbert Ryles would say. But if my body was a machine governed by natural laws, as Descartes had posited, how could I heal mind and body together?

Music would be one way, I hoped. I asked Don and Annie to join me for a concert of sacred music at Notre Dame, though I hesitated briefly when I saw from the program that the theme would be "Les mystères douloureux," the sorrowful mysteries, with Gregorian chants and medieval polyphonies and pieces and improvisations played on the grand *orgue*. We would hear the passion of Christ acted out in sorrowful chants, amplified by the swelling sublimity of the grand organ, with its more than 7,000 pipes. The tableaus would begin with the prayer of Jesus in the Garden of Gethsemane, followed by the flagellation, the crown of thorns, the carrying of the cross, ending with the crucifixion. I wasn't to escape the sorrows of Easter, after all. But where better to experience them than Notre Dame, where even the most prosaic prayers seem to take on an exalted resonance?

As the six robed men of the Ensemble Gregorien de Notre Dame de Paris chanted the melodious words from centuries-old codexes and manuscripts, I was struck by the depiction of Jesus's sense of injustice at what was happening and by his very human questioning of this anguish. "*Moi, je t'ai donné an scepter royal; mais toi tu as placé sur ma tête une couronne d'épines.*" Me, I gave you a royal scepter; but you, you placed on my head a crown of thorns. Again and again, he repeats, *O mon peuple, que t'ai-je fait? En quoi t'ai-je contriste?* O my people, what did I do to you? In what did I sadden you? *Réponds-moi.* Answer me, he almost seems to beg. Jesus appears to be resisting his fate, calling out to his tormentors and to God. But then he lets go. "*Tout est consommé.*" It is finished. It is accomplished.

As I listened to the words of Jesus struggling against his destiny, I couldn't help but think of Gary's battle on the river, as he realized that he was facing his death. Gary's struggle and his death had somehow become entwined in my psyche with the passion story of Jesus. I knew that Gary must have fought mightily. He must have resisted his fate with everything in his mind, body and soul. And then there was a point at which he let go. It was finished. *Tout est consommé.* A universal story, really. As Joseph Campbell and others have told us, there is only one story, with many faces, of the hero whose quest ends finally in sacrifice.

Resisting tears, I wrote a note to Annie Hudson, for whom I was translating: "The next part is about the suffering of Mary, sung by men." And the tenors and baritones did their best. *"Moi qui ne connaissais pas auparavant la peine, je suis fatigué de ma peine, je suis crucifée par ma douleur."* Grief I did not know before, but now I am worn out by grief and tortured by sorrow.

So many songs of love and death. So much sorrow. For a moment I was Mary and all women who have lost their men to a fate they didn't choose. In this 12th-century recitation of her suffering, written by Godefroy de Saint-Victor, Mary resists consolation and asks that she take her son's place in death. *"Mon unique consolation est de vous plaindre."* My only consolation is to weep for you.

On the final page of the program, following the text of Saint-Victor's Planctus, was a photo of Nicholas Coustou's Pietà, one of the glories of Notre Dame. Coustou's rendering of Mary cradling the body of her son, her arms raised in supplication to the heavens, isn't as powerful as Michelangelo's, but Mary's questioning anguish, captured at its peak, is eloquent enough. Like Mary, I had yet to be consoled, nor did I understand why Gary had to die. In a fleeting moment, I did wonder if somehow he had died in order to save others. Including me. And yet seated in this gothic repository of glorious mysteries, I could feel another bundle of grief being lifted away by the music as it rose up through glass and stone on its way skyward.

Chapter 30

Ave Verum Corpus

O n my birthday, at my request, Annie and Don took me
to an Italian rather a French restaurant. La Bocca della
Verita, named for the Mouth of Truth, the famous Roman
sculpture of a river god's face with open mouth, had beckoned to
me from the narrow Rue de Sabot as I walked down St. Germain.
According to legend, liars who placed a hand inside the mouth of
the river god would die. In the movie *Roman Holiday*, Gregory Peck
startled Audrey Hepburn by insouciantly challenging the legend and
placing his hand inside the stone *bocca*. He lived, of course, and won
Audrey's heart. Either he was a truthteller, then, or the river god
made exceptions for those willing to die for love. But then legends
endure only as long as there are believers. Or incurable romantics.

At the small, stylish restaurant I felt as though I were getting Paris and Rome and legendary romance all in one. Its menu,
described on its website as *simples et inventives*, made me think of
all the remarkable dinners Gary and I had enjoyed at Slow Food
establishments in Italy, where dining was a sacrament. I was on the
edge of tears, as I had been the entire time in Paris, and I ached
with longing for Gary. But for once, I was hungry, and as Don reminisced about his good times on the Guadalupe with Gary, I imagined the river god would have given us all a pass for the night.

"You can't fight the current," said Don. "You just have to go
with it."

Was this time in Paris a stage in Slow Grief, I wondered, as I
was beginning to savor life again, even as I felt Gary's absence as

strongly as I ever had, perhaps even more so in a place that called out for love. If there was the promise of Slow Life, a slowing down of pace in order to embrace and share the good things in life, there might be the possibility of Slow Grief, a way to embrace and share life again after loss.

Earlier that day, we had strolled along the fabled Rue du Faubourg St. Honoré, home of the great couturiers, mesmerized by the huge, elaborate chocolate eggs displayed in boutique windows that were as astonishing in their design as the clothes on the racks inside. I couldn't help but think of the amazing journey that chocolate had made, from the heart of Mesoamerica, in remote places like the jungle where Gary had died, all the way around the world. In its bitter form, it had been a sacred food of the gods for Maya and Aztec royalty, while Europeans had later sweetened and lightened it to be used in sweets and desserts. And, of course, Easter eggs, where it had taken on a kind of sacramental quality. In Paris, it had become a sculptural delicacy.

On Easter Sunday, I headed first to the Sainte Chappelle, carrying with me a small container of Gary's ashes, which I was planning to release into the Seine when I felt the time and place were right. Gary and I had both loved the Holy Chapel, with its jeweled stained-glass windows that seem to float above its sturdy narrow base. Louis IX had built it to house his collection of relics of the passion of Christ that were said to include the Crown of Thorns and fragments of the "true cross." As the morning light streamed through the windows, I was reminded of Shelley's beautiful lines from Adonais, his elegy for John Keats:

The One remains, the many change and pass;
Heaven's light forever shines, Earth's shadows fly;
Life, like a dome of many-coloured glass,
Stains the white radiance of Eternity
Until Death tramples it to fragments....

The chapel was getting crowded with jostling tourists and so I walked back to Saint-Germain des-Prés just as mass was beginning.

I was handed a program that announced, *"L'esperance couvre la terre. Il est ressuscité."* Hope covers the earth. He is risen. The sacrifice of Jesus, it said, *"nous plonge dans le don de la vie."* The suffering of Jesus plunges us into the gift of life. A paradox. I received a communion wafer, which I pocketed, then placed in the little silk purse containing Gary's ashes. Perhaps the wafer should have been made of chocolate, I thought.

At the Deux Magots, across the street, I sipped coffee and brought out my notebook, where I found myself writing a note to Gary: "Without you I'm a little brown leaf in the wind." I told him about the communion wafer, which he might have objected to, since he had not been a "believer" in such things.

"I hope you don't mind," I wrote. "It's a promise of resurrection. I know you can't come back in the flesh, but your presence is still with me. As a child, I learned about incorporeal connection through Jesus. I could believe he was with me, even though he was not there in the flesh. Is this so different? Maybe believing in the possibility of resurrection is a preparation for losing the ones we love. Maybe it's just that we can't let you go. We can't give you up for dead."

I decided that it was time to release the ashes, and I remembered a quiet spot along the Seine that was within sight of Notre Dame. I walked along the Quai St. Michel, across from the Ile de la Cité, the island in the Seine dominated by Notre Dame and took some steps down to the edge of the river. I could see the cathedral's monumental dual towers and its three broad portals. I took out my iPhone and selected Mozart's *Ave Verum Corpus*.

As the music soared ever so quietly, the wind wafted the ashes, along with the communion wafer, into the river. The current swirled them briefly before they disappeared beneath the surface. I was mixing the sacraments, the eucharist mingling with a kind of baptism. *Eso nobis praegustatum in mortis examine.* Be for us a foretaste in the test of death.

I then walked to the cathedral in time for Mass, and I was swept up with the crowd past a banner declaring, yet again, *Il est ressuscité.*

If only it were true. If only it could be true. Of Gary and all lost heroes. If only Steve Smith and Barry Day could have proclaimed that day on the river: *Il est ressuscité.*

I sat in a pew and brought out my notebook. But instead of writing on the next blank page, I found myself turning it over to the back page. As the priest intoned the message of resurrection, I started writing from the back page, but it was not in my slanted cursive handwriting. It resembled the neat block print that Gary had used. I watched the letters form as though I were witnessing writing on a wall, even though it was coming from my own hand.

I will love you forever.
I will be with you.
I have always been with you.
I am your soul.
You are my beloved.
Stay strong.
Hold on.
Do it for me and for you.
Love is everything.
Find love again.
You will find happiness.
Watch and wait.

I closed the notebook as the mass ended, not knowing what had happened. The words didn't sound like Gary, and yet they did. It wasn't the Gary of the classroom, the podium, or even of the dinner table. But it was the Gary who had always signed his cards with extravagant messages of love and devotion, almost always saying he would love me forever. It was Gary the incurable romantic. Had I internalized his voice? Was I somehow ventriloquizing his essence? Was this a kind of wish fulfillment? When I had lost him, I had lost the passionate masculine presence in my life, the male pillar of the *hieros gamos*, the sacred marriage of masculine and feminine in which harmony resides. That was one reason, I realized, that I was so out of balance.

In my bewilderment, Wallace Stevens came to my aid yet again. In one of his last poems, "The Final Soliloquy of the Interior Paramour," which one of our friends had read for us during our wedding ceremony, the poet is carrying on an internal monologue, which actually becomes a dialogue within his psyche between masculine and feminine voices. The masculine element, which Stevens portrays as the imagination, has been wedded within his psyche to the female element, representing the earth, or reality. The interior paramour is the part of the poet's psyche who represents, like the Jungian anima, the principle of "otherness."

For the poet and the interior paramour, who make a "dwelling in the evening air," says Stevens, "being there together is enough." Perhaps, then, Gary had somehow become my interior paramour, my interior beloved. My inner comforter. Perhaps these messages in neat block print were more of what Wallace Stevens would have called "useful fictions." If only "being there together" in imagination were enough.

Chapter 31

Pura Vida

Much of the solace I had absorbed in Paris vanished when I arrived back in Austin at the airport, alone, and looked down at the bottom of the escalator next to the baggage carousels, where Gary used to wait for me when I returned home from a journey. The sense of aloneness was overwhelming, and I went through the next few days in jet-lagged insomnia and despair.

One brain-foggy morning, after another miserable sleepless night, I came across an ad for Asclepios, a new wellness center in Costa Rica that seemed too good to be true: *In the country that does not believe in armies, that loves and respects nature and is internationally recognized for protecting its flora, fauna and clean air, we have created a Well Center in harmony with the laws of life.* The center, named for the Greek god of healing, was located near the town of Alajuela, northwest of the capital of San Jose, and close to volcanoes and rain forests. I had no desire to go to a typical spa or resort, where I would be pampered or pounded into shape. But a wellness center with a focus on body, mind and nature sounded better than what the doctor would have ordered.

Suddenly I wanted desperately to be worked on, body and soul, by these specialists who said they had "put together a great understanding and passion for physical and emotional and spiritual health resulting in great well-being." I was intrigued by the center's founder, a Costa Rican lawyer named Marisia Jimenez who had studied naturopathy in Paris and homeopathy in London. I suppose I had something of the incurable cancer patient's blindly optimistic urge to try unconventional cures far from home. And I would also be able to visit my friend Liliana, a convert to Hinduism whom I had met in New Orleans, and who lived on a plantation not far from Alajuela. When Liliana learned of Gary's death on a river, she had given me a small vial of water she had collected from the Brahmaputra River, whose source lies in Tibet and whose lower reaches in India are sacred to Hindus. I emptied the vial into Lake Austin, as she had suggested, as an act of connection.

On my way to San Jose, I made a stop in Guatemala City to change planes. I had thought about whether I wanted to make Guatemala a part of my pilgrimage, but I knew I wasn't ready, nor was I sure I would ever be. So La Aurora airport would be the closest I'd get for now. The airport, which had been renovated since the last time I was there, looked new and bright and full of beautiful weavings for sale. I could see volcanoes in the distance. But as I walked down the terminal walkway, I started shaking, and I couldn't stop. I was having a hard time breathing. Gary's body had been here on its way back to Austin, I thought, and I felt darkness closing in. I was having a textbook panic attack.

I stopped and sat on a bench until the shaking stopped and I could breathe. Still a little unsteady, I walked to one of the vendors along the terminal walkway and picked out a bright turquoise and purple rebozo, or shawl. I paid for it with some of the Guatemalan quetzals I still possessed from changing money in anticipation of the fateful kayak trip six months earlier. I had brought them along, thinking I might need them at the airport. I wrapped the rebozo around my shoulders, like some kind of magic cloak, feeling calm again and ready to resume my journey.

When I arrived in San Jose, the darkness had receded, and I felt relieved when I saw the driver outside the airport waiting with a sign inscribed with my name. I spoke Spanish with Pedro Torres until I realized his English was far better than my Spanish. "Welcome to the country of *pura vida*," he said. "You can translate it either as the pure life or the good life. That's the expression you're going to hear all the time. When someone says it to you, you say it back. *Pura vida.*" Gary would have liked the phrase, I thought, with its similarity to the Italian ideal of *il buon vivere* or the Portuguese *a boa vida*.

We approached the entrance gate to Asclepios, and I was a little daunted to see a tall barbed-wire fence enclosing the grounds. But once inside, the view was of a mist-shrouded volcano and hillside coffee plants. Birds were rustling and singing in the trees. I was shown to my room in the whitewashed residence building. All was quiet, and I didn't see any other guests. This is the "shaman" room, said the young man leading the way. Mine seemed to be the only room with an indigenous-related name. The others evoked various Greek myths. We had passed rooms with the names like Aphrodite, Zeus, Eros. Inside my room, resting on a pedestal on a table, I found a large oval wooden mask, apparently representing the image of a shaman. It looked expressionless, neither friend nor foe.

I called Liliana to see if she could drive over and pick me up so that we could spend the day at her plantation, but her truck had broken down. The next morning I took a taxi over rutted gravel and dirt roads, passing buildings that were still damaged from the horrendous 2009 earthquake, the worst in the region in 150 years. Liliana's rambling stone hacienda had been spared, and she took me on a tour of the grounds, where she had brought back elements of her own journey of recovery a few years earlier. The lush gardens looked a little untidy and overgrown, compared to the well man-icured estates I was used to seeing in prosperous parts of Central America. Several years earlier, Liliana's husband left her for another woman, and following a bitter divorce, she set out for a retreat in India and wound up spending three years there. The seeds from Buddha's Bodhi tree had grown into strong saplings, and the lotus seeds she had brought from Bali had sprouted in a small lake, cov-ering it with blossoms that swayed in the breeze.

We walked the grounds of the estate, picking our way around mango trees so replete with fruit that ripe and overripe mangoes covered the ground like so many fallen leaves. I found it ironic that Liliana had to leave this verdant paradise in order to deal with her grief. Being in a perfect place with a perfect climate, then, was obviously not enough when love ran out. She reached out to cut a lotus blossom for me.

"Traveling after a loss is the best thing you can do," she said. "But you need to be open to what happens. Don't have expectations." She looked at me with a half-smile. "You are lucky in one way. You can take your loved one along with you, at least in your memory, in spirit. So you aren't really alone. I couldn't take my husband along, even in spirit. I was too angry with him."

I mulled over that thought as the taxi brought me back to Asclepios. Was Gary really with me on this journey, in more than memory? At one moment, while Liliana was fixing tea for us, I had absent-mindedly taken out my iPhone to call him. It was the first time I had done that since he died.

Later, I sat beside the small pool adorned by a torii, or traditional Japanese gate, at one end, framing the view of verdant hills and some horses grazing in a field. A torii, usually found at the entrance to a Shinto shrine, symbolically marks the transition from the profane to the sacred, or from the earthly to the heavenly, and in my still shattered, anchorless state, I was neither. But I felt gratitude to be in this beautiful place. I knew I was enormously privileged to be able to choose my own way of grieving. I was not forced by custom or guilt nor doomed by poverty to wear black for the rest of my life, to live life as a shadow.

The next morning, I was no longer the solitary guest at Asclepios. I was joined at breakfast by an elegant woman in her sixties, who had lost her son, and who had come from her home in San Jose for a few days of rest. Her grief was recent, and she had the thousand-mile stare that I knew so well. She was moving slowly and stiffly, like an automaton, just as I had. She had an aura of faded movie-star glamor, but her melancholy smile was coming from the bottom of a well. I knew my voice must have sounded a million miles away. "Estoy muy cansada," she said. I'm very tired.

Sitting at the next table were two friends from Philadelphia, who seemed remarkably different from each other. Maria, a slender Latina in her mid-thirties, was recovering from surgery for breast cancer, while Alice, her plump companion, was pale in the places where she wasn't bright pink from sunburn. Alice explained that she was a therapist who dealt with trauma. "Have you heard of EMDR?" I shook my head. "It stands for Eye Movement Desensitization and Reprocessing." Alice treated people suffering from post-traumatic stress, she said, as well as anxiety and panic. I wanted to learn more, and we met for lunch.

We sat down at the elegantly set table in the small dining room. Alice looked over the single-page menu dismissively. "No meat," she said. "It was bad enough not having coffee this morning." We both ordered salads, and she asked Raul, the waiter, to make sure hers contained no green peppers. "I hate green peppers," she said, with a shudder.

"So how does EMDR work?" I asked.

"We use bilateral stimulation," said Alice. "That's right-left eye movement, moving the eyes back and forth while you relive what's bothering you. It activates the opposite sides of the brain and releases the trauma that's trapped in your nervous system."

I nodded expectantly. I did know something, after all, about feeling lopsided, operating out of one side of the brain. And about pain and suffering being trapped in the body, with the mind looking on, detached and helpless.

Alice paused as Raul brought the salads. Her eyes widened in horror, and she picked up the plate and brought it up closer to her eyes. "Green peppers," she shouted. "I can't stand them. Get them out of here!" She was going into meltdown, and I didn't have a clue how to get her to move her eyes back and forth. Could I do it by waving my fork, like a hypnotist? Obviously, green peppers must have been a source of trauma somewhere in her past. I reached out with the fork, stabbed the single offending slice of pepper that appeared half-buried in a clump of lettuce, and placed it on my own plate. She began to calm down.

"So EMDR is very effective in helping the neurophysiological system deal with mind-body disconnections," she said.

"Oh," I said aloud. Except when it comes to green peppers, I thought.

Chapter 32

The Volcano and the Butterfly

I excused myself to meet Pedro Torres, who had agreed to drive me to Poas Volcano and then to the nature center at La Paz Waterfall. I was looking forward to toucans and butterflies and the sound of falling water.

"I have to warn you, said Pedro, as we set out. "The volcano is usually covered in mist. You can't always see it."

As we wound our way up, I could see yet more evidence of the 2009 earthquake. The main problem, said Francisco, was the mudslides that had covered roads, sent boulders down mountainsides and smothered people in their homes.

"Many people were killed," said Pedro. "No one could get away. And then the roads were gone, so no one could get to them to help them."

And yet the scars were already disappearing. Green shoots were already springing up from the rubble, rewriting the script of loss on the landscape in the natural resilience I could only envy. And as for the people who lost their houses and livelihoods, Pedro said, "No one wants to leave. This is home."

I had seen that stubborn resistance to giving up on a place time and again when I was growing up on the Gulf Coast. Most people, including my parents, cleaned up debris and repaired roofs after each hurricane, rebuilding their lives as though disaster would never happen again. "It's only material things," they would say. "What counts is that we survived." In a sense, I supposed, being human has always meant living on the edge, one way or another — on a storm-

ridden coast, in an earthquake zone, under a volcano, within a violent or besieged culture, or along a tornado alley—but the odds of
staying safe seemed to be shifting.

We parked in a mostly vacant lot and then walked past a brilliant
array of bromeliads lining the path to the volcano. The morning
rain had left drops of water on their leaves that shimmered like
tiny prisms. The earthquake had ravaged the park around the volcano, but the thirsty plants were already disguising the evidence of
upheaval. As Pedro had warned, the mist was so heavy we couldn't
actually see into the crater below, but there was a faint smell of sulphur in the air. I could hear an ominous bubbling sound, as the volcano made itself known.

Out of the blue, I asked Pedro why there was so little evidence of
indigenous culture in Costa Rica. He thought for a moment, then
shrugged. "We only have about 100,000 indigenous left," he said.
"They've all been pushed into little reserves, or they have become no
different from other people. They are losing their languages." That
sounded familiar, I said. I mentioned that my Choctaw ancestors
had been forced to leave their land and travel the Trail of Tears, and
those who stayed had to hide out in the woods for nearly a century.
And now they had a casino and a golf resort on the reservation that
had become big tourist attractions.

"Well, I'm half Chorotega," said Pedro, "but it's not something
I talk about very much. The name Chorotega means 'the fleeing
people.' We came here from Southern Mexico many centuries ago to
keep from being slaves to the Mayan rulers. The Chorotega fought
very hard against the Spanish when they invaded. They had the
most organized resistance here of all the indigenous people. But of
course you know what happened. And now most Chorotega people
live in Guanacaste, up in the north."

"We'll all be the fleeing people," I said, "if global warming
keeps up."

"Mother Earth has a fever," said Pedro, "and she's going to shake
a few of us off."

He suddenly smiled as he spied something glittering that was hidden in a crack on the railing. It was a little gold heart that someone must have left behind as an offering to the volcano, but Pedro had different ideas.

"This is for you," he said, handing me the heart. "I think the volcano wants you to have it."

We waited in vain for the mist to clear and decided to head for the nature center, located on a flank of the volcano, even as it began to rain.

"In a cloud forest, it's always raining," said Pedro.

As we neared the nature center, the roads got worse. Rain was collecting in ruts and deep puddles in the road.

"The epicenter of the earthquake was very close to here," he said. "They had to rescue hundreds of tourists from the area around the waterfall."

Despite the rutted roads, the La Paz nature center, which had been rebuilt, turned out to be something like a theme park, with an elaborate welcome center and a series of exhibits that included a jaguar in a cage, which made me cringe. But I was eager to see the butterfly observatory, which was regarded as the best in the world. As I walked into airy enclosure, I was surrounded by a cloud of fluttering blue morpho butterflies, whose images I had seen everywhere in Costa Rica, emblazoned on T-shirts and postcards.

Along a display board dangled a row of chrysalises from which blue wave butterflies were just beginning to emerge. Blue waves resemble the larger and more numerous blue morphos, but the bright neon blue dorsal sides of their upper wings are patterned with white transversal bands and white spots. I watched as a newly emerged blue wave clung to its empty chrysalis and began to try out its wings, moving them tentatively back and forth, as though it were getting used to the idea of becoming airborne after crawling through the world as a worm.

After a few moments, the blue wave fluttered purposefully into the air, as though it had always known how, aiming toward the flowers and ripe fruit that had been set out as a first feast for the butterflies who now scorned the leaves of the euphorbia plants they had fed on as caterpillars.

On wings of divine deliverance.

Metamorphosis, I thought, appears to be a kind of miracle, though not without an element of pain or trauma in the process of transformation. As Ovid described it in his masterwork of mythic stories, metamorphosis is not a chosen destiny, but rather a drastic, divine-driven, shape-changing transition that becomes inevitable or strangely appropriate—a fearful maiden escaping rape by becoming a tree, or men becoming Circe's pigs that embody their base animal hungers. Humans become less human and more beastly or, in cases of those who are innocent, more rooted in the earth.

A lowly caterpillar endures a kind of death and dissolution in order to become transformed, to change from little more than a voracious eating tube into a delicate winged creature that drinks nectar through a straw. It's a mystery of transformation that scientists have only recently begun to solve, using 3D scans that allow them to see inside the chrysalis as the caterpillar dissolves into a kind of primordial genetic soup of undifferentiated imaginal cells from the which the butterfly takes shape.

I couldn't imagine what it would feel like to emerge with wings from the prison-like dormancy of an earlier, earth-bound, inching-along self. Would we believe in resurrection if there were no butterflies? In thinking of such a delicate winged creature emerging from the mushy remains of a worm, the idea of an immortal soul emerging from a deliquescent body doesn't seem so far-fetched.

In Mexico, the monarchs arrive at their winter home after a long migration by the first of November, which also happens to coincide with the Day of the Dead celebration. Several years ago, I visited the most remote of the monarch sanctuaries in Michohuacan, and as I watched millions of butterflies fill the sky, so many that I could actually hear their wings crackling in a heavenly susurrus, I could understand the traditional belief there that the monarchs are the souls of ancestors who are returning for their annual visit.

Butterflies offer us a symbol and a promise that change is possible. And as I watched the newly emerged blue wave find its way into the air, I knew that out of Gary's death and the end of our life together, I would have to find a new life as a new being if I were going to survive. Somehow, in order to emerge from the darkness, I would have to grow wings.

That evening, I sat in my room with the sliding doors open to the mild air, and I could hear the clay robins rustling and mewing like cats in the trees, going tee-weeooip. I started to doze off in the comfortable chair next to the wooden mask of the shaman, and I found myself revisiting the bend in the river where Gary died. I tried to imagine the scene as he paddled strongly in the current then found himself struggling.

It was a scene I had replayed in my mind, over and over. But this time, the scene shifted into a kind of dream state. I could see a globe of light following Gary, and I watched as it swooped down over Gary's kayak just as it capsized and he was about to slip into the depths. The light hovered there for what seemed a nanosecond, and then there were two globes of light soaring up into the sky. So that's what happened on the river, I thought in my trance-like state. Gary's soul took flight. And he had a guide to show him the way. The scene of struggle that had been haunting me in Paris was supplanted by a vision of deliverance.

Chapter 33

What the Shaman Said

The next morning I went for a walk down the road from Asclepios to a resort located in a sanctuary that was just big enough to get lost in for a while. I followed unmarked trails into denser forest, and I thought I could hear a waterfall. It was like walking a labyrinth as I circled around and around trying to find the source of the sound. Finally I emerged into a clearing, and there was indeed a small waterfall. Nothing as spectacular as those at La Paz, but nevertheless lovely. I was grateful to have found it.

I walked back to Asclepios in time for lunch, and I looked up from my vegetarian plate to see a slender, delicately beautiful blond woman who appeared to be in her late 30s or early 40s heading toward my table. It was Marisia Jimenez, the *maestra*, or queen bee, of Asclepios, who had just returned from her travels. "Can I join you?" she asked.

I was glad to finally meet her, though I wasn't quite prepared for her intensity. Marisia was clearly not one for small talk, as she asked why I had come to Asclepios.

"I'm on a pilgrimage," I said, not knowing exactly how to explain it. "A journey of healing."

"Ah," she said knowingly. "A *peregrinaje*." She paused. "You know you aren't the only one," she said. "I think there are many people who are moving to a more spiritual dimension now. We are obliged to take that step because the energy of the earth is changing. Everything is accelerated. In order to be part of the planet, we have to raise our consciousness. This energy is making us grow. The entire planet is shifting and we are evolving all the time."

"It's evolve or die," I said.

Marisia shook her head at such a black and white picture. "We are struggling and having a hard time. There is so much suffering—that is making people wake up. I think we are trying to confront our problems. But we have to stop and think. If you are following someone to the edge of a cliff, you have to stop."

I asked her how she got off the track of being a lawyer and opened a healing center, which was obviously something of a gamble.

"I didn't know where I was going before this," she said. "My nephew was cured of a fatal disease by natural healing, and I wanted to know more. I said to myself this is something I have to do. It is a mission. I would have thought other people would have been better suited for this than me. But I felt that I had to do it."

I told her my story about losing Gary, and her eyes narrowed appraisingly. She was looking at me the way a doctor would look at a patient. "You think you can find a solution with your mind, but you can't," she said. "You have realized that you are not so powerful, not so strong as you thought you were. Now you have to ask for help. In a way, you have to surrender. You will have to let everything flow."

You can't fight the current. You just have to go with it.

She recommended that I consult a shaman she knew who lived in the countryside but who could make the drive to Asclepios in the morning. Meanwhile I went back to my room and opened the sliding doors to the view of the volcano. The plain clay robins had been joined in the trees by a variety of bright-colored birds. I pulled out my notebook and found myself turning it to the back, as I had done in Paris. I began writing in the block print that resembled Gary's handwriting.

I was with you today at the waterfall. You could hear it with-
out seeing it. You knew it was there before you saw it. You will
see me just as you found the waterfall by following the sound of
the water. I am here with you on your journey. You don't have to

leave me to find your new life. Look, listen for the current. That is
where I will be, waiting for you. My body has dropped away like
the old bodies of the worms that grow wings. Does the butterfly
remember the worm?

I looked at the message, of two minds, as usual. The pilgrim in
me was comforted. But the inner skeptic had the last word, and I
turned the notebook over and wrote:

"I promise you, Gary that I'm not going to turn you into some
kind of neutered New Age image, uttering New Age platitudes."

The next morning I got a call from the front desk that the shaman
had arrived. I wasn't sure what to expect, and I was surprised to see
a small dark-skinned woman with bright blue eyes whose silvery
gray hair was pulled back into a long braid. She was wearing a head-
band and indigenous clothing, but her accent was French rather
than Spanish or Indian. "I grew up in Switzerland," she said. She
had been drawn to indigenous cultures, and after apprenticing to a
shaman in Costa Rica, she decided to stay.

Her movements were quick and birdlike, as she asked me to
follow her to a therapy room, where we were to sit and talk as she
diagnosed what was wrong with me. Well, of course, I already knew
what was wrong. I had lost my husband. But as she looked at me,
she had a troubled expression on her face. She shook her head.

"I'm looking at you, and you are not there," she said. "You are
not in your body."

I looked around, wondering where I might be.

"You separated from your body when your husband died in order
to be with him," she said. "When he was alive, you were not separate. So when he died, you died too."

I had to admit she was right about at least part of myself dying
along with Gary. When I had lost Gary, I had lost my anchor.
Without him, as I had written in my notebook in Paris, I was a
little brown leaf blowing in the wind.

"You are not aligned," she said, "with your soul in your body.
That is what we will work on. You need to bring your soul back into

your body. That does not mean you have to lose your soul connection with your husband. You will still stay connected with him, but it will be with your entire being.

"You will have a new life, and he will be your guide from another dimension. He has no limits in that dimension. And I think you will sometimes also be a guide for him. Because he is now free of the limits of being human on this earth, you can tell him how hard it is to be in this life."

The notion of alternating guidance made me think of the song, "If I Should Fall Behind," that I had asked Gage and Albert to sing at Gary's memorial.

Should we lose each other
In the shadow of the evening trees
I'll wait for you
And should I fall behind
Wait for me

I lay down on the table, and she began to chant and move her hands through the air above my body.

"You will feel heavy once your self, your soul, has re-entered your body," she said.

I lay there after she had finished, and gradually sat up. She looked into my eyes and nodded.

"Yes, you are back," she said.

I did feel heavy, almost cloddish, as though I had weights on my arms and legs and a big stone on my chest. I sensed, though, that I felt leaden because focusing on my loss so intensely was immensely draining, and I had used up all my strength. If this was being back in my body, I wasn't sure I wanted to be there.

"Your life is going to be very different," she said. "It is going to be a life of discovery. Your husband's death has given you a direction you did not have before. This new journey, your mission, could not have been done while your husband was alive. But you are not leaving him behind. He will always be with you."

I remembered a kind of one-sided conversation I had with Gary not long before he died. We were lying in bed, and I asked two of those rhetorical cosmic questions, usually asked by college freshmen in late-night gab sessions, that I had been pondering in recent weeks. "I really want to know who we are and what we're doing here," I said. I wasn't actually expecting an answer, and I could hear Gary beginning the deep breathing that let me know he had drifted off to sleep. He instinctively reached a hand out to touch me. Still with me, though in a different state of consciousness.

The shaman said, as I was leaving, "We are the children of the light. We come from the stars."

Chapter 34

Down to the Shore

I had been thinking about the next stage of my pilgrimage ever since I began corresponding by email with Darwin Horn, Gary's best friend from high school. I first met Darwin at Gary's memorial, and I remembered Gary talking about him and about his famous father, also named Darwin, who had been in the secret service and had written a memoir. I was startled when Dar, as he likes to be called, told me at the memorial that he had traveled to Austin by train from his home in Los Angeles because he didn't like to fly. A tall, powerfully built grizzly bear of a man, he had a surprisingly gentle quality about him, not so different from Gary's. From the brief snippets of bio he sent later, I learned that he had a Ph.D. in anthropology and had worked for years as a teacher, but was now an artist who worked with glass.

Dar had lost his first wife Mary, who had also been a good friend of Gary's, to cancer several years earlier, and he helped to prepare me early on for the emotional rollercoaster I would be facing by laying out his own personal calendar of grief, with no sugar-coating, no shortcuts.

"In my experience," he wrote, "there is a difference between the grief of a sudden, unexpected loss like yours and a long, drawn out one like mine. I had three years to prepare. But the downside was that I was totally spent by the time Mary passed away."

It was Dar who had warned me about the particular intensity of the four-month anniversary of a loved one's death. Grief, Dar told me, had come for him in big, battering waves that swamped him, but the time between waves had gradually grown longer and longer, and the intensity of the waves had diminished. The good news was that he had remarried and rebuilt his life. The portrait of grief that he painted, of a recurring if diminishing tsunami, had scared me. But the messages of hope and encouragement that he sent were like life preservers to a floundering swimmer who couldn't find her way back to the surface.

Corresponding with Dar reminded me of how intrigued I'd been by the stories Gary had told me over the years of his life in California. The images I had formed of his life there were already acquiring a kind of nostalgic aura, like holiday snapshots just beginning to fade: the high school rebel in a tony Los Angeles suburb on the Pacific; the frustrated artist who winds up in the Special Forces; the college firebrand who becomes a scholar of political theory; the activist who envisions technology as a way to change the world.

As I began considering a trip to California to visit Gary's friends, family and colleagues from the different stages of his life before I knew him, Dar encouraged me to come to Los Angeles, to the Palos Verdes Peninsula where he and Gary had grown up and gone to high school together. "I think you'll find that Gary was very much loved in these parts," he said. He and his wife Ellen, also an artist, invited me to stay with them at the loft where they lived and worked in the Los Angeles suburb of San Pedro. Dar warned me that the living quarters in the studio they had converted from an auto parts store might be on the "bohemian side" and not be what I was used to, but that I was welcome to stay as long as I liked.

I had always envisioned Palos Verdes, as Gary had described it to me, as a magical place. He had told me about climbing with his friends down a cliff overlooking the Pacific to a pristine beach, where they would swim, explore tide pools full of starfish, drink beer and tell tall tales. Dar had volunteered to gather as many of Gary's friends from that halcyon era as he could find for dinner and reminiscing.

My plan was to spend a few days with Dar and Ellen in Los Angeles, then drive north to visit Gary's father and stepmother in Solvang, a little town in the Santa Ynez valley east of Santa Barbara. Next I would drive up the coast to Palo Alto, where Gary had attended Stanford as a graduate student and then worked as director of Computer Professionals for Social Responsibility, an organization that drew some of the most brilliant pioneers in computer science and the Internet.

I thought of Palo Alto as yet another magical place, where Gary had first developed his passion for technology's potential as a means of transformation. I would be staying with his old friends Severo Ornstein and Laura Gould, both visionary computer scientists who had worked with Gary when he headed CPSR. Like Dar, Severo had suggested a gathering of Gary's old friends in a kind of impromptu memorial dinner.

I arrived in Los Angeles on a warm, sunny day in late June and drove south from the airport to San Pedro, the port district of Los Angeles, which lies at the southern end of the Palos Verdes Peninsula, on the west side of San Pedro Bay. Dar and Ellen's building would have been difficult to distinguish from the other industrial and commercial buildings in the neighborhood except for its wild turquoise color and the large, brilliantly hued glass sculptures visible on their pedestals from the front windows.

Before I rang the bell, Dar raised the chain-metal curtain over the front door and welcomed me with a big hug. He led me like a spellbound Alice into a large studio/workshop that was a wild, eclectic labyrinth of objects, with narrow pathways through his and Ellen's works in progress as well as stacks and stacks of found objects that Ellen used in her sculptures. They had created a little niche of a guest room along one side of the studio, separated by a curtain. It reminded me of a cocoon. Their own cozy living space was at the front of the studio, with kitchen, living room and bedroom, all neatly arranged like the living quarters on a ship.

As I looked at the array of ukuleles displayed on the wall, a legacy of Ellen's sojourn in Hawaii, I could feel my layers of reserve melting away rapidly, as though I were standing next to a crackling fire. I had felt some initial trepidation at intruding into Gary's world, but I immediately felt at home in this welter of eccentric creativity, as though I had known Dar and Ellen all my life.

Dar gave me a thumbnail preview of the guests who were coming for a barbecue dinner he and Ellen were putting together. Ellen was making a salad, while Dar fired up the grill on the back patio behind the studio to cook a big pile of steaks. Most of the guys I would meet, he said, had been on the swim team with he and Gary. Apparently California high school swim teams were turning out prodigies in those days. I remembered Gary saying that he had competed in at least one meet against Mark Spitz before Spitz went on to become an Olympic superstar. Gary's specialty was the breaststroke, and he said he lost miserably to Spitz. When I first met Gary, he still had the broad shoulders and sculpted torso of a swimmer, though he stopped competing after high school.

As Dar talked about the swim team, I had the impression that they had become an extended family whose lives entwined more closely than those of most high school buddies. Perhaps the most unusual member of the team had been Bruce Shimizu, whom Dar remembered as being the only Asian student at school. "Bruce was a little bewildered," said Dar. "He met Gary through Eagle Scouts and Gary encouraged him to join the swim team. At the end of every semester, the Shimizus would have us over to the house, and his mom and sister would cook sukiyaki and serve us like we were grownup men. It was very Japanese. We loved it!"

Another swim team cohort was Ted Abresch, who had actually moved away to Chicago after their freshman year, according to Dar, but who had stayed in contact and eventually moved back for a few years. Ted was now working as a research scientist at UC Davis, and he would be flying in from San Francisco. His father had been in the merchant marine during World War II and had been on several ships that were torpedoed. Dar, who was a history buff, had found a record of one of his rescues by an ocean liner in the Atlantic. Ted's mother had an equally dramatic story. She had escaped from Holland on the last boat that allowed Jews to leave the country. "Ted's mom was a great friend to us all," said Dar. "We spent a lot of time at her apartment, and she treated us like adults. We never took advantage of that."

As it turned out, the first guest to arrive at the studio was Dar's sister Diane, who had been a year behind Gary and Dar in school. Diane had a story she wanted to tell me about Gary and one of his heroic rescues. She had been held for detention after school one day as punishment for bringing only one pencil to a class where everyone was supposed to have at least two pencils. She was feeling angry and humiliated until Gary told her, Solomon-like, that she should have snapped her pencil in two so she would have been in compliance with the rule. It was so like Gary, I thought, who was already learning as a preteen to think his way around arbitrary rules. After Diane left the detention hall, she said, her day got worse when she realized she would have to walk home, a considerable distance, because the school bus had already left. But then she saw Gary, who had waited for her in order to walk her home because, he said, she was Dar's sister.

In the meantime Bruce Shimuzu and Ted Abresch arrived, as well as Rob Hollister, another former swim team member, who was in a wheelchair. He was barely able to speak, and I had to lean close to hear him. I could tell that Dar was shocked at how frail Rob looked. Rob was a filmmaker who had worked at the Museum of Contemporary Art in Los Angeles until his colon cancer worsened.

The last to arrive was Jim Roberts, making a surprise appearance. He and Gary had been close during high school, and I remembered Gary saying that Jim's family had essentially adopted him when he was having trouble at home. Jim married an Italian woman who lived in Milan, and he traveled back and forth to Italy for his business, which had to do with intellectual property law. He and Gary roomed together in San Francisco after Gary returned from the military, and he came to our wedding in Austin. Jim, who looks a little like George Clooney, and who dresses impeccably, on the preppie side, always struck me as a kind of buttoned-down merry prankster.

Bruce Shimizu said that he, too, had something he wanted to tell me. "Gary saved my life," he said. I wondered if it had to do with drowning, but he shook his head. "When I got to high school, I didn't know anyone, and I didn't know how to fit in. Gary just took me under his wing," he said. "He was always there for me."

Jim Roberts wanted to change the sacral tone of the reminiscences. He and Gary had cut class to drive Gary's rattling, smoking old station wagon up to Haight-Ashbury, where they intended to get high, if possible. The car broke down on the highway, and they hitched the rest of the way. Jim's recollection got a little foggy at that point. He also remembered visiting Gary a few months after graduation at the hippie compound in Puget Sound where Gary was living. Gary, who had been at the top of his class, surprised everyone by enrolling in the University of Puget Sound as an art student.

"He had this huge Afro," said Jim. "And there were all these followers of Meher Baba around."

Meher Baba, who had reportedly taken a vow of silence for most of his life, had claimed to be an avatar of the divine. I could hardly imagine super-rational Gary surrounded by members of a mystical cult. I remembered Gary telling me about his time at the commune, when he was hanging out with an heir to the Morton's Salt fortune who was trying adorn a psychedelic bus with stained-glass windows. By then Gary had essentially dropped out of college, and the draft loomed.

"The next thing we knew Gary was wearing an Army uniform," said Jim. "We didn't know if it was for real."

Feeling miffed by Jim's jocular tone, I told him that yes, it was for real. A little defensively, I told him that I had thought about going to Italy as part of my pilgrimage, but I thought it would be too painful. I explained that it was the place we had loved the most, where we had gone nearly every summer. We had even entertained fantasies about retiring there. Gary would check out the online real estate section of the *Corriere della Serra* every morning and sigh at the prices. He had put together a collection of photos we had taken in and around Verona on his 58th birthday, four months before he died, and titled it "A Perfect Day in Italy." I feared that if I did get up the gumption to go to Italy, I would arrive in Verona or Torri del Benaco, where we had spent so many perfect days, and simply collapse from grief.

Jim looked at me askance, as if I had said I was afraid of the sun or the moon. A man of impulse, he had little patience with my apprehensions. "Just gut it up and go," he said.

I was still stinging from Jim's lack of sensitivity after everyone had left, and I had curled up in my little loft cocoon, which was surprisingly comfortable. I dozed off quickly, despite all the memories that had been stirred up, and I slept soundly all night for the first time I could remember.

I slipped out just after dawn to go for a walk on Cabrillo beach, which was adjacent to the harbor just a couple of miles away from the studio. I watched cargo ships chug back and forth as I walked out on the jetties. I glanced over past the jetties as one big ship seemed to be following me out toward the sea on a parallel course. I then did a double take when I saw the name on its side. *Italia*. So the good ship *Italia* shadowed me as I walked all the way out to the final point and had to turn back. Well, I thought, if that's not synchronicity, I don't know what is. And I had a feeling I'd be getting to Italy one way or another, ready or not.

When I got back to the studio, Dar volunteered to take me to visit Miraleste, where he and Gary went to high school. It had since been converted into a middle school because of the peninsula's changing demographics. Compared to my plain, serviceable high school in Brazosport, Miraleste was a posh country club, with airy classrooms, professional landscaping, lots of comfortable outdoor spaces, and, of course, a first-class swimming pool.

I was trying to imagine Gary walking the halls there—tall, skinny, curly-haired and quietly brazen. A kid with a big heart and overreaching dreams. I recalled a scene that Gary told me about when he had been selected as Miraleste's Marauder, the rakish mascot that Gary himself had designed as a cross between a pirate and a matador. At halftime during a football game, he was supposed to charge boldly across the football field on a galloping horse, wearing a mask, cape and tight toreador pants. He had hardly started galloping when the pants split, and he found himself dismounting backward, the Marauder too bold for his britches.

As Dar and I leaned against the rail on one of the outdoor walkways, he pointed to the roof of the gym, where he and Gary had perched and talked all night after graduation, dodging the night watchman, sharing dreams of what they wanted to do and who they wanted to be.

"Gary wanted to change the world, and I wanted to be an anthropologist," he said. "That was the last long talk I had with Gary," said Dar.

I was taken aback because I had assumed they had remained close. They went their separate ways after that night, he said, but somehow remained soul brothers despite the distance. I suppose it was a guy thing. Getting back together was one of those things always on the plate, but it never happened.

It wasn't until I returned to Austin that I located Gary's 1970 Miraleste yearbook, *El Mirador*, and found messages inscribed on its pages from a number of Gary's friends, including Ted Abresch, who wrote,

"Believe it or not, I may be a bit sentimental in this. I would hardly start to recall all of the good times and hardships we've each had during our friendship....Friendship is a great thing, and I've been proud to have you as a friend."

I was reminded of the observation from Gary's friend Stan about Gary's ability to inspire deep and enduring love in his friends. I realized that the tribe of Gary was already being formed early on, and that it had always been diverse and inclusive.

There were several notes thanking Gary for various kindnesses. And there were lots of long messages written with a flourish from girls who obviously had big crushes on him. Someone named Betty Ann wrote, "You've got a way about you that everything turns to gold." A girl named Karen, who told Gary that she loved him, described the "eager excited look" he would get when he was "explaining a new plan"—a trait he never lost. One of his male friends called him a "pied piper."

Although there was no message in the yearbook from Dar, there was one from his late wife Mary, which I could hardly read through my tears:

"Gary, I respect you and admire you for your strong qualities of leadership and quiet deliberation. But more than that, you're a warm, sympathetic, unique person who like all of us is just trying to figure out who he is and where he's going. I know you'll find what you're looking for."

That afternoon, Ted Abresch joined Dar and Ellen and me for a commemorative walk down to the fabled beach that Gary had told me about, where they had spent so many days and nights doing the things that teenagers do on a beach. "We used to dig deep holes to sit in so no one could see us," said Dar. I was bringing some of Gary's ashes for us to release into the Pacific. I thought Dar had been joking when he called it Rat Beach, but the sign on the cliff above the beach announced "RAT Beach," which Dar told me stood for "Right after Torrance" Beach. "This is all part of the oldest stratified site in California," he said, pointing out various rocks of interest.

There are no roads to RAT beach, which is a protected cove, and it requires a long walk from Torrance Beach along a cliff and then down a gradual sandy incline, lined by wildflowers. The waves of the Pacific were pounding away, not strongly enough for serious surfers, but enough for serious atmosphere.

"This must have been paradise," I said.

Dar nodded. "At one time you could find everything you needed here to live on—the indigenous people who were here gathered abalone and caught halibut," he said. "Look at all the edible plants: wild radishes, quail bush, the tobacco tree that hummingbirds get addicted to, wild nasturtiums, the wild mustard that came from the mustard seeds scattered by the mission-building padres to build a 'golden' road between the missions in California."

On the way down from the cliff, Ellen picked wild nasturtiums and other flowers. On the beach, I saw a long, thick strand of kelp that had drifted in from an offshore kelp forest. It looked like a huge brown discarded lei, and I thought we could use it as an organic altar right above the moving water line. We each gathered stones, shells and other "found" beach ornaments and placed them along with the wildflowers on the seaweed altar, as the waves came closer and closer. I passed out portions of Gary's ashes to Ted, Dar and Ellen, and as we cupped them in our hands, I thought of William Blake's vision. *To see a world in a grain of sand, and heaven in a wild flower, hold infinity in the palm of your hand, and eternity in an hour.*

As the waves finally arrived and collected our offerings, taking them back out to sea, we released the ashes and watched them disappear into the current flowing back out into the Pacific, taking along with them small grains of our grief. We stood and listened to the song of the waves, heads bowed, as the ashes of the one joined the waters of the many. Then Ellen recited a poem she had just composed spontaneously:

Down to the ocean
Let me out to sea
Let all the fishes have what's left of me
I have my freedom now to really be
You who I have left
Will join me eventually

Ted said that he had felt an electric charge as he released the ashes. "Gary always knew how to hold an audience," he said.

Our attention was caught by two boys in low-slung board shorts who were wading out into the surf, laughing and splashing. They were about the age when Gary and Dar and Ted first started coming down to the beach to dig their holes and ponder questions about life, but not yet about death.

"That could be us 40 years ago," said Dar. "Life goes on."

A few weeks later, after I had returned to Austin, Dar sent an email that Rob Hollister had passed away. The ceremony we held for Gary at the beach had made such a strong impression, he said, that he and his friends had decided to take Rob's ashes down to RAT Beach, just as we had with Gary's, to release them into the Pacific with flowers, stones, shells and songs.

He has never left for ever.

Chapter 35

Along the Valley

As I headed north to Solvang the next morning, I was pondering how much of Gary's life had been determined by the time and place where he grew up. I had never known anyone like him — the compassionate warrior and passionate music lover with a scholar's vision of philosophy and a geek's grasp of technology. Because I didn't meet him until he was in his late thirties, I sometimes thought of him as springing forth from the earth that way, full grown and formidable. My women friends had often told me that Gary seemed almost too good to be true. But I was learning that he had followed a long, twisting road to get there, and lhe had paid a price along the way. There had always been chinks in the armor.

I was thinking of how strongly the winds of change had blown into that sheltered cove, where he and his young tribe had traded dreams, bringing with it harbingers of war and calls for rebellion and reinvention. The counterculture, Vietnam, rock music had all swirled into the currents there, making it difficult for someone like Gary, with his desire to make an unconventional mark on the world, to follow the usual patterns of growing into manhood.

Jim's remarks about Gary's strange interlude after he graduated from high school made me wonder what had really happened during his time in Puget Sound, when he had apparently tuned in and dropped out. And maybe screwed up. It must have been something extreme in order for him to make an about-face from the counterculture and join the army, where he would presumably have had to march in step with authority.

Shortly after his death, I had gotten a teary call from one of his friends from the University of Puget Sound named Roberta, who wanted to reminisce about that time. I gathered that she had been in love with him.

"I met Gary in art class," she said. "He's the kind of person you never forget." Like Jim, she had been struck by Gary's hair. "He had the wildest hair," she said. "He also started the trend of low-rider pants. He was always extremely independent."

She also remembered the old rattletrap of a station wagon he had gotten from his dad and the stained-glass windows he was helping to make for the psychedelic bus, which she said was to be a "moving church." But she had also implied something darker, which I had been too shell-shocked at the time to register.

"His amazingness took flight," she said. "He was like that god who went too close to the sun and crashed and burned. Icarus."

I didn't know then what she meant by falling to earth. But I did know that Gary had clashed often with his parents during those years and that the man he became remained something of a stranger to them for the rest of his life. When we visited them at their home in Solvang over the years, it was always a little awkward, as though everyone had to get reacquainted all over again. I sensed at Gary's memorial that Art's grief at losing his son was compounded by a realization of how much he had yet to learn about him. The out-pouring of love and admiration for Gary at the service had surprised him and touched him deeply.

I learned from Art that Gary's stepmother was ill, so I was reluctant to impose on them for very long. I had reserved a room at a hotel in Solvang for a single night. But Art had been a stalwart supporter for me ever since the day he made that fateful call in December that changed everything, and I wanted to see face-to-face how he was faring. He was always stoic when we talked on the phone, but I imagined that his grief was unfathomable.

Art wrote me an extraordinary email before I left for Paris in which he advised me to begin thinking about writing something that would be meaningful for my nephew Chase and niece Maddie, whom he had met at Gary's memorial. The two of them spent a considerable amount of time texting on their iPhones during the dinner following the memorial, and Art felt that they could use some mentoring from an older family member. Me.

"Facebook, Twitter and other formats on the computer along with iPhone dialogue are exceptionally poor references for meaningful interpersonal relationships that all persons will need to experience in time. You have at your disposal experiences that are quite different from most people. Sometimes the transfer of information by known family members can help a lot to format other junior family members' minds as long as the information is honest; they will also remember the issues for the rest of their lives."

Although the email was written in Art's rather stiff, ex-engineer style, it was heartfelt and generous, and I felt that he was essentially giving me his blessing to move on with my life. It was almost an echo of Gary, with insistence that I "get in gear."

"I want to convince you that you need to spend more time in writing your own accomplishments while letting Gary's history fade slowly away over time," he concluded.

It was advice that I wasn't ready yet to hear, feeling that it was far too early, particularly since writing about anything at all had become so painful. And I had no intention of letting Gary or his history fade away from my life, ever. But Art had planted an idea that would slowly take root, though it would take a far different form than what he envisioned. *Not fade away*, I thought, echoing Buddy Holly. *Not fade away.*

I swung east from the coast into bucolic Santa Ynez Valley, where horse farms were rapidly being displaced by vineyards and mansionettes. I drove onto San Marcos Pass, with its splendid views of Cachuma Lake and the wooded hills made famous by Ronald Reagan's Rancho Del Cielo, which served as the Western White House during his presidency. As I drove through Solvang, I felt, as always, that I was entering a kind of Disney version of a Danish village, with half-timbered houses and hotels, decorative windmills, restaurants that serve aebleskiver (Danish pastries), and a copy of Copenhagen's statue of The Little Mermaid, the Hans Christian Anderson heroine. The town was founded in 1911 by Danes from the midwestern U.S. who were seeking a better climate, and its identity as a picturesque Danish colony quickly began to attract tourists.

Outside town, the Danish influence gave way to evidence of the region's older cultures. I drove past historic Mission Santa Ines, thinking about the mustard seeds Dar told me about that had been scattered by the mission-building *padres* to create a golden road between their settlements. That golden road had meant anything but prosperity for the Native Americans in California. The Chumash Indians, who had once numbered in the tens of thousands and ranged from the beaches of Malibu to Paso Robles and inland to the San Joaquin Valley, had been granted a thumbnail-sized reservation in Santa Ynez and tribal recognition only in 1901, ten years before the Danes arrived.

Along Mission Road were signs for the Chumash Indian Casino, which lay a few miles out of town within the confines of the tiny Chumash reservation, where I remembered there had been some bingo games when I first started coming to Solvang. The size of the new casino, Art had told me, had grown in inverse proportion to the small numbers of the remaining Chumash tribe. His house lay about halfway between Solvang and the casino, and I could tell that traffic on the once quiet road had picked up.

I pulled into the driveway of Art and Pierrette's tidy little one-story ranch house, which he had built after his retirement in a deliberately modest style that seemed a rebuke to the oversized estates springing up around him. The shades inside were pulled down to keep out the heat, but it also seemed as though the house itself was in mourning. Art had taken up sculpting after he retired from his engineering job at Hughes, and he was quite good at it. He had finished a bust of Gary as a boy that he began before Gary died, and it now had the look of a memorial sculpture.

Art was his usual dry, laconic self, and Gary's stepmother Pierrette had valiantly pulled herself together for my visit, though she clearly was not feeling well. Art wanted to know what I was working on, whether I had any new writing projects. "I think it's time you started thinking more about Carol and less about Gary," he said, echoing his email message.

I told him about the reunion of Gary's high school friends in Los Angeles, and he said that he wished he and Gary had not been so much at odds in those years. And without prompting, he began talking about Gary's time in Puget Sound. "There are single events that are turning points in someone's life," he said. "They are like a key to how you live your life." Art had decided that the key event in Gary's life had to do with the death of a dog. At some point Gary had apparently stopped going to class, and he had lost his scholarship and run out of money. According to Art, no one in the hippie compound where he was living was willing or able to help him out, and the dog he had adopted there wound up starving to death. Art said that burying the dog that died from neglect had been the turning point for Gary.

Gary had never told me that part of the story about his life as a hippie dropout, possibly because of shame. That is, if it were true. I wasn't sure that Art had the whole story. He had heard and seen what he expected to hear and see. "Dropping out" was a disaster, from Art's point of view. Though the dog's death had undoubtedly been traumatic, had it occurred the way Art thought it had, it might have propelled Gary into the army. But I didn't agree with Art that a single event like that was the key to Gary's life from then on.

I wasn't going to bring it up, but I felt that Gary's loss of his mother to a terrible accident at such a young age was undoubtedly a bigger piece of the puzzle. I knew that it must have been a key for Art, too, who had told me in his understated way that it had been difficult for him after Gary's mother died. At Gary's memorial, he told me that from his own experience, it would take me "at least six months" to recover. Even then, however, I knew that six months would mark only an early stage of my journey of healing.

I wasn't sure that Art had ever acknowledged the depth of his own grief, in part because he had been so concerned with sheltering Gary from the enormity of what had happened. He had not taken Gary to visit his mother's grave, and Gary told me that he didn't know for many years where she was buried. Art gave me a bundle of photographs that included a photo of himself and Gary taken before Gary's mother died. He had built a small plane for Gary, and in the photo, Gary is grinning happily as he poses in the plane, with Art looking on without a care in the world. A golden moment before their world was shattered.

Art said that he and Pierrette were still losing sleep thinking about Gary, but they were following their everyday routines in order to keep going.

"We have a lot of small but important tasks that keep us occupied and that help us focus on the issues of growing older," he said.

They each had serious health problems, and Art was concerned about passing his forthcoming driving test in order to retain his driver's license. He had resumed painstakingly typing up Gary's Digital Nation columns that had appeared over the years in the *Los Angeles Times*. He wanted to turn the columns into a format so that it could be easily reproduced as a book.

My heart ached for Art, and I remembered that Gary told me once that his father had suffered the trials of Job. Gary's much younger half brother Duane, who had been considered a math genius, and who had been a promising student at Cal Tech, had suffered a mental breakdown and had been in a halfway house for many years, unable to live on his own. After learning about Gary's death, he had stopped speaking to his parents, and it was as though they had now lost both sons.

The next morning I accompanied Art to his favorite donut shop, which he wanted me to see. It was his special place, his refuge every morning before he started the day. The proprietor greeted Art like a family member, and he hugged me as a new addition. There were photos of his children and grandchildren tacked on the wall, and there was a slightly yellowing notice of one of Gary's awards still posted prominently, as Gary had apparently been adopted in absentia into the donut maker's family as well.

"I've been watching these kids grow up," said Art, pointing to the photos of the children on the walls. "It gives me comfort watching a new generation, seeing how they turn out."

I hoped that a little piece of his grief would be lifted away each day as he followed his routine in this ever-changing green-and-gold valley, where no one could lay permanent claim.

A little while later, I was in my car, driving toward the coast to join mythical Highway 1 en route to Palo Alto and points north. It was such a beautiful day that I pushed a button to roll the windows down and let the wind ruffle my hair. I could already smell the sea. I was planning to spend the night in the tiny coastal town of Cambria, which Ellen and Dar had recommended. They said I'd be able to see the sea otters playing in the tide pools there. And I could dine at a wonderful café they recommended called the Black Cat.

As I felt my spirits lift in anticipation of watching the otters, I had a flashback to the moment when "The Age of Miracles" appeared abruptly on my iPhone, startling me with its iconic image of the woman in the convertible. She had been heading out on the road with the wind blowing in her hair, leaving behind the house with the picket fence. At that moment of deepest despair, when I felt so utterly lost, the woman behind the wheel had seemed impossibly far ahead of me, her eyes focused on the open road awaiting her. But here I was, heading out on a beckoning road, though in a compact rental car, the wind blowing in my hair, leaving behind not a picket fence but a trail of memories. I was catching up with the woman in the convertible, and maybe I would pass her in the mountains.

Chapter 36

Recapitulation

The next day, as I drove north toward Palo Alto after communing with beguiling otters and languid, grunting elephant seals, I felt as though I were fast-forwarding to Gary's life after the military. I took in Big Sur in a kind of delirious blur, as though I were speeding through time as well as space. In a sense, I had been engaged in a kind of reenactment of Gary's life in California—as though I had watched part of his life story flash before my eyes, in a slower, piecemeal version of the life review that people who experience a near–death experience describe.

I had no idea if Gary experienced an instant panoramic recapitulation of his life as he capsized in the river. But if he had, I imagined that some of the scenes that I had relived vicariously with his friends and his father would have been part of it. I hoped that there had been no business left unfinished, that there would have been a resolution of anything left unresolved, that there would have been nothing but peace in all the peaks and valleys of his life. And I hoped that above all, he knew how much he had been loved.

I was not all convinced that a dying dog was the key to who Gary became as a man—as a teacher, as a leader, or as a husband. I was coming to think that he had found in the military a way to be a warrior, to act out the heroic, larger-than-life instincts he had always shown, and that he had managed to maintain for the rest of his life the kind of youthful bravado and idealism that most of us tend to lose in the daily grind. But I also thought his high expectations of himself as well as of me had brought him a great deal of pain and disappointment.

In retrospect, Art had given me a key piece to the puzzle of why Gary and I had begun to feel as though we were growing apart. And a key to understanding why he had become so impatient with me when I seemed to be getting off track in my career—getting lost in my assignments or exploring ideas that didn't pan out—and particularly when I ventured anywhere close to the world of woo woo, a category that for Gary included pretty much anything spiritual.

During his time in Puget Sound, Gary's attempt at being an artist and free spirit, communing with ashram types with their heads in the clouds, had not ended well. As his friend told me, he had crashed and burned, like Icarus. In a sense, he had been rescued by the order and discipline of the military. He had been a gifted artist, but as far as I knew, he never picked up a paintbrush or palette again.

I could remember only once during our time together that Gary had actually picked up a couple of the colored pencils I had lying around to draw something. It was a quick, almost desultory sketch of our cat Gizmo. It was as though drawing was painful for him, maybe reminding him of a squandered gift. Which was perhaps why he kept telling me to "get in gear," and why I so often felt that I had fallen short. He didn't want me to crash and burn, as he had. But for me, intermittent failure was part of the creative process. It was something I accepted, however painfully. But then, I was no Icarus. I'm not sure I ever soared high enough to fall as hard as Gary had.

Gary told his friend Amon Burton a story about his early days as a raw recruit, when his unit's drill sergeant divided the guys into three groups, with Gary leading one of the groups. The sergeant called everyone to attention and abruptly commanded them to strip.

"Take off your clothes, men. Everything off."

The young men, most of whom were gangly, inexperienced draftees fresh out of small towns, farms or the poor side of town, looked around incredulously, but two of the groups complied with the order. Gary had conferred with his men and told them that he thought the order was unreasonable, and that they should refuse to obey it. So they simply remained there in line, standing at attention in their fatigues, as the other recruits stood nervously in formation, buck naked and embarrassed.

"As you were," commanded the sergeant. He then came up to Gary and said sternly, "We'll discuss this later."

As Gary told the story, the sergeant informed him later that issuing the bizarre order had been a test of character, and that Gary's group was the only one that day that passed. The order had indeed been unreasonable.

After leaving the army, Gary made a splash at Occidental College, founding an anti-apartheid group on campus that had influenced a young Barack Obama, who arrived at Oxy the year after Gary graduated. One of Gary's friends from Occidental, Andrew, had called me shortly after his death, shaken to the core.

"Gary can't be dead," he said, his voice breaking. "He wasn't supposed to die. He was Aragorn," he said, referring to the swashbuckling hero of *Lord of the Rings*.

Andrew told me that Oxy had flown flags at half-staff the day after Gary died.

Gary made a similar mark at Stanford, where he enrolled as a graduate student in political science. But the time at Stanford had been more problematic. He had been a star, but he had clashed bitterly with the ultra-conservative head of the department, and by the time he heard about a new activist organization being formed by some of the most brilliant computer scientists in Silicon Valley, he was ready to leave academia for a more warrior-like role again. He told me he later regretted not staying to get his Ph.D., partly because it had kept him off the tenure track at the LBJ School, leaving him always insecure about his job. But the causes that Computer Professionals for Social Responsibility was taking up seemed more urgent to him at the time than defending his honor in an academic duel.

Severo Ornstein was already something of a legend by the time he and a handful of colleagues founded CPSR. He had been an eyewitness and key participant during what he called in his memoir the "middle ages" of computing, including the birth of the Internet from the defense department's Advanced Research Projects Agency Network, known as ARPAnet. Severo, though, readily admits that when first presented with the possibility that computers could be used to create a communications network, he responded, "Who would want such a thing?"

Severo and his pioneering computer cohorts had been concerned about the proliferation of nuclear weapons and by the increasing influence by the Department of Defense on important computer research and development. CPSR's mission, as Gary explained it to me, was not to put the brakes on the fast-developing new technology, but to ensure that it was being used in the best interest of the public. The founders had already chosen a candidate as the first director of CPSR, but after interviewing Gary, who had essentially elbowed his way into their offices in Palo Alto, they gave him the job.

Severo and Laura kept their ties to CPSR even after they retired to their secluded home in Woodside that they dubbed Poon Hill, after a famous viewpoint in Nepal to which they had trekked. Although I had been to Poon Hill once before with Gary, I was awed yet again by the towering redwood forest that survived in the hills above Palo Alto. Poon Hill fit seamlessly into the surrounding forest. But many of their neighbors were not as concerned with blending into their surroundings. After their retirement, Laura and Severo watched as Woodside became a kind of wooded Valhalla for rock musicians, inventors who had done extremely well by their patents, and tech titans who had made their mark in Silicon Valley.

Neil Young lived on a 1500-acre ranch down the road from Laura and Severo. Larry Ellison, CEO of Oracle, had spent nine years building an architecturally authentic Japanese feudal castle in Woodside, and Steve Jobs had demolished the historic Jackling House after a prolonged court battle and was in the process of replacing it before his death.

I arrived just in time to join Laura and Severo and their neighborhood friends in a fireworks-watching party at an estate on the highest hill in the area, with a distant but dramatic view of lower San Francisco Bay, where the fireworks were being launched. When we returned to their lovely, quiet house, Laura asked if I wanted to sleep outside under the stars, on a bed they had placed on a porch, under a mosquito net. I said yes, enthusiastically, and I slept soundly in my outdoor cocoon, until I was awakened after dawn by their two cats, who wanted to come inside the net and cuddle.

The next morning, we went for a walk in the golden hills above the Pacific where their neighbor Carl Djurassi, best known as the inventor of the birth control pill, had established an artists' colony and vast, panoramic outdoor sculpture garden. I posed for a photo under the landmark Torii gate where Gary and I had posed during our previous visit more than a decade earlier. As with the Torii at Asclepios, it seemed to promise a possible transition to sacred ground, if you could leave your baggage behind and walk through it with the lightest of footsteps.

That afternoon, another of Gary's friends, Bob Taylor, arrived to drive me to a spa for a massage and then to dinner at the best restaurant in town. Gary had told me that Taylor, now in his 80s, had presided over the team at the Department of Defense that had developed the ARPAnet and had co-written a breakthrough paper in 1968 titled "The Computer as a Communications Device." Severo noted in his frank, lively memoir that Taylor and his mentor J.C.R. Licklider "provided the principal impetus for networking in the U.S."

When Bob Taylor, who had gotten to know Gary through CPSR, heard I was coming for a visit, he wrote that he wanted to reciprocate the hospitality Gary had shown him when he had come to Austin to accept an award from the University of Texas. Taylor was known as something of a recluse, who reportedly never left his home in Woodside, and it was a surprise when Gary was able to talk him into traveling to Texas to accept the award.

Gary would have loved the idea of one of the fathers of the Internet chauffeuring me around Woodside, though Taylor drove his souped-up Audi so fast around the curves on the narrow mountain roads, I wasn't sure we'd make it back for the group picnic Severo had planned the next day.

Our friends Pete and Kathryn Lewis drove in for the gathering from Palo Alto, joining a group of about 30 of Gary's old CPSR friends, including Bob Taylor. Severo hadn't planned a formal program, but Pete gave a moving speech, as did Severo and Terry Winograd, another of CPSR's early founders. A professor of computer science at Stanford, Terry had served as adviser to then-PhD student Larry Page, who was working on a research project involving Web search. Page took a leave of absence from Stanford to co-found Google, bringing Terry onboard as an advisor.

Like Severo, many of the group had essentially retired from the fray, and they had begun watching the technology revolution from the sidelines. CPSR itself was on its way to being disbanded after its near-three-decade run. I could sense a kind of nostalgia among the older members of the group for those heady, pivotal days just before computer technology began to accelerate in its incredibly rapid and relentless transformation of everyday lives, when its possibilities as well as its dangers seemed limitless.

I told the group that they were honorary members of the ever-growing global and digital tribe of Gary. And then I told them about the tradition of the second line that I had learned in New Orleans, about the point where mourning the loss of a loved one turns into a celebration of the life and the memories that remain. So they were not just a tribe, I said, but a second line, with a mission not only to carry on the ideals they had shared with Gary, but to carry on "full bore."

I looked around at faces that were sympathetic but puzzled. Gary had understood the second line, in all its bittersweet soulfulness, but I wasn't sure that his friends, living in this cool, rarefied climate of wealth and accomplishment, could absorb a message of hope and joy that had arisen from the hot, swampy depths of New Orleans, bubbling up from the depths of poverty. But if I had managed to bring along parasols and a jazz band, I said to myself, they would have gotten it.

Later, one of Gary's friends, a woman in her 60s named Miriam, who had been a brilliant engineer, pulled me aside, her face a hard mask of focused intensity.

"You'll never get over losing Gary," she told me, in the husky familiar voice of rebuke I recognized from the unmerry widow in Austin.

"I lost my son, and it still haunts me every day," she said. "The pain never goes away. You'll always feel it. You'll always feel alone."

Her air of finality was daunting, but I wasn't ready to grant her the last word on loss. I smiled at her, almost reflexively, not knowing yet how to explain the many ways Gary was still with me despite the pain. Even in a world of virtual community and electronic communications, where actual physical presence isn't necessary, the notion of feeling connected to Gary in an incorporeal way was difficult to describe. I wasn't sure myself what it was all about.

He has never left for ever.

The next day, I drove into San Francisco and stopped at the Asian Art Museum, which had always been one of my favorite places in the city. And it was there that I found a way I could have explained to Miriam how Gary could be gone and yet present—there and yet not there. For an exhibit called "Here/Not Here," eight artists had made works expressing their interpretation of "Buddha presence" and the theme of impermanence. For the artists, Buddha presence is everywhere, though the Buddha himself has gone.

A Thai artist named Jakkai Siributr created the empty silhouette of a Buddha image, a Buddha that is visible in its absence, by using a web of stitched mantras, loosely connected with safety pins, to suggest the outline. And so it was that the space Gary had occupied with his body was empty. Gary was gone. And yet, for me, Gary's presence was everywhere. There and not there. The web of people who had loved him had created a firm and lasting silhouette of who he was and where he had been.

Chapter 37

Saudades

Coming back to Austin, which was simmering in record heat, I had a week to gird myself for the next stage of my pilgrimage, which I both dreaded and anticipated. I would be going to Portugal and stirring up memories that I knew would be painful, but which I needed to face. I dug up some CDs Gary and I had found in Lisbon, and I envisioned myself as a fado singer of a certain age, draped in black lace, posturing in a smoky dive of a nightclub, belting out my regrets and unrequited longing for the beloved voyager who had sailed out into unknown seas, never to return.

Along with their genius for navigation, the Portuguese know all too well about stories with sad endings. My own personal fado song, though, would have to include a stanza about my own regrettable behavior and my yearning for a chance to live it over again and change it.

I had been invited to Porto for the weeklong International School on Digital Transformation, known as ISDT, which Gary started two years earlier as part of an ongoing collaboration between the University of Texas and the University of Porto. Despite my misgivings, I felt strongly that I needed to go, particularly after I had learned from Sharon Strover, Gary's colleague at the University of Texas who was overseeing the collaboration between the two universities, that the school had been renamed for him. It was now the Gary Chapman International School on Digital Transformation.

Sharon had asked if I would give a speech on Gary's behalf as part
of the opening session.

ISDT had been a kind of dream come true for Gary, who had
become intrigued with Portugal in the summer of 2008, when he
spent a week there as a visiting professor in Lisbon and Porto. I
had joined him there for a few days, as he conjured up the idea of
an annual summer school, similar to the ISODARCO program in
Italy that had been such an important part of his life. By the following summer, ISDT had become a reality, and the ISDT banner
was flying triumphantly from the roof of the Retoria, a rambling,
atmospheric stone building on the University of Porto campus
whose walls were adorned with distinguished-looking portraits of
professors of yesteryear. In its first year, the school had drawn students from around the world, and it had been a dazzling success.

We had fallen in love with Porto, with the ancient vineyards
lining the Douro Valley, with the dramatic view of Vila Nova de
Gaia from the Pia Maria Bridge designed by Gustave Eiffel, with
the historic Zona Ribeirinha, or riverfront, lined with *barcos rabelos*,
flat-bottomed boats that had transported casks of port. We loved
the quirkiness of the Casa de Musica, the concert hall designed by
Rem Koolhaus that resembled a giant meteor that had landed in the
middle of the city. We had become close friends with the Portuguese participants in the school, who treated us like family.

I was fascinated by the Portuguese notion of *saudade*, of the kind
of sadness beyond nostalgia evoked in fado, finding in it some of the
bittersweet consolations of the New Orleans second line. The previous summer in Portugal, the school's second year, had been something of a disaster for me, beginning with a freak accident that put
me on crutches and in debilitating pain. A week before we were to
leave, we took our dogs to the park by the lake in our neighborhood,
where an imbecile had let his two large dogs loose to run around. I
was nervously watching them career around at high speed, and I
froze when one of them made a beeline towards me, running full
blast. His head slammed into my right knee, sending me flying into

the air. I landed flat on my face, my knee bent at an unnatural angle beneath me.

The doctor in the emergency room and the specialist at Austin Sports Medicine agreed that nothing was broken, but that I would need to be on crutches for at least a month, and I would need physical therapy. But we were scheduled to leave for Porto in a week, and I was determined to go, even as I thought with foreboding about Porto's steep cobbled streets. I bought a metal hiking stick as a substitute for crutches, and I loaded up on Ibuprofen, as I was allergic to the hydrocodone the doctor had prescribed.

And so I arrived in Porto the summer before Gary died as a cripple, as I dubbed myself, in constant and excruciating pain. If this had been a test of character, I failed miserably. I hobbled up and down the streets determinedly, but occasionally I would step in a crack and yell involuntarily. I could see Gary wince, and I knew it bothered him, but I couldn't help myself. The heat was getting to me as well. Although Porto's weather is usually ideal, the temperatures rose above 100, and everyone in Porto was out in the streets at night to escape their hot, un-air-conditioned apartments. When we stopped at a bar or restaurant, I would ask for a bag of ice to put on my knee, which was constantly throbbing. What a wimp, I told myself.

I kept running out of Ibuprofen, and feeling like an addict, I would send Gary to get more. At one point, I hobbled past a blind man, who asked me for money, and I wondered indignantly why he would beg for money from a cripple. I was taking so much of the painkiller that I could almost excuse myself for the craziness of my behavior, which culminated in my telling Gary in the height of a quarrel that I never wanted to see him again. And though I immediately took it back, I had said the unsayable, and it had haunted me ever since. It had felt like a curse that needed to be erased. And forgiven.

And so I had a lot on my mind as I changed planes in New York, en route to Porto. I was feeling as much like a penitent as a pilgrim at this stage. I had brought along some of Gary's ashes to release in the Douro if I felt that there was an appropriate time and place. I had been ever more tense than usual going through security, as many countries require elaborate documentation in order to transport and release cremated ashes.

I was wide awake on most of the flight, and I decided to watch the single movie that was offered on the plane, one that had not actually been released yet in the states. It was called *The Way*, starring Martin Sheen, and as I realized that it was about a pilgrimage, I was getting that familiar flummoxed feeling of being caught up in synchronicity. In the movie, Sheen gets a phone call, much like mine.

"Is this the father of Daniel Avery?"

The son of Sheen's character has been killed in an accident while on the pilgrimage trail to Santiago de Compostela, and Sheen vows to finish the pilgrimage, taking along his son's ashes, which he releases at points along the way. He also lets go of bits and pieces of grief and anger, as he encounters saints and sinners on the trail and learns as much about himself as about his son.

At the end of the movie, Sheen's character was much further along in acceptance of his loss than I was of my own loss as I watched it. I arrived in Porto this time with a far more grievous injury than a bum knee, and I was bringing with me a great emptiness. I was bringing my own *saudades*. But in some ways I felt far stronger than I had the previous summer, and I had some ideas about what I wanted to say in my opening remarks to the school. I walked from the hotel to the gardens surrounding the Crystal Palace, the old stone-and-glass exhibition hall, where Gary and I had whiled away an afternoon, and jotted down some notes.

That evening, I looked out at familiar and friendly faces in the audience at the opening session, and I knew I was in yet another gathering of the global tribe of Gary. I wanted to tell our Portuguese hosts how much Gary had loved Portugal, not only for its fado music, its azulejo tiles, its warm hospitality, its hold on the past. But also for its quirkiness and whimsicality, which made Portugal more open than most places to ideas of change and transformation, the theme of the school. Porto, I said, was the perfect place to think about the Good Life, as Gary had envisioned it—the *Boa Vida*, as it was called in Portuguese.

What Gary was calling for, I said, was not only a vision of how to preserve local traditions of food and culture, but ways we could join together to harness technology and tools like social media to help bring the Good Life to all. And then I suggested one way to label the seeming contradiction between technology and traditional culture: Slow Food and Speedy Communication. I said that I hoped everyone there would work towards their own vision of the good life, the *Boa Vida*.

I was going to read a quote from a paper Gary had written abut the Good Life, but I could feel myself on the edge of tears, so I handed the quote to Sharon Strover to read:

People who hope for a better world feel the need for a shared vision of the good life that is flexible enough for innumerable individual circumstances but comprehensive enough to unite people in optimistic, deliberate, progressive social change.

After my talk, I walked with Diego Gomez, a community activist from Bogota, Colombia, to the restaurant where we were all to gather for dinner. We heard music coming from somewhere. We both looked around for the source of the music until I realized it was coming from my iPhone, which was inside my purse. It had switched on, and it was playing a song called "Vida." Life. It could have been the theme song of my talk. The song was from an album by an Austin band named Del Castillo, and the image of the album cover that had appeared on the iPhone was of a circle of haloed beings seated around a circular table. A woman is seated next to an empty seat that is filled with a radiant light. I listened to the lyrics, which, translated from the Spanish, said: "I'm waiting for you." Or alternately, "I'm hoping for you."

Diego was shaking his head at the coincidence. "That is a good song for us to hear tonight," he said.

That night I sent my friend Elizabeth an email, telling her about the song that had apparently come from Gary's cosmic playlist and about the image of the woman sitting next to the empty seat filled with light.

"I'm in the middle of a mystery," I said. "I'm not only in a different country, but sometimes on a different plane from ordinary life. It's unknown terrain. But of course that's what being a pilgrim is all about, I suppose. Even if it's a sidewalk I've walked before, it's new."

Chapter 38

On the Wings of a Heron

One morning in July, before the heat of the day had taken hold, I decided to take one of our kayaks out on Lake Austin. I had developed a dread of kayaking, and I hadn't even looked at our kayaks after Gary died. I was having some bad days and nights, feeling as though I were sinking back down into the depths. But if I was ever going to fully reclaim my life, I realized, it was about time to mark that taboo involving kayaks off the list of things I thought I might not ever do again.

The battered old Delta Dagger, which was big enough that Gary had paddled it with Zip wedged in the cockpit, had been sitting unused in the communal rack by the lake. The Dagger is so wide and heavy it wouldn't overturn in a tidal wave, which also made it difficult for me to maneuver while out of the water. Huffing and puffing, I emptied it of stagnant water and debris, including an empty bird's nest. I hauled it to the dock, edged it into the water and paddled my way upstream to an inlet known as Panther Creek, where Gary and I had often lazed along and watched sunbathing turtles dive from the muddy bank into the water. We would often see great blue herons wading along the shore and deer grazing in the overgrown meadow alongside the creek.

Developers had begun to clear one side of the creek, but on this quiet morning, I saw a great blue that held his ground as I paddled by, then took off and flew beside me companionably for a moment. Great blues put me in mind of pterodactyls, and this one in particular seemed to hark back to prehistoric times. I reached the undeveloped stretch of the shore that had always reminded me of a jungle, much like the thicketed banks of Oyster Creek when I was growing up, and I said to myself, without really thinking about it, this looks like Vietnam. I imagined myself paddling through the Mekong Delta, much as I had imagined plying the Amazon when I was a kid rowing on Oyster Creek.

Vietnam. I held the name in my mind like a banner as I paddled back home, wondering why I had made an imaginary plunge into Southeast Asia, where I had never been. I thought about it for a while after I got back to the house and realized that Vietnam was a part of the puzzle I was putting together of Gary's life that was still missing. It felt like unfinished business—not just for Gary, but also for our generation.

At my college graduation, a group of my tech-savvy classmates rigged a loudspeaker that was hidden behind the dais where we were to receive our diplomas. As the name of the first graduate was called, the twangy protest song by Country Joe and the Fish, "I Feel Like I'm Fixin' to Die Rag," rang out over the campus:

> *And it's one, two, three, what are we fighting for?*
> *Don't ask me, I don't give a damn*
> *Next stop is Vietnam.*

The baffled school authorities couldn't find the source of the music, and it continued on through the sound of machine guns going rat-tat-tat and a final explosion, which made everyone jump out of their seats.

Vietnam terrified us all. I didn't know anyone who had actually enlisted, as Gary had. Some of my friends and classmates did crazy, drastic things to avoid going. One friend shot himself in the foot with a shotgun. Another gained a hundred pounds. Another took so much speed he nearly died. Yet another took off for the Mexican border, while another headed north. Most of my friends, in fact, managed to evade the draft, one way or another. Some, however, of the few who were drafted, died there, and some came back with something missing. Some regretted not going; at least one stayed in

Canada. I don't think anyone was ever quite the same, whether they went or not.

Gary had never been able to bring himself to visit the Vietnam War Memorial in Washington D.C., and he made a point of steering around it as widely as possible when we were walking on the national mall. At the time, I considered the act of walking up to the curving black wall as the equivalent of encountering the dragon, and I had always wondered why Gary hadn't been able to face that particular beast. He was extremely touchy about it and didn't want to discuss it. He had always been uncomfortable when he saw a homeless veteran holding up a cardboard sign on a street corner asking for money, and he resented the image of the Vietnam veteran as the tattered loser who had never been able to adjust to normal life back in the U.S.

Gary despised most of the movies about Vietnam, particularly *The Deerhunter*, which he said reinforced false stereotypes about innocent Americans and depraved Vietnamese. There had been brutality on both sides, he told me emphatically. No one was innocent. He had serious reservations about Francis Ford Coppola's *Apocalypse Now* as well, which he saw as depicting Vietnam as the mysterious Heart of Darkness, which tainted the souls of American soldiers who fell apart there or turned into murderous psychopaths without the restraints of civilization. Some Americans brought the darkness with them, he told me once.

The Iraq war had brought it all back to the surface, and it had created ripples in the mostly smooth current of our lives. In retrospect, it was the beginning of an unsettling feeling of distance between us. I remember looking at a photo a friend had taken of him unaware, and there was a sad, haunted look on his face, which I attributed then to the tinnitus that constantly bothered him.

As Bill Broyles wrote in his brilliant *Brothers in Arms*, later republished as *Goodbye Vietnam*, "For so many of us Americans, the war, whether a source of pride and strength or shame and despair, was like a piece of shrapnel, still working its way to the surface, troubling our sleep." One night, not long before Gary died, we were watching a report about Iraq, and I said something to him, thoughtlessly, that upset him and sent him out of the house for a walk to cool down. When we send young people to war, I said, we aren't just asking them to risk their lives. We're asking them to risk their souls.

I was actually thinking about someone else at the time—my sweet, brilliant, slightly geeky high school friend David, who had beaten me out in a couple of scholarships. He had been like a big brother, smiling indulgently at my antics in Chemistry Club, offering a shoulder to cry on when some jerk broke my heart. David, who had tousled red hair and beautiful blue eyes, and who sang like an angel in the school choir, was drafted after leaving Cal Tech. We had lost touch by then. And when I learned what happened, I couldn't imagine why a science genius had been sent into war as a grunt. From what his best friend told me, David had the top of his head blown off by a round fired from a sniper on his second day on patrol in Vietnam. He hadn't died, but the pain and suffering turned him into a drug addict when he came back home. He was killed by a bullet several years later during a drug deal gone wrong. His name wasn't on the black wall, but it should have been.

I knew little of Gary's experience as a medic except that his time in the line of fire had been brief because he had joined the Army as the war was winding down. When I asked him once how long he had been in Southeast Asia, he muttered, "Five months" and didn't want to go into it. He told me only that some of his experiences had involved parachuting behind the lines—possibly into Laos and Cambodia, from what I gathered—and that his missions had been classified, which I confirmed from the records I had requested from the National Personnel Records Center in St. Louis. Some of the information had been blacked out.

I found one of his notebooks from his training days at Fort Bragg, and much of it was devoted to strategies in gathering intelligence, and there was a lengthy, highly technical section on sniper training. "Gentlemen, there is no point in firing your weapon if you do not have a meaningful target," he had written. "And there is no point in engaging that target unless you plan to use your weapon efficiently and accurately."

I had a long talk with Cliff, Gary's best friend during his Special Forces medical training, who had remained in the military and only recently retired. Cliff had left a message on Gary's iPhone after his death, saying simply, "I just wanted to say goodbye, buddy." Gary had been the star of their class, he said, by far the best student. "That was a kick-ass course," he said.

Gary had been "cocky," according to Cliff. He sent me via email a group photo of the class. It wasn't hard to find Gary in the photo, with his cocky pose and lopsided grin. But he looked incredibly skinny. I knew from his records that he weighed a wispy 156 pounds at his physical exam after recruitment, and he couldn't have been much more than that when the photo was taken. Not long after we met, he gave me an old camouflage jacket that he had kept from those days, and it fit me. It was almost too tight. His waist had been tiny.

Cliff also warned me that Gary might have exaggerated his experiences in Special Forces, as Green Berets were wont to do, he said. But Gary had never actually bragged about his exploits. His stories usually focused on his eccentric commanding officers or fellow soldiers, including recruits from the ghetto who had no knowledge of human anatomy and who had to learn where to locate their lungs, livers or kidneys. They had so much to learn, Gary said. So much to do to catch up.

Although Gary showed little sympathy for veterans who blamed their ordeals in the military for not being able to cope with civilian life, I knew that he was not at peace with what he himself had witnessed. During one heated argument in which, absurdly, we were trading stories of dealing with danger, he blurted out, "I put bullets in people." It was a strange way to imply that he had shot or killed in the course of duty, but it was the most he had ever said about feeling guilt or regret from his experiences.

Though Cliff and Gary hadn't stayed in touch, and they had
shifted to opposite sides of the political spectrum, Cliff had been
just as shaken up by Gary's death as his friends from other periods
in his life. He said that Gary had introduced him to his favorite
musicians, including Bruce Springsteen, whom Gary had gone to
hear in New Jersey when he was stationed at Fort Dix and Springsteen was beginning to create a buzz from his gigs at the Stone Pony
in Asbury Park.

"There are still traces of Gary in me when I listen to those
artists," Cliff said.

Cliff also told me about one of the less admirable incidents during
Gary's off-duty adventures, when he borrowed Cliff's Camaro to
drive with some buddies down to Boystown in Nuevo Laredo, just
across the border, where so many Texas boys, including several I
knew in high school and college, had made their rite of passage into
manhood. Gary had told me about the incident, which put him in
the hospital with an injury that was not from combat. An old ker-
osene room heater had apparently exploded before anything much
could happen, and Gary wound up losing most of the cartilage in
one of his knees. I had never been able to figure out how that had
transpired, but I didn't really want to know the details.

"Gary loved life," said Cliff. "He wanted to experience it all.
There are some people who live a whole life and don't really live
at all." Cliff sighed heavily. "My universe is a lot smaller now that
Gary isn't in it," he said.

After he hung up, I looked at the young man in the photo he
sent me, with the cocky stance and crooked smile and the feverish
hunger for life, and I decided that I needed to make Vietnam part
of my pilgrimage. Later that night, as I was looking at my calendar,
I picked up my notebook in a kind of daze and began writing in the
block print that was becoming so familiar.

*"Yes I was there with you on the creek. I was the wings of the blue
heron. I was the wind blowing against the current. I brushed
against your face.*

Vietnam.

Yes you should go. I was so young. You will go with knowledge of what was to happen.

The jungle was so green. The rain was so hot. There was blood. I was supposed to heal but I could not stop the blood. I felt I had to pay for all of that blood. Blood on the land. Why? For what purpose when we could have met and shaken hands and shared a meal.

I have seen their souls, and they, too, are free. We are free of hatred and greed and hunger and pain and suffering. If only we could have seen the light in each other's eyes.

I love you Carol. The light is there for you. I will always be here for you. Look for me in the wind, in the water, in the wings of birds and butterflies. Go on your great adventure, my darling wife. I will be by your side when you need me.

As I had asked before, I asked yet again, whether these were simply my own words, the lines of dialogue my subconscious was conjuring up, like lines in a movie I was improvising—more useful fictions. Was this the voice of my interior beloved, my inner comforter? Or was I sensing his presence in the wind and in the wings of birds because I couldn't let him go, and I had to locate him somewhere, had to invent his presence in some tangible way? Was I a child again talking to Jesus?

I was having an argument yet again with the Gary who would have been skeptical of such things. But because he was not there to present his side, except as an imagined voice, I was arguing with myself. My inner skeptic wasn't nearly as persuasive as my inner longing, and I couldn't possibly win either way.

The neatly printed words, yet again, felt comforting in a truncated, poetic way but somehow too clichéd and corny to be Gary's words. Gary, who loved Machiavelli and hard-boiled mysteries, would never have described himself as being manifest on the wings

of a heron, I thought. Or would he, if he were free of all constraints? If these were Gary's words coming through the ether, maybe it was I as the cliché-ridden transcriber who was the problem.

I vaguely remembered some quote from Wittgenstein that if lions could speak, how could we, not being lions, really know what they were saying? If the departed, freed of all the frailties of the flesh, could actually speak to us from some über realm, some energy level beyond ours, some higher frequency of consciousness than ours, could we, as mere mortals, really understand where they were coming from?

What I did know was that I needed to go to Vietnam, whether it was for me or for Gary. I had a dragon to face myself and a few demons of my own to deal with.

On wings of divine deliverance.

A few days later, on Gary's birthday, I got a call from the dean's office at the LBJ School saying that there was a package for me, that it was a present for me from Gary that someone had dropped off. I held the phone away from my ear, trying not to freak out. Of course they knew that Gary had died the previous December. Nobody would joke about a thing like that. Calm down, Carol. Take a breath. The Angel Gabriel doesn't do personal package delivery, even in the movies.

Apparently the package had been dropped off by a student who said that Gary had bid on a necklace in a silent auction that was a benefit for the student association the previous December, just days before he died, and he had won it. The deal was that the winner would tell the student what name to have engraved in Arabic on a silver necklace when the student went to Cairo over the holidays. Gary had given the student my name, but he had died before she returned, and she hadn't known what to do with the necklace when she got home and learned that he had died. Finally, months later, she dropped the package off at the dean's office on the day that happened to be Gary's birthday. And so it was that my late husband presented me with a silver necklace on his birthday, tied up in a ribbon of synchronicity.

Okay, Gary, the rationalist, how would you account for that? Well, Gary, the ultimate romantic of extravagant gestures, you've outdone yourself this time. Carol, the skeptic, pipe down. Carol, the permeable believer, you've won a round.

Chapter 39

Blessings from the Jade Emperor

Mai Ngoc, my Vietnamese guide, could hardly believe it when I arrived at the airport in Ho Chi Minh City (aka Saigon) with only a small carry-on bag and without jet lag. I had been traveling for 36 hours, but I was pumped with adrenaline and probably buzzing like an alarm clock.

"We are going to have to keep you busy," she said, sizing me up with a sly smile that I would get to know and love in the next few days.

My hotel room wouldn't be ready yet for a couple of hours, so Mai decided we'd make an unscheduled stop at a special pagoda before checking in at the hotel.

"That way you can start your journey with a blessing," she said.

It was my introduction to Mai's uncanny ability to read my moods and energy levels and to improvise as we went along. She always seemed to know where I needed to go next. Mai knew that I had lost my husband, and that he had been an army veteran. But she clearly wasn't out to coddle me. I had found her through a California travel company called Classic Journeys that specializes in personalized walking tours that focus on culture rather than adventure. But I could tell already that with Mai, who was small but feisty, I'd have both. Mai and her family had been among the boat people who had evacuated South Vietnam after Saigon fell to the North Vietnamese. She had grown up in Canada but returned to Vietnam when opportunity knocked for guides with fluent English and leadership skills.

I decided to put myself in her hands, and because I was traveling as a pilgrim rather than as war veteran, I wanted to travel with as little baggage as possible. Which meant that I tried not to bring along with me the familiar, tangled litany of names, images, phrases, slogans, platitudes, historical ironies, lines in movies and song lyrics that had helped to make Vietnam the nightmare that wouldn't go away: the domino theory, the Tonkin Gulf resolution, Vietnamization, the Tet offensive, free-fire zone, Operation Rolling Thunder, My Lai, Agent Orange, the smell of napalm in the morning, "Run Through the Jungle," the Hanoi Hilton, tiger cages, punji sticks, "Have You Ever Seen the Rain." Inevitably, I would encounter vestiges of war on my journey, but for now I knew them only second-hand. I didn't need to bring them along with me as shrapnel embedded in my psyche, clouding my vision.

Mai hailed a taxi to take us to Phuoc Hai Tu, the Emperor of Jade Pagoda. The Emperor of Jade, she said, was the supreme god of the Taoists, but the temple held figures from other faiths, including a Sakyamuni Buddha, in case I wanted to get blessings from them as well. Mai herself was a Buddhist, she said. We walked past low, unassuming pink walls and a modest gate guarded by ceramic Fu lions, into a busy courtyard. Hawkers were plying their wares, including live turtles, firecrackers, lottery tickets and joss stocks to burn in honor of the departed. A small fetid pond, surrounded by people tossing coins, was full of turtles crawling over each other. They had been placed there as good luck offerings, said Mai. Turtles symbolized a long life, but the turtles themselves, I surmised, would not enjoy a long life under their crowded conditions.

Already, I was wilting from the intense heat. I knew it would be hot in Vietnam, and I was prepared to deal with it, having lived in sweltering Houston and torrid New Orleans, at times without air conditioning. But this was heat and humidity of a different order. I realized I was going to have to take the heat as a given and get on with it. This was just a small taste of what it would have been like as a soldier humping the five-pound metal helmets, seven-pound flak jackets and the 20-pound medic satchels, not to mention the weapon of choice and ammunition of the day, which Tim O'Brien had described in his masterful *The Things They Carried*, the book about Vietnam that had been Gary's favorite.

Smoke and incense were billowing out of the temple as we entered the first of several inner sanctums. I gathered that the large carved bearded figure in embroidered silk who looked like Confucius, though with a stern, judgmental look about him, was the Jade Emperor himself. The emperor acts as a kind of filter at heaven's gate, deciding who gets in and who gets rejected and sent to the Realm of Hell—which Mai said we'd visit in another room of the temple. Mai suggested that I buy a bottle of some kind of holy water as an offering. The bottle in question appeared to be a soda pop bottle filled with an unidentified liquid. I hoped it wasn't highly combustible.

"Tell him who you want to have blessed," she said, as I handed the bottle to the priest.

"Gary," I said.

The youngish priest, who appeared a little harried by the number of supplicants that day, looked at me fiercely, as though looks could pierce the skin, and repeated, "Gary," as he poured the liquid over the flames burning on the altar. The flames flickered but kept burning brightly. The priest nodded. So Gary had apparently passed muster with the Jade Emperor.

I speed-walked through the Realm of Hell, presided over by carved wooden figures of the Chief of Hell and his retinue, who appeared to be administering various sorts of torture to the rejectees from heaven. I stopped, however, to rub the legs of a large wooden horse, which would apparently carry my wishes to heaven if I rubbed hard enough and wished intently enough. If wishes were horses, I thought, this would be my steed.

I hardly had time to drop my bags off at the hotel and catch my breath before we headed to the Museum of War Remnants, which was apparently a *de rigueur* stop for American visitors. Mai was uncharacteristically apologetic as walked up to the entrance. She stopped at the front door, saying that she would wait for me here, that this was something that I should experience on my own.

"I think some of these are photoshopped," she said, "to exaggerate. You know, for propaganda."

I wasn't so sure, however, as I entered exhibits called "Historical Truths" and "Aggressive War Crimes." So here they were, in color and in black-and-white, the vestiges, the shrapnel, that I hadn't wanted to bring along with me. The museum was a collection of the horrors of the Vietnam War from the perspective of the Vietnamese. There were photographs that showed the effects of napalm and phosphorous on human flesh and the effects of the defoliant Agent Orange on the environment. Annihilation.

There was a room titled "Requiem" devoted to combat as seen through the lens of war photographers on both sides who had themselves died. On the wall were indelible visions of hell—of mud, mangled bodies, and twisted metal—that no painter of perdition, not even Hieronymus Bosch at his most tortuous, has ever captured. Highlighted in the display were photos developed from the legendary Robert Capa's last roll of film. The photos had been taken in 1954, when the combatants had been the French and Vietnamese, shortly before Capa was blown apart by a landmine.

I walked slowly, with a strange detachment, through these rooms that spoke of unimaginable horror, as though I had seen it all before. I felt nothing, or so I thought. When I reached the exit, I smiled when I saw Mai, who was waiting for me with an apprehensive look on her face.

"All OK?" she asked.

"All OK," I said. "What's for lunch?"

That evening, Mai took me on the back of her motorbike to her neighborhood of narrow streets and alleyways to meet a seamstress who lived just down the alley from her apartment. I had admired Mai's beautiful black silk jacket, which was her official guide uniform, and she asked if I wanted one. Well, of course I did. So no problem. The seamstress, who had been sitting out in the narrow, crowded alley on a plastic chair, taking a break, beckoned us into a small room full of remnants of silk fabric. A cat was sleeping beneath a table that supported a small sewing machine. A few quick measurements, and the seamstress said the jacket would be ready first thing in the morning.

Sure enough, the next morning, Mai arrived at my hotel lobby with the jacket carefully folded and neatly wrapped in colorful gift paper. I immediately went to my room and put it on and didn't want to take off for the rest of the time I was in Vietnam. I washed it every night and let it dry so that it would be fresh each day. The beautifully tailored jacket, which was a cross between the traditional *Ao baba*, or working pajamas of the peasant, and the *Ao gam*, or formal tunic of the upper class, fit like a second skin. It felt to me like protective camouflage, which was a silly thought, given my long, blond-streaked hair and pale skin. I wasn't fooling anybody.

Our next stop was the Cu Chi Tunnels, another reminder of the horrors of war that had become a popular tourist attraction for Vietnamese and Americans alike. My strange detachment from the day before reappeared, and I wondered if perhaps my soul had taken another vacation from my body. The tour of the tunnels began in a large hall with a miniature replica of the tunnels and some spoon-like tools that had been used to carve out the approximately 130 miles of tunnels that contained the basic elements of life underground, including sleeping quarters, hospitals and schoolrooms. A small section of the tunnels, which were originally only about 31 inches high, had been widened to allow access to Westerners, with their greater height and wider girth.

A uniformed photographer snapped pictures as I popped up from a hole in the ground and posed with a grin, holding up the camouflage divot above my head, and again inside a narrow tunnel as I crawled with my hands touching each side. Why is this woman smiling? This is not Fantasyland, damn it! I wondered if someone in charge of transforming the tunnels into a tourist attraction had visited Disneyland. Visit the Haunted Tunnel, the Burrow of Horrors. When I later looked at the prints I was presented with in a tidy envelope, my smile looked strained and a little demented.

Scattered around the grounds were living-history-style exhibits, a sort of Williamsburg of life underground. At one stand, a woman in *ao baba* pajamas was serving samples of rice cakes and tapioca, the staple food of the tunnels. At another, a woman was measuring out little paper cups of rice wine. It all seemed rather cheery until I came to an exhibit of the low-tech torture devices the Viet Cong had used on American soldiers, including the dreaded pits and pungi sticks that had been adapted from traditional methods of hunting and trapping large animals.

Against the greater firepower of the Americans, the Viet Cong had used whatever was at hand, to terrifying effect. They would emerge from the tunnels to set booby traps, planting trip wires that would set off grenades or overturn boxes of scorpions onto the heads of patrolling GIs.

"The tunnels were part of the special terror of Vietnam," Bill Broyles had written. "In our minds the enemy wasn't another soldier, a man like us. He was mysterious and elusive – a vision from the unknown, a bogeyman with terrible powers rising up out of the earth."

And yet the Viet Cong, who had dug these tunnels with little more than glorified spoons and their fingernails, were relying on the simplest of strategies. When Americans trained dogs to sniff out the openings of the tunnels, the VC would smear the openings with garlic. The VC lived underground like rats for months at a time. They had suffered malaria, dysentery and other diseases. More than 45,000 Vietnamese were said to have died in the tunnels or in protecting them.

As we reached the exit, I turned down the chance to fire a weapon of my choice—an AK47, an M16, or a Russian SKS. But when we stopped at a souvenir stand, I bought a green VC hat proclaiming that I had survived the Cu Chi Tunnels. It was clear to me that you had to go no further than the Cu Chi Tunnels to understand why the Vietnam War had been unwinnable for the U.S.

It was a relief to head south to the Mekong Delta, the land of the Nine Dragons, where the Mekong River divides into nine mouths reaching toward the sea. The rice paddies in the fertile delta can produce three or four crops a year, said Mai, as we passed men and women in conical hats, bent over the green shoots, with the occasional tethered water buffalo grazing nearby. The lush tropical landscape, cut through with waterways, reminded me of the Louisiana bayou country, an impression that grew stronger as I watched fishermen ply their nets. At one point, we clambered into a small wooden-hulled boat, and as we poled our way through a narrow waterway, lined by thick undergrowth, I suddenly realized this was very close to the scene of Vietnam I had imagined on Panther Creek. It was here, I thought, that the wings of the heron had brought me.

On wings of divine deliverance.

We reached a bridge at a settlement called Cam Son, where Mai had arranged for bicycles to ride into the delta along paths and levees, past farms, orchards and small villages. Mai, who had grown up in the delta, and seemed to know every plant and tree, would occasionally stop and pluck leaves used as seasoning for cooking for me to smell or edible berries for me to taste.

We stopped at an orchard, where the owner, a small, elderly man named Hai Cu, had prepared a platter of fruit for me to sample. Hai Cu, said Mai, had been a VC combatant, but after the war he had returned to his previous life as a farmer. I was bewildered by the variety of colors and textures on the platter: the translucent white meat of the longan, known as the dragon eye; the seed-packed meat of the sweet-sop, or sugar apple; the rambutan, or hairy cherry, with its thick hide peeled away; and my favorite, the pitaya, or dragon fruit, whose bright red scaly exterior did indeed bring a dragon to mind. Hai Cu invited me to try out a hammock to rest before resuming my journey, and he playfully waved a palm frond over my face to generate a wisp of a breeze.

We continued on our bikes along a pathway until we reached a crowd of people who were spilling out of a small house, where a tent had been set up in the garden for shade. Musicians were banging out a rhythm on drums and other percussion instruments, and I assumed it was a wedding.

"Oh, no, this is a funeral," said Mai.

She spoke to one of the guests, who smiled at me and waved me into the enclosure under the tent.

"They would like you to join them," said Mai.

I was seated next to two elderly gentlemen, who passed me a plate of candies and urged me to take some. They explained to Mai, who translated for me, that they were celebrating the life of the family matriarch, who had passed away at age 85, and that this was not a sad occasion, but a happy one to think that she had lived such a long life.

I toasted the health of the family and joined in the ritual of holding burning joss sticks in honor of the matriarch, as we were all blessed by a priest with a bandana tied around his head. As the drums played on, and incense wafted across the garden, it was difficult to think of this edenic place, with its ripe overhanging fruit, its kindly elders, its hospitable villages and its placid canals as the locale of notoriously savage fighting between VC guerrillas and units of the U.S. Navy's swift boats and hovercrafts.

American GIs in Vietnam, whose average age had been 19, wrote Bill Broyles, had found themselves in "a war of exceptional brutality, waged at times by old men, women, and children, who would treat them with exaggerated kindness during the day and try to kill them at night."

Yes. And yet swords had been beaten into ploughshares, battlefields had turned green again, and bomb craters had been transformed into fish ponds. The smiles and the welcome now seemed genuine. Looking at my growing collection of photos of myself taken with smiling crones with blackened, betelnut-stained teeth, with grinning children proffering the peace sign, with young women giggling as we posed together, with elderly men offering tea, I remembered what Tim O'Brien had written when he returned to Vietnam in 1995.

"Dear God. We should've bombed these people with love."

The next two days passed in a jumble of postcard impressions. I jogged on the sands of China Beach, past posh new hotels and resorts, on the stretch of shore where Americans had once concocted their fantasy retreat from the horrors of the war; had a slinky dress made in the sleepy but chic town of Hoi An, known for its exquisite tailoring; and handed out candy to school children in the tiny settlement of Hoa Chau, after teaching them a song about numbers in English. And now I was on my way through the Hai Van tunnels, which cut through the Truong Son Mountains, which divide north and south Vietnam, to the former Imperial capital of Hue, which had suffered some of the bloodiest battles of the war and had nearly been demolished.

Hue had been the capital of the Nguyan dynasty, which once controlled the land from southern China to the Gulf of Siam. The building of the Imperial City began in 1804, but by 1945, when the last emperor abdicated, the French influence had prevailed. The Imperial City, like Beijing's Forbidden City, had become a historical relic. During the Vietnam War, the Americans were reluctant to raze a historical treasure, but the ferocity of the Tet offensive had overcome that forbearance. The brutality on both sides took a heavy toll on Hue and on its population. Much of the Imperial City was destroyed by U.S. bombing, and the Viet Cong slaughtered some 3,000 civilians after taking over the city.

Mai had arranged for us to arrive at the Imperial City by dragon boat after a ride down the Perfume River. I was wearing my now standard outfit of custom silk tunic, khaki pants and a straw conical hat I had bought at a market. We walked over a moat through the Hien Nhon and Chuong Duc gates, past nine antique bronze "holy cannons" never actually fired and past the flag tower, from which the Viet Cong flew their flag for 24 days after taking the city during the Tet offensive.

We headed toward Thai Hoa palace, the Palace of Supreme Harmony, one of only two surviving palaces, where visitors can don imperial-era costumes and play emperor for the camera. We stopped beside two enormous bronze urns, known as Vac Dong, decorated with birds, plants and animals, and took pictures of each other, smiling, with our arms around each other's shoulders.

We walked back toward the Temple of Generations, which contains carved stone stelae and life-sized statues honoring various emperors, including one who was incredibly short. We took silly photos trying to look as short as the midget-sized emperor.

As we headed back toward the entrance gates, I looked over to the plaza where we had admired the urns, and I saw a tour group, listening to a guide, who was gesturing toward Thai Hoa palace. They were dressed in olive green and some were wearing hats like the one I had bought at the Cu Chi Tunnels. Most of them had grey hair.

"Those are VC veterans," said Mai. "They're taking a tour, just like you are."

I looked and looked at this group of about 30 VC veterans, who must have been about Gary's age, and suddenly, I collapsed. My legs gave out, and I was on the ground, sobbing uncontrollably. It was as though the fragile wall of resistance I had built against feeling all the sorrow and horror of the war had given way, and I couldn't stop the flood. I felt as though I had been swept into a tsunami, and I was drowning in grief as wide and deep as the ocean. I was gone.

Mai lifted me to my feet and led me to a stone ledge, sat me down, and put her arm around my shoulders, as I continued to weep. I couldn't stop. But after a moment I looked up and found that I was now surrounded by the group of VC veterans, who were looking at me with worried, concerned faces. There were two women in the group, their long grey hair tied into braids. The tour guide asked

Mai what was wrong, and she explained that I was here in Vietnam because of my late husband, who had been in the army.

"Please tell them I'm sorry," I said, and the tears started again.

I just couldn't stop. I wasn't sure I could ever stop crying. For Gary, for my classmates who died here, for the terrible loss of innocence, for all the useless suffering, for all the wounds and cruelty on both sides, for the beautiful green land ravaged by our savage chemicals, by the revelations of human depravity and corruption this war had revealed. It was too much to bear.

Later, I couldn't even imagine what a spectacle I must have made, a pale American with long blond hair, wearing a conical peasant hat and silk pajama top, sobbing her heart out, clinging to a small Vietnamese woman wearing an identical silk jacket, hers with Classic Journeys embroidered on the pocket.

One of the women took my hand, and she held it tightly for what must have been a good ten minutes, before I could control my crying. Others in the group came up to touch my shoulder or my arm. They formed a close circle around me, and it must have resembled one of those scenes where the invalid on her deathbed is surrounded by family. Surely they must be related somehow, a puzzled onlooker would have thought.

The woman who was holding my hand spoke to me softly in Vietnamese, and the tour guide said that they all wanted me to know that they had no bad feelings towards Americans. The war is over for them, she said, and they were glad that I had come.

"They want me to tell you that are very sorry for the loss of your husband," she said.

One of the men in the group looked at me with such utter kindness that I felt as though I were looking into the face of the Buddha. *If only we could have seen the light in each other's eyes.*

Eventually they left, and Mai and I sat there for a while. Neither one of us knew what to make of what happened. As we walked slowly back to the entrance gates, Mai bought a little bag of fish food for me to drop into the moat, causing a small feeding frenzy among the golden koi carp below. As I watched the flashes of gold in the water, I began to calm down, and a young man standing beside me along the rail smiled and gave me a thumbs up. Another Buddha smile for my collection.

It wasn't until later that I realized I had found a group of necessary angels in a most unlikely place. Or was it that they had found me? More synchronicity, I supposed. Was it more than a fortunate coincidence? I couldn't help but wonder whether the gray-haired veterans, like the young sergeant at the Austin airport, had harkened to some call of duty that ordinary mortals can't hear. I hoped that they, too, had gotten some solace from our meeting. They had taken along with them a large measure of my grief, which I hoped they had dispersed to the four winds.

If a small, riven nation could heal from such grievous wounds, did that mean that I could heal as well? One of my friends, a Vietnam vet, told me that he liked to visit old Civil War battlefields. He had always found it comforting that grass grows over the most scarred of battlegrounds.

Chapter 40

The Gecko and the Dragon

hen I look back now on the photographs that Mai took of me, and that friendly strangers took of the two of us together during that time, I can see an almost childlike joy in my smile — as though I am rediscovering something I had lost a long time ago. Why is this woman smiling? The smile was indiscriminate. There I am in Hanoi, smiling with a group of young college graduates in front of the ancient Temple of Literature and its tranquil Well of Heavenly Clarity; smiling in front of the Hoa lo Prison — the Hanoi Hilton — for heaven's sake; smiling in front of Ho Chi Minh's modest house on the edge of a small lake; smiling coyly behind the fan-shaped menu at Indochine, where I had one of the best meals of my life; smiling as I hold up the Chinese character for Happiness that I have drawn on a napkin at Mai's instruction, and that I can now recognize when I see it.

I'm particularly fond of the video Mai took of me at the Tay Pagoda, located on a hill deep in the countryside outside Hanoi. We are still breathless from climbing, and she is instructing me, off camera, in the proper etiquette of asking a favor of the Buddha. I am kneeling, bowing, and praying awkwardly on a linoleum rug in front of a carved gilded Buddha. I feel obliged to explain that I'm not a Buddhist, and so I am just going through the motions. Okay, well, I guess I've dabbled a little in hope of finding detachment, but I'm not a devotee, I say, equivocating.

"Don't worry," says Mai. "It doesn't matter as long as your heart is pure."

She has me repeat the motions and words over and over until I get it right. I ask for love, past, present and future, though I speak softly so that she can't hear the words.

We were both smiling when she handed back my iPhone. Just as we stepped outside the pagoda, we heard a loud, scary shrieking noise that seemed to come from an adjacent building, and I jumped. I had thought we were all alone on the hilltop. Mai got a serious look on her face and shook her head. I thought she was going to tell me about bad omens.

"You are very, very lucky," she said. "That is the leopard gecko, and he is giving you his blessing. I have never heard one here before, in all the time I have been coming here. So the Buddha has answered you. You will get your wishes."

On the day before I left Vietnam, Mai took me to the gangplank of a large sailing junk that would take me on an overnight cruise around Halong Bay, one of the most strange and beautiful places on earth. I was distraught when I learned she wouldn't be coming along. But when I got on board, the boat hostess took over Mai's role of big sister. She explained that Halong means "dragon coming down to earth," and that according to legend, an enormous dragon had descended into the sea, carving the fantastical rock formations that jut out from the water with its thrashing tail.

The boat was laden with happy young couples, many of whom appeared to be honeymooners. I was the only lone traveller on the boat, and at dinner, the hostess came to sit with me at my solitary table. She asked me why I had come to Vietnam, and I said it was because I had lost my husband. She said that she, too, had lost her husband a few years earlier.

"Here in Vietnam," she said, "we believe that even if your husband dies, he will still be with you, that he will be at your back."

"I'm beginning to believe that too," I replied.

He has never left for ever.

The next morning, as the sun illumined the jagged rocks in shades of impossibly beautiful purple, pink and pearl, I decided to take out one of the kayaks that were available for rent on the boat. The rental attendant apologized that all they had were tandem kayaks. Did I still want to go? Yes, I did. And so I paddled my way from the junk through an opening between two towering limestone rocks that seemed to form a gateway from the bay to the South China Sea. I was alone on the water, in my kayak built for two, with the misty horizon ahead of me. I could just keep going, I thought, all the way to China. I had lost my fear of dragons, and I had learned the symbol for happiness. But it was time to go home.

On my flight back to the U.S. one of the featured movies on my Korean Airlines fight was on the subject of pilgrimage. It was a documentary set in Tibet about pilgrims who come to Mount Kailash, which has been identified in Hindu and Buddhist scriptures as the mystic heart of the universe. These pilgrims wore protective gloves and aprons as they circled the sacred mountain, flinging themselves along in a kind of mobile prostration. They would stretch out facedown on the often icy ground, then get up and step to the point where their hands were touching the ground just before, then prostrate themselves again. They appeared to be in a daze as they inched along.

The pilgrims spoke about how prostration made the journey more intense and increased the possibility of reaching the goal of their pilgrimage, whether it was to overcome grief, to acquire better luck in their lives, or to up their chances of a good rebirth into the next life.

It occurred to me that what appeared to be an agonizingly slow way of finding relief from suffering might actually have seemed to these pilgrims as a shortcut. Or at least a way to simplify the task. Circling the mountain put a boundary on the limitless. Follow the ancient footsteps, lose all distractions, quash the ego, feel at one with the sacred, mission accomplished.

Chapter 41

Return of the Hawk

As the first anniversary of Gary's death approached, I wasn't sure how I wanted to spend the day. How do you observe the anniversary of a death? I wasn't ready for any kind of formal ritual, but I wanted the day to be special. A friend I hadn't seen in a long time was in town, and I suddenly got the urge to cook dinner for the two of us. I hadn't even gotten a pan out of the cupboard after Gary died, but I started thinking about jambalaya, one of the standard dishes I learned to make in New Orleans. Gary had usually done the cooking for the two of us, but jambalaya and gumbo had been my forte.

There are different theories about the origin of the name jambalaya. Even in New Orleans, no one agrees on whether it came from the Provencal word "jambalaia," meaning a mishmash, or mixup of ingredients, or whether it was a combination of jambon, the French word for ham, the French words *à la*, and "ya," thought to be an African word for rice. In any case, when I made gumbo or jambalaya, stirring up a spicy mishmash of ingredients, I felt something like a voodoo priestess conjuring up a magic healing potion.

I set out to buy the ingredients, including shrimp and andouille, a Cajun sausage, and the makings of a salad, but I realized I didn't have implements to toss and serve the salad. I stopped at a little "hippie" convenience store, with various organic products, and bought some organic bamboo "hands" for the salad.

As I started chopping the ingredients, I put on some New Orleans music, a collection of our favorites on a CD that Gary had put together for me, with Professor Longhair, the Neville Brothers and others, and I found myself dancing around the kitchen, second-lining, and thinking about the day so many years ago in New Orleans, before we had even touched, when Gary had told me on the phone that he was on his way from Boston to see me.

After caramelizing the onions and stirring in the chopped green pepper and celery, I broke open the package containing the new bamboo salad hands. A small piece of paper fluttered to the floor, similar to the fortune in a fortune cookie. I picked it up and read: "You allow love in."

Later that day, my sister Ellen called, saying that something strange had happened that morning. She drove to work, and as she pulled into the parking lot, she looked over to a pole where she had seen a hawk perching quietly for the past several mornings. He wasn't there, and she looked over and saw him flying over an adjacent field. She had thought to herself, "Look, that's Gary, now flying free," and as the thought came into her mind, something happened to the music that was coming from her iPod. It had been playing a pop song that she hadn't been paying much attention to, but she heard a strange scratching sound. The iPod switched in mid-song to the chorus of another song, this one by Christina Perri, and she heard the words, "I have loved you for a thousand years." And then the words, "I'll love you for a thousand more."

"I thought right away that this was a message for you from Gary," said Ellen. From the cosmic playlist.

On wings of divine deliverance.

Part IV

When the Light Came Back

We shall not cease from exploration
And the end of all our exploring
Will be to arrive where we started.
And know the place for the first time...

~ T. S. Eliot

Chapter 42

Oculus

A week later I was on my way to Rome. I would be arriving on the morning of the solstice, December 21, which was not only the darkest day of the year, but also the day when light would begin to return. It would be the second winter solstice since Gary's death. I had decided that I would spend the holidays in the Eternal City and that I would end my pilgrimage there if I felt that I had finally found what I was looking for. There would be no shrine, sanctuary or sacred rock marking the end of the trek. And without a map, or a well-worn pathway, I wouldn't have the certainty of the pilgrim circling the mountain that I had reached the endpoint of my journey. But I hoped that I would know when I had come full circle — that I would know the moment when the end had become my beginning, to borrow from Eliot.

If being in Italy without Gary had once seemed impossible, it now it seemed inevitable. I had conquered my fear of dragons, I thought, so why would I fear the country that Gary loved most, where he had found the source of the Good Life, and the place where he had envisioned himself growing old? If he had lived, I thought, this was the place where we could have grown old together, enjoying delectable Slow Food dinners and arguing crankily about humanism, religion and science, amid the ruins of antiquity. Or at least that was the fantasy that Gary woke up with on many mornings as he looked at real estate listings in Italy before heading off to another day at UT, where impervious, sleep-deprived 18-year-olds in his freshman class nodded out or texted as he tried to convey his own passion for learning.

I had a reservation at the Del Senato, located within a stone's throw of the Pantheon, the best preserved building of the ancient world, where Gary and I had stayed during our last trip to Rome eight years earlier. I chose the Del Senato this time, though, for the light as much as for the memory. I wanted to be inside the Pantheon at noon on the solstice, at the moment when the light coming through the oculus, the opening at the top of the dome, points precisely over the main doorway.

I wasn't quite sure why this seemed so important, but I knew that I wanted to be there at that pivotal moment. Maybe it was something like the shift from loss to joy in a second line, although this would be more of a cosmic second line — or alignment, that is. At last year's solstice, I was to have joined Gary in Tikal, to watch the light deliver its message on the pyramids. And so perhaps this was a substitute of one ancient monument for another. But that wasn't quite right. Gary had died in a place whose history and whose ancient gods were alien to him. It was Italy, I knew, that he would have chosen as the place to watch the last light of the day.

As I told the cab driver at the train station where I wanted to go, I glanced down at the book he had placed next to the driver's seat: *La Verita Sta Sul Limite.* Truth is the Limit. Well, of course, what else would one expect on a pilgrimage?

"What's it about?" I asked.

Pleased by my interest, he replied that it was about mathematics, about calculus, about how truth shouldn't be left to professors.

"*È bellissimo,*" he said.

Beautiful. Maybe I should read it too, I said, as the driver took a geometrically improbable route to my hotel.

Already I was absorbing the light and the colors of the city, which are like no other — as art critic Robert Hughes had described them, "the warm organic colors of the ancient earth and stone of which the city is composed, the colors of limestone, the ruddy gray of tufa, the warm discoloration of once-white marble, and the speckled, rich surface of the marble known as *pavonazzo*, dappled with white spots and inclusions like the fat in a slice of mortadella." In its very stones, Rome conveys the contradictions of decay and permanence.

Arriving at the Piazza della Rotunda, which spread out in grand welcome in front of the 2000-year-old Pantheon, made me feel a little intimidated, since I had no royal retinue or anything more than a small suitcase along with me. The concierge at the Del Senato asked if I was alone.

"Yes, I'm alone," I said.

I must have looked forlorn as I said it. The concierge smiled at me conspiratorially.

"We say it is better to be good alone than in bad company," he said with a wink.

Soon I was I looking out the window of my room toward the Pantheon, remembering the last time Gary and I were at the Del Senato, almost exactly eight years earlier, looking out on a surreal scene taking place on the piazza. A group of royalists were welcoming Prince Vittorio Emmanuel, son of the late King Umberto, on his first visit back to Italy since 1946, when he had been sent into exile. The constitutional law prohibiting the return of male descendants of the King of Italy had just been abolished, and after the prince had forsworn any claim to the throne or to the crown jewels, he was allowed to return, though it was only for a day. He had been to see the Pope and now he had come to the Pantheon, a shrine built to honor multiple divinities, in a visit full of symbolism that was not appreciated by all. His small group of supporters was surrounded by angry protestors with signs denouncing the late King Umberto's tacit collusion with Fascism.

The Pantheon, which had been built during the rule of the temperamental emperor Hadrian, was given its name, implying a reverence for all gods, because its "vaulted roof resembles the heavens," a Roman Senator had written. Byron had described it as the "pride of Rome" and "relic of nobler days" in his hyperbolic poetic travelogue

"Childe Harolde's Pilgrimage." Byron's wandering pilgrim, disillu-
sioned by a life of revelry, and a thinly disguised alter ego of Byron
himself, had been chastened by viewing Rome's antiquities, as he
searched for something that would endure amid the rise and fall of
empires. The Pantheon, he wrote, was:

> *simple, erect, severe, austere, sublime —*
> *Shrine of all saints and temple of all gods,*
> *From Jove to Jesus — spared and blest by time.*

I looked at my watch and hurried downstairs. It was 15 minutes
before noon. I was surprised that the Pantheon was relatively empty
of visitors, and I had the floor directly under the oculus to myself.
The dome of the Pantheon, made of concrete that has lasted for two
millennia, is considered one of the greatest achievements in the history of architecture and engineering, and the oculus, which appears
small from the perspective of the ground, actually has a diameter of
more than 27 feet. As I looked upward, it appeared not only to let in
the light but also a portion of the very sky itself.

"Glory sheds/Her light through thy sole aperture," Byron
had gushed.

With no other windows in the building, the light entering the
oculus becomes a kind of spotlight being cast onto the interior of
the Pantheon. In recent years, historians have speculated that the
Pantheon acts as a kind of sundial, with the direction of the light
indicating the change of seasons rather than the time of day. At
noon, the sun is to the south, so the spotlight falls on the northern
half of the temple. In winter, when the sun is low in the sky, the
spotlight falls higher up on the interior. And on the winter solstice,
the spotlight points due north, directly over the front entrance.

Sure enough, as I watched, the spotlight, moving almost imper-
ceptibly, arrived at a point that appeared to be directly over the door.
I wanted to applaud: heaven and earth and human endeavor coming
together in a ballet of light and stone. *Bellissimo.*

The Pantheon, however, was not the only scene for a seasonal
light show. A friend sent me a note later that night about the phe-

nomenon of Bianchini's Meridian, a remarkable sundial built by astronomer and mathematician Francesco Bianchini inside Santa Maria degli Angeli, the church designed by Michelangelo that lies within the ruins of the Baths of Diocletian.

At the beginning of the 18th century, Pope Clement XI commissioned Bianchini to build a device that could track time and the seasons in order to check the accuracy of the Gregorian calendar and thus to predict the date of Easter precisely every year. Bianchini designed a line cast in bronze, enclosed by marble, along which the sun would cast a narrow spotlight from a small hole in the wall, indicating the arrival, down to the minute, of the winter or summer solstice. This I had to see. By comparison, the Pantheon's broad spotlight seemed a bit primitive.

I was afraid that I was a day late to watch the show, but apparently the exact time of the phenomenon varies from year to year and is determined by astronomical measurements. I made my way to the grounds of the baths, but I had a difficult time finding the entrance to the church, which was not so surprising. Michelangelo's unusual church, with no obvious façade or grand entrance, seems to lurk as a gorgeous surprise within the baths. I learned that it was chosen for the meridian because the baths, and thus the church, were oriented to receive unobstructed exposure to the sun — and because it was built within a pagan structure, it would represent a victory of the Christian over the pagan calendar.

I looked around impatiently inside the church for something to indicate an astonishing event, but didn't see a crowd gathered anywhere. I asked a group of priests who were milling about if they knew about the solstice, but not knowing the Italian for solstice, I mimed in ridiculous but apparently effective body language the sun shining on a particular spot. "*Si*," said one of the priests. "*Certo*." Certainly. The professor will arrive shortly, he said in Italian. I was just in time.

I saw a scholarly-looking middle-aged man walking briskly toward an area near the church altar, carrying a bulging canvas bag full of instruments, and I gleaned that this was the *Professore* because he was followed by a group of young people that could only be students. I finally noticed the 120-foot-long line of bronze on the floor of the church that had already been marked with tape by the *Professore* to indicate the crucial places to watch as the sun's spotlight made its way to a point just in front of an inlaid altar with the image of what appeared to be a royal deer—an image of Christ, I assumed.

And make its way it did, indeed, until the three-foot-long oval spotlight arrived at the exact point where the long bronze line intersected a horizontal endpoint line. *Bellissimo.* And this time, there was applause, as the students looked a little awestruck at the reliability, measurability, predictability and precision of the laws that appear to govern the universe. This was a universe made intelligible to us by light, with a little help from a brilliant scientist. I don't know about the students, but I suspected they were as grateful as I was to watch the light return, keeping its annual promise. In a seemingly chaotic world with an uncertain future, we have that, at least, to count on.

Chapter 43

The Empty Manger

I had never seen a city as gaudily and gorgeously bedecked for Christmas as Rome. There were twinkling lights, nativity scenes, artful Christmas trees made of everything but the kitchen sink, and eye-popping displays in shop windows wherever I looked. Green, white and red lights replicating the stripes of the Italian flag had been strung up on the Via del Corso all the way from the Piazza del Popolo to the Piazza Venezia adjacent to the awful Monumento a Vittorio Emanuele II, also known as the Wedding Cake.

One afternoon I made my way up the Corso to the chic shopping streets that lead to the Piazza di Spagna and the Spanish Steps, where I wanted to visit the Keats-Shelley House, overlooking the steps, and pay my respects to John Keats, whose poems I revered, and whose death had been shockingly untimely. He had wasted away of tuberculosis at age 25 in that house, and every time I came to Rome, I morbidly wanted to look out the window of the room where he died, trying to envision what he had seen, to imagine what he had felt, to thank him for his poems.

On his deathbed, Keats told his friend Shelley that the only epitaph he wanted on his gravestone was this: "Here lies one whose name was writ in water." It is difficult to gauge the irony and sadness of this request, as it was Shelley himself who was to die of drowning a year later. Standing in this small prison cell of a room with a view, surrounded with all the mementos of a life that had touched so many, I couldn't help but think that Gary, too, who had died in a river, would have wanted such an epitaph.

Keats's friends added a small plaque on the cemetery wall near his tomb with these words:

Keats! If thy cherished name be 'writ in water'
Each drop had fallen from some mourner's cheek
A sacred tribute such as heroes seek,
Though oft in vain — for dazzling deeds of slaughter
Sleep on! Not honoured less for Epitaph so meek!

On Christmas Eve, I gave myself over to following the lights and the sounds of the Roman Christmas, with the notion of winding up at Santa Maria in Trastavere, a small church known for its unusual nativity scenes. From the Pantheon, which had become a familiar and beloved old friend, I headed to the sublime Piazza Navona, a short walk away, which had been transformed into a giant Christmas market, complete with merry-go-round, where you could perch on a levitating wooden horse or unicorn and gaze dizzily at Bernini's fabulous Fountain of the Four Rivers, trying to match the rivers, representing the four continents, to the godlike marble figures. One of the river gods, the one identified with the Rio de la Plata, appears to be cowering over a pile of coins, representing the riches America could bring to Europe, apparently afraid of the coiled snake that could take it all away.

The circling carousel horses were appropriate, I thought, since the piazza was built atop the ruins of the Stadium of Domitium, where chariot races had been held in the days of Imperial Rome. At one end of the piazza was a sleigh with Father Christmas beckoning children to go for a ride, or at least to have their photos taken with him.

Gradually I made my way down to the Campo de Fiori, presided over by the gloomy statue of the martyr Giordano Bruno, philosopher, astronomer and mathematician, who loomed as a grim reprimand over the bustling daily market of fruit and flowers. Bruno, who speculated in the late 16th century that the universe was infinitely large, composed of world after world, had been burned at the stake for disturbing the far smaller and more theologically navigable medieval cosmogony of the time. As he was led to the pyre that would consume him, he defiantly told his persecutors, "Perhaps you pronounce this sentence against me with greater fear than I receive it."

I made my way through the old Jewish Quarter, no longer gated, which also demanded further acknowledgments of wrongful persecutions and long overdue apologies, to the Ponte Sisto, which took me over the Tiber into Trastevere, whose rough charm as a medieval working class suburb, with narrow curving streets, had been overly discovered but not yet spoiled. I did some semi-lost winding and wandering before arriving at the Piazza di Santa Maria in Trastavere, where a small crowd was beginning to gather in front of the church.

I was able to catch a glimpse of the multiple nativity scenes on display before the church closed in preparation for midnight mass, and it was clear why the church had become famous for them. There were lively scenes of everyday life in Italy, including one of a carpenter in a wheelchair and another of an artist standing in front of an easel painting a seascape. The main nativity scene, with manger and shepherds, however, was puzzling. The manger was empty. I asked a priest who was passing by why there was no baby Jesus in the manger and he replied, "He hasn't been born yet." Well, of course. Still Christmas Eve.

I walked across to the legendary restaurant Sabatini, which I remembered fondly from a previous visit, and was lucky to get an outdoor table looking onto the piazza, where I was able to linger until midnight. I was determined to watch for the stealthy arrival of the baby Jesus. Fortunately the proprietor Sylvester Sabatini, age 85, was on the premises, making his way around the tables, charming his customers with jokes and songs. He still had a good tenor voice, and he entertained two lovebirds at the table next to mine with a passionate rendition of "Arrivederci Roma."

Meanwhile I had seen a police vehicle pull up to the front of
the church and park, with lights flashing. No baby Jesus in evidence. I lingered over my glass of house red, which was quite good,
and finally indulged in a dessert of raspberry sorbetto. By now, the
church bells were ringing. I paid the check and walked into the
church on the stroke of midnight. And there he was. Baby Jesus was
now lying in the manger. The feeling of the fulfillment of a promise
was something like watching the light arrive at its preordered destinations on the solstice.

Chapter 44

Ashes to Ashes at Santa Croce

The day after Christmas I took a train to Florence to visit the Franciscan Basilica of Santa Croce, also known as the Temple of Italian Glories because of the great artists and thinkers who are buried there. I wanted to pay homage to two of Gary's heroes in his own personal pantheon, whose tombs I had never visited. I had a thought of leaving some of Gary's ashes there if it were possible. He had revered Machiavelli and Galileo, giants of science and ideas, as though they were his personal mentors, looking over his shoulder, always enlarging his frame of reference to a far older and broader world than the contentious politics of the Texas Legislature and the day-to-day issues of technology that had commanded so much of his energy. And while I was there at Santa Croce, I would also pay my respects to my own hero Dante, whose visions of heaven and hell—particularly of the sinners caught in descending circles of the inferno—I often found relevant to people and events in contemporary life.

As I was walking toward the 14th-century basilica, with its unexpectedly gaudy Gothic Revival façade, added in the 19th century, my iPhone beeped with a message. It was from my sister Ellen, who said that her computer was crashing, and that she wanted to make sure that I got a photo of Gary and her kids that she feared would be lost. She had appended the photo, which had been taken several years earlier. It was of Gary and me, posing with Chase and Maddie, dressed in their costumes from a school production of The Wizard of Oz. Maddie was a munchkin, and Chase was a flying monkey. That had been a happy day, and it was a comforting image of Gary to be taking along with me into the Temple of Italian Glories. I wouldn't feel as though I were walking in alone.

I was also taking along Byron's description of Santa Croce, and his own tributes to Gary's heroes (and to Michelangelo and the dramatist Vittorio Alfieri as well):

In Santa Croce's holy precincts lie
Ashes which make it holier, dust which is
Even in itself an immortality,
Though there were nothing save the past, and this,
The particle of those sublimities
Which have relapsed to chaos: — here repose
Angelo's, Alfieri's bones, and his,
The starry Galileo, with his woes;
Here Machiavelli's earth return'd to whence it rose.

These are four minds, which, like the elements,
Might furnish forth creation: — Italy!

As I surveyed the basilica, it was clear that I wouldn't be able to sprinkle ashes on the tombs, as it would have simply looked like someone had dropped cigarette ashes on the immaculate marble floors. And so I would be placing virtual ashes on the cenotaphs of Gary's heroes.

It was Machiavelli's tomb that I saw first, located midway along the south wall of the main sanctuary. The inscription there reads: *Tanto nomini nullum par elogium* (for such a great name there is no adequate praise). Ironic, of course, for someone who spent so much time in exile and whose name has become synonymous with political scheming, cynicism and the manipulation of power. For Gary, though, Machiavelli was the father of political science, the first modern thinker about the uses and abuses of power. Machiavelli, in his view, was a realist and brilliant political strategist who was unhampered by Utopian fantasies or by religious idealism. *The*

Prince, he said, was as much a warning of what tyrants were capable of as it was a pragmatic handbook of how to gain and keep power.

In the far northwest corner was the tomb of "starry Galileo," who had also suffered for offering a view of the world that clashed with the powers-that-be of his time. In 1633, the church tried him as a heretic for daring to assert that the earth revolved around the sun and forced him to recant—though some have said the recanting was done with fingers crossed.

With the trial of Galileo, two worlds came into cosmic conflict: Galileo's world of science and humanism and the Church's world of faith and absolutism. The end of Galileo's liberty, as Gary had described it, meant the end of the Italian Renaissance—the Italian Glories. In 2008, he had called me with some news that he found incredibly ironic: that the Vatican was changing Galileo's status from that of a heretic to that of a hero of faith and science—just in time for the 400th anniversary of the invention of his telescope and the International Year of Astronomy that had been designated by the U.N. A little late to tell Galileo that all was forgiven, said Gary.

I looked around for Dante and found his cenotaph adjacent to Michelangelo's on the south wall of the basilica. The Florentines had made numerous efforts to get Dante's remains back from Ravenna, where he died, probably of malaria, but his tomb in Santa Croce remains empty. However, it wasn't until 2008 that Florence finally revoked a death sentence against Dante lodged during his lifetime that had resulted from trumped-up charges against him leveled by political enemies during a time of partisan wars and vendettas. It's little wonder that Dante placed divisive political partisanship in the next-to-lowest circle of hell in *The Divine Comedy*.

It was Dante's *La Vita Nuova*, The New Life, however, that had become the most meaningful of his works for me. The death of his beloved Beatrice, who was also his guide in the Paradiso section of *The Divine Comedy*, inspired Dante to search for consolation by transforming the notion of earthly love into a yearning for a love that transcends death—for a kind of divine love. He envisions Beatrice as the clear river that consoles the dejected pilgrim, becoming love and water all at once. For Dante, water, like love, can surround one, but it can't be grasped.

He addresses his fellow pilgrims:

O pilgrims who walk lost in thought, do you know where you are? The street? The house you are near?

. . .

If you would pause in your travels, I could tell the story my sighing heart reiterates day and night, and you would weep with us.

In the final words of *La Vita Nuova*, Dante says of Beatrice that he will "*say of her what has never been said of any woman.*"

That evening, I wrote in a little journal I had bought for its covers made of Florentine paper that if I were a poet on the order of Dante, or a thinker on the order of Machiavelli, or a scientist on the order of Galileo, I would say of Gary what has never been said of any man. Because I, too, was looking for a new life, a *vita nuova*, a new way of looking at love and death, a way of making a place for Gary in the starry heavens, of remembering him in a beautiful poem, of giving him his rightful place in the ongoing story of those who would be heroes and pay a price. I would not carve his name in stone, but I would write his name in water.

Each drop had fallen from some mourner's cheek
A sacred tribute such as heroes seek.

Chapter 45

A Second Line All the Way from Rome

I was back in Rome for New Year's Eve, which I discovered is spent on the streets as a kind of moveable feast for the masses, a greatly magnified version of the ritual of the Sunday evening *passegiata*, the neighborly, gossipy stroll along the streets of a city's *centro storico*, or historic center. As the sun went down, I decided to join the ever-widening stream of people who were heading up the Via del Corso toward the Piazza del Popolo. Young men were walking in clumps, some of them wearing identical soccer-team jackets, singing and chanting support for their teams, with AS Roma fans trying to outshout Lazio boosters.

The widening stream reached the Piazza del Popolo, then circled back down the Corso, which had once been the scene of bizarre races, known as the *corsi dei barberi* (races of the barbarians) run by riderless horses, donkeys, and street urchins during Carnival. Many of the celebrants were wearing blinking headgear—flashing tiaras, horns, insect antennae—to light the way. I asked a young woman walking beside me where everyone was going, and she just shrugged. Anywhere, nowhere. Just going with the flow. But her companion said the main goal was a concert being held on the Via dei Fori Imperiali, on the stretch from the Roman Forum to the Coliseum. The featured band, she said, was Negramaro, a pop group named after a wine produced in the Salento region. They were expecting more than 100,000 people to show up, she said.

The river of people was now moving so efficiently, without bumping or shoving, that it felt like a school of fish, moving in concert, in harmonious patterns. When the stream reached a barricade, preventing access to streets that had been closed off for the concert, it simply regrouped smoothly and moved along to a different street.

Eventually we were moving alongside the forum, which was illumined spookily by red lights. It was as though we had descended into one of Dante's circles, gazing at forgotten monuments, at the ruins of pride and ambition, at everything that decays and falls. But there was such joy and laughter that it was impossible to feel sad for more than a moment before the current swept us along.

We could hear the music in the distance, but we never actually arrived at its source, as the crowds in front of the Coliseum had grown too dense. We were moving along small, dark side streets, and I had no idea where we were or how I'd get back, but I felt utterly safe, in the way I had once felt safe when I was tucked into a second line in New Orleans, moving through streets I couldn't have walked alone.

I began to imagine that I had become a part of some boundless second line, and that it was inevitable that my pilgrimage had brought me here, into this flowing current of humanity. I could imagine everyone I had encountered on my pilgrimage joining in this inclusive second line, bobbing along in the current. I could even envision a skeptical Machiavelli looking on, commenting wryly on the apparent lack of leadership in this unruly mob, with Bruce Springsteen providing the music from Gary's cosmic playlist.

In his "Land of Hope and Dreams," Springsteen had envisioned a train carrying the broken-hearted as well as "sweet souls departed." And so, too, I imagined later, it would carry all of the tribe of Gary, electronic and in the flesh—young and old, geeks, techies, soldiers, artists, soul singers, opera divas, and kayak paddlers. They were all part of Gary's story, of the ever-widening current that had been his life. And now they were part of mine.

I was dancing in the street with strangers who had become a river of necessary angels, sweeping me along with the current into that ineffable turn from sorrow and loss into contagious celebration.

I let go. I knew it was momentary, but simply being immersed like a baptized child in this vital flowing river, in safe and sweet oblivion, offered the possibility of a new life, *la vita nuova*.

Water, like love, can surround one, but it cannot be grasped.

When I finally broke away, I had no trouble navigating my way back to the Del Senato, where I found the Piazza della Rotunda full of revelers. One of them handed me a sparkler. I reached my room and opened the window just in time to watch fireworks booming and showering down over the Pantheon, as though it were under siege by a vast army of joy-seekers.

For a moment, I wondered if the men with torches on the plaza beneath my window would manage to set the Pantheon—or the hotel—on fire. There was smoke everywhere. But as I watched the enduring old stones lit up by starbursts in the night, my heart seemed to crack open with such force that I felt it must have exploded like the fireworks.

You allow love in.

I could never have imagined a pilgrimage ending so dramatically, with rockets shooting over the Pantheon, sparks flying, the sound of mortar shells exploding, the smell of smoke and sulphur in the air, glowing ashes drifting down from the sky. It was as though the sights and sounds of war had been transformed into peaceable if high-decibel celebration. I suppose it was more an epiphany of pyrotechnics than of spiritual enlightenment. But I knew that Gary would have loved the idea of going out with a bang rather than a whimper, in this city of the eternal return of light, with a rousing toast to life rather than with aching tears of sorrow.

The real paradox of being a pilgrim is that you mistakenly believe that as you put one foot in front of the other, over and over, you are moving forward. But for most of the journey, you are actually looking back. And when you finally come full circle, there you are, startled to be back at the place where you began. You are still a lone pilgrim. But you are now aware of all the footsteps that were beside you along the way. Lone, but not alone. And now you

can see those walking in front of you, and you can hear those following behind you.

When Orpheus returned from the underworld, he failed to bring
Eurydice back with him. And even if he could have brought her
back, whole, to the land of the living, she would no longer be the
same Eurydice, just as he would no longer be the same Orpheus.
Death had changed everything. But he wasn't coming back to the
world of light and life entirely alone. He was bringing her back as
memory, as a voice in his psyche, as his interior paramour and comforter. As a Eurydice presence, there and not there. Always.

As there is a Gary presence, there and not there. Always.

Where the Cool Water Flows

The fireworks marked the penultimate moment of my journey following Gary's death. I knew then that I was coming back to life, that I had made the crucial turn, the one where the doctor knows that the patient will survive. But with the passage of time, I found that I could never actually pinpoint an official end to my pilgrimage, as I kept encountering thin places and necessary angels in the months and years that followed.

I have found that once you've begun walking deliberately on a chosen road, whether it's a pilgrimage, a second line, a labyrinth, a bright path, or a pattern of stones in your backyard, you never really depart from it. Although the circles of my journey have become smaller, I still hear the current of the river that took Gary away from me but brought him back to me in glimmers. There and not there.

I've continued my dialogue with Gary, though what goes on inside my head on the subject of miracles and synchronicity is more like a multi-part conversation. I watch and listen as Gary the rational skeptic takes on Gary the romantic and Gary the interior comforter, while Carol the sometime skeptic challenges Carol the would-be believer. They all get a word in.

No one actually wins, of course, because some things just remain in the air. When I see a hawk, it could be just a hawk. Or it could be something more, depending on the angle of vision. If, as Wallace Stevens wrote, there are 13 ways of looking at a blackbird, there must be many more ways of looking at a hawk. And they might all be right, depending on the eye of the beholder.

The second Easter following Gary's death, I drove into the Hill Country with my parents, my sister and her husband and my niece and nephew to the banks of the Guadalupe River, where Gary had often launched his kayak with his friends for a day of paddling. He loved the Guadalupe, with its clear green water and occasional exciting ripples. We thought about how he loved to wow his friends with the chilled bottle of wine and a wineglass he had tucked into a cooler, along with slices of prosciutto and mozzarella, to outclass the cold beers and ham sandwiches they had brought along.

We released some of Gary's ashes into the river, each of us saying something in our own way about how much we missed him. My mother, who is frail and doesn't see well anymore, said quietly, "We'll all be going down the river some day. Some of us sooner than others. Gary just went before us so he could show us the way."

As I drove home, I turned on Gary's iPod, which had been set, as usual, on shuffle. And the song that came on was "Green River," by Creedence Clearwater Revival.

Well, take me back down where cool water flows
Let me remember things I love.

"Oh, really?" you ask, incredulously. I can almost see you shaking your head. Not again. So you'll have to take my word for it and maybe start a dialogue between your inner skeptic and your inner mystic. Because the cosmic playlist plays on, and all our names are written in water.

Made in the USA
Lexington, KY
26 March 2015